T0323508

Monarch: Resilience through Evolution

Monarch: Resilience through Evolution is a comprehensive guide on strategy across the industry life cycle, taking readers on an insightful journey through the dynamic world of business. Drawing inspiration from the resilient and adaptive nature of the monarch butterfly, this book offers a fresh perspective on strategic decision-making in today's ever-changing business environment.

Central to the narrative is the concept of the industry life cycle, which serves as the foundational context for strategy development and deployment in organizations. It considers the complexities of organizations as adaptive systems and industries as aggregates of organizations, emphasizing the importance of adaptability, persistence, and strategic agility. Monarch advocates for approaching strategy as a living process aligned with this perspective.

Through insightful analyses and real-world examples, the book illustrates how organizations can navigate uncertainty and thrive in the face of adversity. At each phase of the life cycle, guidance on organizational self-assessment, strategy development, strategy deployment, and common pitfalls to avoid is provided. An innovative approach to the strategy cascade is introduced, using the notion of "magnifying lenses" to ensure strategic alignment across corporate, business, and functional-levels. The book then transitions into pursuing strategy as a negotiation and concludes with a special note on the *strategic imperative* and considerations for leadership.

Monarch: Resilience through Evolution

A Book on Strategy Across the Industry Life Cycle

Hanan Alhaddi

Routledge
Taylor & Francis Group

A PRODUCTIVITY PRESS BOOK

First published 2025
by Routledge
605 Third Avenue, New York, NY 10158

and by Routledge
4 Park Square, Milton Park, Abingdon, Oxon, OX14 4RN

Routledge is an imprint of the Taylor & Francis Group, an informa business

ISBN: 978-1-032-91601-9 (hbk)
ISBN: 978-1-032-90770-3 (pbk)
ISBN: 978-1-003-56413-3 (ebk)

DOI: 10.4324/9781003564133

Typeset in Adobe Garamond
by SPi Technologies India Pvt Ltd (Straive)

To my late father and my loving family.

Contents

Prelude

So what triggered writing this book?

For years, my experiences in the industry have provided me with invaluable insights into how decisions are made within organizations. However, as I taught and researched strategy, I became acutely aware of the widening gap between academic theory and practical application. While textbooks and case studies offered a foundation, it sounded closer to Nirvana than a reflection of the realities of how strategies are implemented in the corporate world, the "real world"! I also noticed a concerning trend: many "strategy" teams lacked a deep understanding of corporate, business, and functional-level strategies. The word strategy is often inserted in sentences, liberally. Strategies were becoming mere "flavors of the month," adopted superficially without a genuine grasp of their implications or alignment with the organization's current position in the industry life cycle.

These disconnects underscored the need for a comprehensive work that not only acknowledges the industry life cycle as the backdrop, but also recognizes that organizations are composed of people and industries are composed of organizations....and so, there was the common thread of natural evolution. It became clear that strategy is not merely about choosing the latest buzzword; it is fundamentally about making informed trade-offs and engaging in negotiation, all while ensuring strategic alignment while strategies are deployed from corporate-level down to functional-level.

So, what about the negotiation aspect? Well, if business leaders are going to compete for organizational resources as these trade-offs are (or should be) made, then negotiation is an essential mechanism to successful strategy implementation

Lastly, you might be wondering why I use "we" throughout this book. My intention is to cultivate a sense of camaraderie as we embark on this exploration together. By fostering a collaborative environment, I invite you to join me on this journey of understanding and applying strategic concepts as you navigate the pages of Monarch.

Preface

Monarch: Resilience through Evolution is a book on strategy inspired by the monarch butterfly's resilience and adaptability. Just as the monarch navigates thousands of miles to reach its destination, effective strategy guides organizations through evolving business environments.

Central to the book is the concept of the industry life cycle, which serves as the foundational context for strategy development and deployment in organizations. The book begins by defining what strategy is and is not, emphasizing the importance of understanding the macroenvironment—external factors that influence an organization's operations. Recognizing organizations as complex adaptive systems (CAS), we view them as dynamic entities that must continuously adjust to maintain their competitive edge.

In Part I, we explore the ecosystem in which organizations operate, discussing the need for strategy to be responsive and adaptive. We then examine the notion of the industry life cycle through the various stages (from embryonic through growth, shakeout, maturity, and decline), illustrating how strategies must evolve to meet new challenges and seize opportunities.

Part II provides practical strategies for each stage of the industry life cycle. We discuss how to disrupt during the embryonic phase, differentiate or lead in cost during growth, adapt to survive the shakeout, compete fiercely during maturity, and decide whether to end the game or pivot during decline. Aligning strategies with these phases helps organizations navigate the industry landscape more effectively and achieve sustained success.

In the final part, we focus on implementing strategy. We introduce the concept of viewing strategy through three magnifying lenses—corporate, business, and functional-levels—ensuring strategic alignment throughout the organization. We also discuss pursuing strategy as a negotiation where trade-offs and stakeholder alignment through continuous dialogues are crucial for success.

Monarch aims to provide a practical guide for business leaders and students, blending theoretical insights with real-world applications. By drawing on well-established strategy concepts and frameworks, we offer a comprehensive approach to understanding and applying strategic principles across various industry contexts.

Much like the monarch butterfly's journey, the path to effective strategy involves persistence, adaptation, and resilience. This book equips you with the tools and knowledge to navigate this journey, ensuring your organization remains dynamic and competitive in an ever-changing business landscape.

About the Author

Dr. Hanan Alhaddi is an industry expert and academic practitioner with nearly 20 years of experience in corporate strategy, enterprise transformation, and process re-engineering. She is a guest lecturer on strategy and the director of integrative cases on AI at Oxford University's Saïd Business School. She holds advanced degrees in strategy and innovation from Oxford University and Harvard University and professional credentials in AI and GenAI from MIT and IBM. Dr. Alhaddi has published extensively on strategy and business management and regularly speaks at industry and academic conferences, contributing to the advancement of new knowledge in the field. She is the CEO of Alhaddi Consulting Group, serves on the board of directors of the Connected Vehicle Trade Association, and an Associate Editor for the *Journal of Management and Strategy*.

Dr. Alhaddi completed her doctorate in business administration with a focus on strategic positioning and differentiation from Lawrence Technological University and her engineering degree from Wayne State University.

STRATEGY AND THE ECOSYSTEM

Chapter 1

What Strategy Is and Is Not

A Monarch embarks on an extraordinary journey spanning thousands of miles from North America to Central Mexico, navigating complex terrains, and overcoming some of nature's toughest challenges....a journey executed over multiple generations and one that showcases its innate ability to adapt, persist, and thrive.

    ...a journey relevant to its size is equivalent to a person walking around the earth 8 times
    ...a potent of resilience
    ...an exemplar of how strategy is supposed to work

What Is Strategy?

At the center of every successful organization lies a well-crafted strategy that guides its direction and actions. Strategy, in essence, is a compass. And just like one, it is dynamic and responsive to where you are, but should always lead your organization toward its north star. Because organizations are arguably living entities, they impact and are impacted by the surrounding environment (known as the macroenvironment). This ongoing dynamic results in changes in the positions

DOI: 10.4324/9781003564133-2

of the organizations from time to time and, hence, continuously relying on the compass for direction. As the compass shows which way is north, the organizations respond by making trade-offs to adjust their paths. The response manifests itself in deliberate choices and exchanges that organizations make as they strive to implement their strategies.

In business terms, these ongoing adjustments yield a competitive position among rivals as the organization sets its strategic goals and embarks on a journey to accomplish them. In other words, strategy is about making decisions that align with the organization's purpose, values, and desired outcomes while considering the constraints and opportunities presented by the external environment.

Effective strategies are born from carefully evaluating alternatives and selecting the most promising path forward. This necessitates recognizing the inevitability of trade-offs, as resources are inherently scarce. By carefully allocating resources to areas that offer the greatest potential for success, organizations can strategically differentiate themselves from competitors and achieve sustainable growth.

A well-defined strategy provides a roadmap for navigating complexity and uncertainty. It involves a thorough understanding of the organization's internal capabilities and external landscape, including market dynamics, customer needs, technological advancements, regulatory factors, and other competitive forces. By conducting comprehensive analyses and assessments, organizations can identify opportunities, assess risks, and develop a clear understanding of their competitive advantages.

Strategy is not a static document or a one-time exercise but an ongoing process. It requires continuous monitoring and adaptation to changing circumstances. As the external environment evolves, organizations must remain agile and responsive, adjusting their strategies to maintain relevance and capitalize on emerging opportunities. Flexibility and the ability to pivot when necessary are vital elements of successful strategy execution.

Needless to say, effective strategy involves effective communication and alignment throughout the organization. It is not solely the responsibility of top-level executives or strategy departments but should permeate throughout all levels and functions. Every employee should understand the organization's strategic objectives, their role in achieving them, and how their daily work contributes to the overall strategy.

Apple

Apple, under the visionary leadership of Steve Jobs and Tim Cook, exemplifies a company that has strategically differentiated itself in the technology industry. Apple's strategy is deeply rooted in innovation, user experience, and premium product offerings. By leveraging its core competencies in design, software integration, and branding, Apple has *consistently* introduced groundbreaking products that resonate with consumers worldwide. The introduction of the iPhone revolutionized the smartphone industry, merging functionality and aesthetics in a way that redefined user expectations. Apple's strategic choices, including the development of intuitive user interfaces, seamless integration across devices, and a robust ecosystem of services, have solidified its position as a global technology leader. An effective strategy could change from time to time depending on the ever-changing macroenvironment, but it will likely produce *consistent* results.

Southwest Airlines

Southwest Airlines has carved out a unique position in the highly competitive airline industry through its relentless pursuit of a cost leadership strategy. The company has focused on operational efficiency and low-cost operations as key differentiators. By implementing strategies such as point-to-point routes, high aircraft utilization, and streamlined processes, Southwest has been able to offer affordable fares while maintaining profitability. Their approach to cost reduction extends to their customer-centric service model, as they prioritize quick turnarounds, efficient boarding processes, and friendly customer interactions. Southwest's strategic choices have enabled it to attract price-sensitive customers, build customer loyalty, and expand its market presence.

Progress Over the Years

Over the years, the concept of strategy has undergone a remarkable transformation. It has shifted from being perceived as a static plan to becoming a dynamic and adaptive process that propels organizations toward success. This evolution is evident when we examine the various strategy books included in our list, considering their publication dates and the ideas they present.

In earlier times, strategy was often viewed as a rigid and pre-defined plan that aimed to achieve long-term objectives. Books like *Competitive Strategy* by Michael E. Porter, published in 1980, highlighted the importance of analyzing industries and competitors to formulate effective strategies. It laid the foundation for understanding the competitive landscape and positioning an organization advantageously. However, this approach largely focused on a relatively stable business environment, where strategic plans could be formulated and executed over extended periods.

As the business landscape became more complex and dynamic, new perspectives emerged. "The Art of the Long View" by Peter Schwartz, published in 1996, introduced the concept of scenario planning and emphasized the need to anticipate and respond to future uncertainties. This marked a shift from static planning to a more flexible and forward-thinking approach to strategy.

In the early 2000s, books like *Good to Great* by Jim Collins (published in 2001) and *Blue Ocean Strategy* by W. Chan Kim and Renée Mauborgne (published in 2005) challenged traditional notions of strategy. They focused on differentiating organizations from competitors by creating unique value propositions. These books emphasized the importance of market positioning, innovation, and identifying uncontested market spaces.

In more recent years, strategy has evolved further, taking into account the dynamic nature of industries and the need for continuous adaptation. *Your Strategy Needs a Strategy* by Martin Reeves, Knut Haanaes, and Janmejaya Sinha (published in 2015) introduced the concept of a "strategy palette," which emphasized the need for organizations to tailor their strategies to different business environments. This book highlighted the importance of adopting multiple strategic approaches and being agile in response to changing circumstances.

Additionally, *Playing to Win* by A.G. Lafley and Roger L. Martin (published in 2013) emphasized the role of strategic choices in defining an organization's success. It focused on the importance of making clear and deliberate choices, aligning resources, and creating a unique and valuable position in the market.

These examples demonstrate the progression of strategy from a static plan to a dynamic and adaptive process. Strategy today requires a continuous learning mindset, flexibility to respond to emerging trends, and the ability to navigate complexity. Organizations must embrace a range of strategic approaches and adapt their strategies to suit different business environments.

By integrating insights from these books, we gain a comprehensive understanding of how strategy has evolved over time (see Table 1.1). The lessons learned from each publication contribute to a more nuanced and contemporary approach to strategy, one that acknowledges the complexity and dynamism of the business landscape. In our journey through this book, we will build upon these valuable insights to develop a holistic understanding of strategy and its practical implementation across the industry life cycle.

Strategy and Complexity: Where the Two Meet

Strategy has come a long way from being a static plan to becoming a dynamic and adaptive process that can propel organizations toward success. This evolution becomes even more compelling when we consider organizations as complex adaptive systems (CASs).

Think of your organization as a living, breathing entity that constantly evolves and adapts to its environment. It's like a vibrant ecosystem where various elements interact, influence each other, and respond to changes. This fresh perspective adds depth to our understanding of strategy and enables us to navigate the intricacies of the business world.

Gone are the days when strategies were set in stone and executed without question. We now realize that the business environment is anything but predictable. It's complex, uncertain, and interconnected. As we embrace the concept of organizations as CASs, we recognize the need for agility, responsiveness, and continuous learning in our strategic endeavors.

In this book, we explore different perspectives on strategy (and yes, we will borrow from the wisdom in some of the renowned strategy books) while we anchor ourselves in our industries. Why? Because our industries are nothing but clusters of our organizations that produce similar products and services and play by similar rules. We draw insights from various sources to help us navigate the complexity of our macroenvironments, effectively.

With the realization that strategies cannot be one-size-fits-all (hence, trade-offs and choice-making), we emphasize the need to tailor them to our organizations' unique context and industry dynamics (a simplified articulation of Porter's notion of "fit and coordination among activities"). By embracing this mindset, we can seize opportunities and gain a competitive edge.

Embracing the idea of organizations as CASs also means embracing a culture of experimentation and adaptation. It's about empowering individuals at all levels to contribute their insights, ideas, and expertise to drive innovation. By fostering an environment where collaboration and diversity of thought flourish, we encourage creativity and ensure our strategies remain dynamic and relevant…and by integrating the concept of organizations as CASs into our understanding of the evolution of strategy, we foster a proactive mindset—one that embraces change, uncertainty, and interdependencies; one that harnesses the power of agility, resilience, and innovation to propel our organizations toward sustainable success in today's ever-evolving business landscape.

What You Might Read About Strategy

Table 1.1 Comparative Analysis of Common Strategy Books

Book Title	Monarch	Your Strategy Needs a Strategy	Exploring Strategy	The Art of the Long View	Blue Ocean Strategy	Playing to Win	Good to Great	Competitive Strategy	The Art of Strategy	Good Strategy Bad Strategy
Definition of Strategy	Strategy is an ongoing and adaptive process that responds to the industry life cycle phase in which the organization competes. It must consider the evolution of the industry across its life cycle and should be developed & deployed in line with that.	Strategy is viewed as a dynamic and adaptive process that aligns with different contexts. It emphasizes the importance of considering multiple perspectives and utilizing different strategic approaches.	Strategy is understood from various perspectives, combining different strategic theories and concepts. It involves analyzing and formulating strategies by considering the five Ps: plan, ploy, pattern, position, and perspective.	Strategy is seen as a future-oriented approach that involves scenario planning. It emphasizes the consideration of long-term perspectives and the exploration of different possible futures.	Strategy is perceived as the creation of new markets by focusing on value innovation. It involves looking across industries, strategic groups, buyer groups, complementary products and services, and functional-emotional orientation over time.	Strategy is defined as a choice made based on five key questions: What is our winning aspiration, where to play, how to win, core capabilities, and management systems. It involves aligning resources, actions, and systems to execute the chosen strategic direction.	Strategy is emphasized as a disciplined approach to achieving greatness. It involves disciplined action, focusing on finding what an organization can excel at, what drives its economic engine, and what it is deeply passionate about.	Strategy is approached by analyzing competitive forces and positioning opportunities. It involves choosing among three generic strategies: cost leadership, differentiation, and focus.	Strategy is viewed as an integrative approach that considers various factors and trade-offs. It involves analyzing seven key elements: arenas, differentiators, vehicles, staging, economic logic, mastery, and core competencies.	Strategy is perceived as a diagnosis and action approach. It involves identifying obstacles, focusing on key areas, and formulating a guiding policy for effective strategic action.

Approach to Strategy									
Emphasizes the synergy between organizations and industries as dynamic and alive experiencing evolution across their various stages, and so should strategy. As a guiding compass, the strategy should always aim toward the organization's north star and therefore should be adaptive as strategy is developed and deployed. Monarch applies a magnifying lens perspective to the three common tiers of strategy (corporate-level, business-level, and functional-level) to ensure strategic alignment. As the strategy is developed, it should be perceived as a negotiation.	The approach to strategy in this book is integrative, combining different strategic theories and concepts. It encourages analyzing and formulating strategies by considering various perspectives and the five Ps: plan, ploy, pattern, position, and perspective.	The approach to strategy in this book is future-oriented, focusing on long-term perspectives. It emphasizes the importance of scenario planning to anticipate and prepare for future uncertainties. The book suggests developing future maps, exploring different scenarios, engaging in strategic conversations, making informed decisions, defining relevant metrics, and committing to actions.	The approach to strategy in this book is centered around value innovation. It suggests exploring new market spaces by challenging existing industry boundaries. The book introduces six paths for creating blue oceans, which involve looking across industries, strategic groups, buyer groups, complementary products and services, functional-emotional orientation, and time.	The book advocates for a disciplined approach to strategy, based on answering five key questions. It emphasizes the importance of making strategic choices, aligning resources, and executing the chosen strategic direction. The approach involves defining a winning aspiration, determining where to play, identifying how to win, leveraging core capabilities, and aligning management systems to support the chosen strategy.	The approach in this book is to pursue greatness through disciplined action. It emphasizes finding what an organization can excel at, identifying its economic engine, and aligning passion and purpose. The book explores the importance of disciplined people and thought in driving sustained greatness.	The approach in this book is focused on competitive positioning. It suggests analyzing the competitive environment and choosing among three generic strategies: cost leadership, differentiation, and focus. The book introduces the five forces framework for analyzing competitive forces and highlights the importance of effective implementation to gain a competitive advantage.	The approach in this book is integrative, considering various factors and trade-offs. It involves analyzing seven key elements of strategy, including arenas, differentiators, vehicles, staging, economic logic, mastery, and core competencies. The book introduces the strategy diamond framework, which helps organizations holistically evaluate and shape their strategies based on these elements.	The approach in this book is diagnosis and action. It emphasizes identifying obstacles, focusing on key areas, and formulating a guiding policy to address the challenges. The book introduces the kernel of strategy, which consists of proximate objectives, fundamental diagnosis, and a guiding policy. It encourages overcoming obstacles and formulating effective strategies through a clear understanding of the organization's context and the industry dynamics.

(Continued)

TABLE 1.1 (Continued)

Book Title	Monarch	Your Strategy Needs a Strategy	Exploring Strategy	The Art of the Long View	Blue Ocean Strategy	Playing to Win	Good to Great	Competitive Strategy	The Art of Strategy	Good Strategy Bad Strategy
Elements of Strategy	Highlights the five phases of an industry life cycle and the applicable strategic approach organizations should consider at each phase—embryonic: disrupt your way through; growth: emerge as a differentiator or cost leader; shakeout: adapt to survive; maturity: compete until blue oceans turn red, decline: end your game or play another one	Identifies five key strategies that organizations can consider: classical, adaptive, visionary, shaping, and renewal. Each strategy corresponds to different business contexts and demands. The strategies provide a framework for organizations to navigate industry dynamics and life cycle stages effectively.	Emphasizes the importance of considering various elements when formulating strategies. It highlights the five Ps of strategy: plan, ploy, pattern, position, and perspective. These elements help organizations analyze the internal and external environment, identify opportunities and threats, and formulate effective strategies based on their unique context.	Introduces six key elements that contribute to effective strategy development: future maps, scenarios, strategic conversation, decisions, metrics, and commitments. These elements help organizations anticipate and shape the future, make informed decisions, and commit to actions that align with their long-term objectives.	Outlines six paths that organizations can explore to create blue oceans: look across industries, strategic groups, buyer groups, complementary products and services, functional-emotional orientation, and time. These paths provide a systematic approach to uncovering new market spaces and redefining industry boundaries, enabling organizations to capture uncontested market space and drive growth.	Emphasizes five strategic choices that organizations should consider: What is our winning aspiration, where to play, how to win, core capabilities, and management systems. These choices guide organizations in determining their strategic direction, competitive positioning, and resource allocation. By making thoughtful choices, organizations can align their actions and resources to achieve strategic goals effectively.	Identifies disciplined action as a key element of achieving greatness. It emphasizes the importance of disciplined people and thought in driving sustainable success. While the book does not explicitly outline specific elements of strategy, it highlights the significance of disciplined execution, focusing on what an organization can excel at, and aligning its economic engine with its passion and purpose.	Highlights three generic strategies that organizations can pursue: cost leadership, differentiation, and focus. These strategies help organizations gain a competitive advantage by positioning themselves effectively in the market. The book introduces the five forces framework, which analyzes the competitive environment and identifies opportunities for organizations to gain a strategic edge over their rivals.	Presents seven elements that organizations should consider in their strategy: arenas, differentiators, vehicles, staging, economic logic, mastery, and core competencies. These elements help organizations evaluate their strategies and make informed choices. By considering these elements, organizations can develop a comprehensive strategy that aligns with their goals and leverages their core capabilities effectively.	Emphasizes the importance of diagnosing the challenges and formulating effective strategies. It introduces the kernel of strategy which consists of proximate objectives, fundamental diagnosis, and a guiding policy. By understanding the organization's context, obstacles, and key areas, organizations can formulate strategies that address the challenges and align with their goals effectively.

Frameworks										
Introduces Monarch Grid: a guiding framework for an organizational approach toward strategy at each phase of the industry life cycle to ensure resilience through the evolution of the industry. There are assessments, guidance, and pitfalls for each phase.	Introduces the STRATAPLEX framework, which includes the Strategic Fitness Process, Strategic Planning, and Strategy in Action. This framework helps organizations assess their strategic fitness, plan their strategies, and execute them effectively.	Presents a strategy development process that guides organizations in formulating effective strategies. It involves analyzing the internal and external environment, formulating strategic options, and implementing the chosen strategies.	Emphasizes the use of scenario planning as a framework for developing alternative futures. By creating future maps, exploring different scenarios, engaging in strategic conversations, and making informed decisions, organizations can navigate industry dynamics and anticipate future trends.	Introduces the Strategy Canvas as a framework for creating blue ocean strategies. It helps organizations identify key factors that drive value for customers and differentiate their offerings from competitors. The Strategy Canvas enables organizations to systematically explore new market spaces and redefine industry boundaries.	Introduces the Strategy Choice Cascade: a framework that helps organizations align their resources, actions, and systems with the chosen strategic direction. It involves defining a winning aspiration, determining where to play, identifying how to win, leveraging core capabilities, and aligning management systems. The Strategy Choice Cascade provides a structured approach to strategy alignment and execution.	Does not explicitly introduce a specific framework, but emphasizes a disciplined approach to strategy execution. It emphasizes the importance of disciplined action, disciplined people, and disciplined thought in achieving sustained greatness.	Introduces the five forces framework as a tool for analyzing the competitive environment. It helps organizations understand the competitive forces at play, such as the threat of new entrants, bargaining power of buyers and suppliers, threat of substitutes, and intensity of rivalry. This framework assists organizations in making strategic choices and implementing effective strategies to gain a competitive advantage.	Introduces the Strategy Diamond as a framework for developing comprehensive strategies. It involves analyzing seven elements of strategy: arenas, differentiators, vehicles, staging, economic logic, mastery, and core competencies. The Strategy Diamond helps organizations evaluate their strategic choices, consider various trade-offs, and develop strategies that align with their objectives and capabilities.	Does not introduce a specific framework but emphasizes the importance of a clear diagnosis and guiding policy. It highlights the kernel of strategy as a framework that helps organizations overcome obstacles, focus on key areas, and formulate strategies that align with their goals and the industry dynamics.

(Continued)

TABLE 1.1 (Continued)

Book Title	Monarch	Your Strategy Needs a Strategy	Exploring Strategy	The Art of the Long View	Blue Ocean Strategy	Playing to Win	Good to Great	Competitive Strategy	The Art of Strategy	Good Strategy Bad Strategy
Process	Suggests a process that starts assessing the phase of the industry life cycle in which the organization competes followed by steps to develop, then to deploy the appropriate strategy.	Suggests a process that involves defining, shaping, choosing, and testing strategies. This iterative process helps organizations adapt their strategies to different contexts and evolving industry dynamics.	Outlines an analysis, formulation, and implementation process for strategy development. It involves analyzing the internal and external environment, formulating strategic options, and implementing the chosen strategies.	Highlights the process of developing alternative futures by creating future maps, exploring scenarios, engaging in strategic conversations, making decisions, defining metrics, and committing to actions. This process helps organizations anticipate long-term trends, make informed decisions, and align their strategies with future possibilities.	Suggests a process that involves using the Strategy Canvas to identify value drivers and differentiators, formulating strategic options, and executing the chosen strategies. The process of developing a blue ocean strategy includes strategy formulation and execution, focusing on redefining industry boundaries and capturing new demand.	Presents a process known as the Strategy Choice Cascade, which involves defining a winning aspiration, determining where to play, identifying how to win, leveraging core capabilities, and aligning management systems. This process helps organizations align their resources, actions, and systems with the chosen strategic direction, ensuring effective execution of the strategy.	Emphasizes a disciplined process of building greatness through disciplined action. It highlights the importance of disciplined people and thought in executing strategies effectively.	Outlines an analysis, choice, and implementation process for competitive strategy. It involves analyzing the competitive environment using the five forces framework, making strategic choices, and implementing the chosen strategies. This process enables organizations to gain a competitive advantage by effectively positioning themselves within the competitive landscape.	Suggests an analysis, choice, and action process for strategy development. It involves analyzing the seven elements of strategy, making strategic choices, and taking action to implement the chosen strategies. This process helps organizations develop holistic strategies that consider various factors and trade-offs.	Highlights the importance of diagnosis, guiding policy, and overcoming obstacles. It emphasizes the process of diagnosing the challenges, formulating a guiding policy, and taking action to address the obstacles. This process helps organizations overcome hurdles, focus on key areas, and formulate effective strategies for success.

Practical Implementation	Monarch is written for practitioners and practice academics. Although research-based, it offers practical understanding and insights for organizations. The practical implementation tools include the organizational self-assessment, guides to develop and deploy strategies.	Provides practical tools for strategic analysis and decision-making. It encourages organizations to adapt their strategies to fit changing circumstances and different industry life cycle stages. The practical implementation involves utilizing the STRATAPLEX framework, conducting strategic analysis, and making informed decisions.	Emphasizes the application of theories and concepts to real-world cases. It helps readers develop strategic thinking skills and understand different perspectives on strategy. The practical implementation involves analyzing case studies, applying strategic theories and concepts, and developing a deeper understanding of strategy in action.	Emphasizes applying theories and concepts to develop strategic thinking skills. It encourages readers to understand different perspectives on strategy and apply them to real-world scenarios. The practical implementation involves analyzing case studies, formulating strategies, and understanding the impact of long-term trends on strategy development.	Provides practical guidance on strategy formulation and execution. It offers tools, such as the Strategy Canvas, to help organizations redefine industry boundaries, create uncontested market space, and capture new demand. The practical implementation involves utilizing these tools to develop innovative strategies, implementing them effectively, and driving market success.	Provides practical guidance on aligning resources, actions, and systems to execute the chosen strategic direction. It involves aligning the organization's structure, processes, and people with the strategic goals. The practical implementation focuses on developing alignment mechanisms, establishing performance metrics, and continuously monitoring and adjusting strategies to ensure effective execution.	Provides practical insights on leadership and disciplined execution. It emphasizes the importance of disciplined action, disciplined people, and disciplined thought in achieving sustained greatness. The practical implementation involves developing leadership skills, fostering a culture of discipline, and aligning actions with the organization's purpose and goals.	Provides practical guidance on gaining a competitive advantage through strategic positioning and resource allocation. It involves analyzing the competitive environment, making strategic choices, and implementing strategies effectively. The practical implementation focuses on understanding the competitive forces, developing strategic positioning, and aligning resources to outperform rivals.	Offers practical guidance on developing comprehensive strategies that consider various factors and trade-offs. It involves analyzing the seven elements of strategy, making strategic choices, and implementing the chosen strategies. The practical implementation focuses on evaluating arenas, identifying differentiators, selecting vehicles, and staging strategies effectively.	Provides practical guidance on overcoming obstacles, focusing on key areas, and formulating a guiding policy for effective strategic action. The practical implementation involves diagnosing challenges, formulating strategies, and aligning actions with the guiding policy. It emphasizes adapting strategies to the organization's context and industry dynamics to overcome obstacles and achieve strategic success.

(Continued)

TABLE 1.1 (Continued)

Book Title	Monarch	Your Strategy Needs a Strategy	Exploring Strategy	The Art of the Long View	Blue Ocean Strategy	Playing to Win	Good to Great	Competitive Strategy	The Art of Strategy	Good Strategy Bad Strategy
Perception on Industry Life Cycle	Perceives the industry life cycle as the primary backdrop for strategy development and deployment due to its implications and ongoing dynamic with organizations (industries are clusters of organizations).	Acknowledges that industry life cycle stages and context influence the choice and application of different strategies. It suggests that organizations consider the industry life cycle as a contextual factor when formulating strategies using the STRATAPLEX framework. By understanding the dynamics of the industry life cycle, organizations can adapt their strategies effectively and navigate the challenges and opportunities of each stage.	References the industry life cycle as part of the strategic analysis process but relies on the "business environment" as the contextual framing. It encourages organizations to consider the industry life cycle and its implications for strategy formulation. By understanding the industry life cycle dynamics, organizations can develop strategies that align with the specific stage and context they operate in, maximizing their competitive advantage and growth potential.	Recognizes the importance of understanding the industry life cycle in scenario planning and long-term strategic thinking. It suggests that organizations consider the industry life cycle when developing alternative futures. By anticipating the changes and challenges associated with each stage of the industry life cycle, organizations can develop flexible strategies and make informed decisions that align with the future industry landscape.	Emphasizes considering the industry life cycle when identifying new market opportunities. By understanding the industry life cycle and the specific dynamics of each stage, organizations can identify blue ocean opportunities and create new markets. It suggests that organizations explore industry boundaries and market space across different industry life cycle stages to drive innovation and capture new demand.	Recognizes the industry life cycle as a crucial consideration when making strategic choices. By understanding the industry life cycle stage, organizations can identify winning aspirations, determine where to compete, and devise strategies to outperform competitors. It suggests that organizations align their strategic choices with the specific industry life cycle stage to maximize their competitive advantage and drive success.	Does not explicitly focus on the industry life cycle, but emphasizes the importance of disciplined execution and finding what an organization can excel at. Organizations can leverage their strengths and unique capabilities to succeed in different industry life cycle stages. The book highlights the need for sustained focus, disciplined people, and aligned actions to drive long-term success, regardless of the specific industry life cycle stage.	Considers the industry life cycle within the analysis of competitive forces and positioning opportunities. By understanding the industry life cycle dynamics, organizations can identify strategic opportunities and determine effective competitive positioning. It suggests that organizations analyze the competitive forces within the context of the industry life cycle to develop strategies that leverage industry dynamics and gain a competitive advantage.	Recognizes the importance of understanding industry dynamics, including the industry life cycle, to develop a comprehensive strategy. By incorporating the industry life cycle into the analysis, organizations can assess the dynamics of each stage and position themselves strategically. It suggests that organizations consider various elements of strategy within the context of the industry life cycle to achieve competitive advantage and drive success.	Recognizes the industry life cycle as a key factor in formulating effective strategies. By diagnosing the challenges within the context of the industry life cycle stage, organizations can overcome obstacles and develop strategies that align with the specific dynamics of each stage. It emphasizes the importance of understanding the organization's context and the industry dynamics to formulate effective strategies that drive success throughout the industry life cycle.

How This Book Perceives Strategy and Why?

In this book, we approach strategy by establishing a profound linkage between the organization as a living organism (CAS) and the industry life cycle, which exhibits similar living traits. This "living" aspect of organizations and industries underscores their organic, dynamic, and interconnected nature. This recognition encourages business leaders to view their organizations and industries as adaptive systems that require ongoing strategic attention and a proactive approach to remain competitive and successful.

By perceiving strategy as what an organization needs to do to survive and thrive in an industry, we recognize that strategies should be informed by the phase of the industry life cycle in which the organization operates and competes.

Just as living organisms go through various stages of growth, maturity, and decline, industries also exhibit similar patterns of evolution. Each phase of the industry life cycle presents distinct challenges and opportunities that organizations must navigate strategically. By aligning our strategies with the specific phase of the industry life cycle, we can enhance our chances of survival and maximize our potential for success.

So, let's hone in on this idea....

Organization and the Industry, They Breath Similarly

Let's consider the analogy of an organization as a living organism within the context of the industry life cycle. In the embryonic phase, the organization is like a newborn, full of potential but vulnerable to external forces. It requires strategies that focus on disruption and innovation to establish a strong position in the market. This aligns with the concept of the organization as a CAS, capable of adapting and learning in a rapidly changing environment.

As the industry enters the growth phase, the organization gains strength and begins to flourish. It is analogous to an adolescent organism experiencing growth spurts. Here, strategies must focus on differentiation or cost leadership to establish a competitive advantage. This requires an understanding of the dynamic interplay of internal capabilities and external market forces.

As the industry progresses, it enters the shakeout phase, similar to an organism experiencing a period of intense competition for resources. During this stage, weaker players are often eliminated, and the focus shifts to optimizing efficiency and scaling operations. Strategies must emphasize consolidation, cost control, and strengthening competitive positioning to survive this critical transition and prepare for long-term sustainability.

As the industry matures, the organization reaches its prime, much like an mature organism in its prime years. Strategies in the maturity phase should emphasize sustaining and expanding market share by refining the value proposition, exploring new market spaces, or entering new segments. The organization must navigate the competitive landscape and changes in customer preferences.

Eventually, industries enter the decline phase, like the aging process of a living organism. Strategies during this phase should focus on managing decline gracefully, exploring opportunities in related industries, or reinventing the organization's purpose. By recognizing the signs of decline and proactively adapting strategies, organizations can extend their life cycle and transition to new phases.

Fitbit and the Wearable Technology Industry

The wearable technology and fitness industry, at its inception in the late 2000s, represented a transformative force in merging technology with health and fitness. This burgeoning industry would witness significant evolution through five distinct phases, paralleling the journey of organizations within it.

- Embryonic Phase (Late 2000s—Early 2010s): As the industry took its initial steps, Fitbit emerged as a trailblazer during the embryonic phase. Introducing the first generation of fitness trackers, Fitbit's early focus on basic activity tracking laid the foundation for what would become a transformative era for wearable technology.
- Growth Phase (Mid-2010s): Fitbit, amidst the industry's growth, experienced a meteoric rise. The mid-2010s marked a period of rapid market acceptance, with Fitbit expanding its product line to include more advanced features. The introduction of heart rate monitoring and sleep tracking showcased the organization's commitment to innovation in response to increasing consumer demands.
- Shakeout Phase (Late-2010s): However, as the industry matured, the late 2010s brought challenges. Intensified competition from tech giants such as Apple and Samsung marked the shakeout phase. Fitbit, like its counterparts, faced the need to navigate market consolidation and adapt to the changing landscape, leading to strategic responses to maintain its position.
- Maturity Phase (2020s): Entering the 2020s, Fitbit found itself in a solidified position within the mature wearable technology market. Continuous product enhancements and strategic partnerships characterized this phase, reflecting the organization's resilience and adaptability. The industry, now stable, boasted a variety of wearables offered by established players.
- Decline Phase (2020+): Hypothetically, during a decline phase, challenges would likely emerge for Fitbit and the wearable technology industry.

Potential market saturation and shifting consumer preferences may prompt Fitbit to explore new markets or integrate with broader health ecosystems. Navigating the decline phase requires strategic decisions to address challenges posed by emerging technologies.

Each phase has characteristics and implications that might not be identical between organizations and the industries they compete (and thrive) within, but this commonality is informed by several realities. In other words, in synergizing dynamics and evolution of organizations and industries we start to see that they evolve in tandem; they influence and shape each other. This interplay can be understood through several key dynamics, listed as follows, that illustrate how organizations and industries co-evolve, adapting to external forces and internal capabilities:

- *Adaptation to Environment*: Just like living organisms, organizations and industries must adapt to their changing environments to survive and thrive. Organizations must respond to shifts in consumer preferences, technological advancements, and regulatory changes. Similarly, industries need to evolve to meet new demands, market trends, and disruptive innovations.
- *Evolution and Growth*: Both organizations and industries go through stages of growth, maturity, and decline. Organizations start as small start-ups, mature into established companies, and some eventually decline or reinvent themselves. Similarly, industries emerge, grow, and may eventually become saturated or replaced by new ones.
- *Learning and Knowledge Acquisition*: Living entities continuously learn and acquire new skills and knowledge, the same applies to organizations and industries. Organizations invest in research, training, and development to stay competitive. Industries foster innovation, encourage knowledge-sharing, and often collaborate to tackle shared challenges.
- *Competitive Interactions*: Just as living organisms compete for resources, organizations compete for market share, talent, and customers. Similarly, industries experience competitive dynamics, where companies compete for dominance, leading to strategic moves, mergers, and acquisitions.
- *Resilience and Adaptability*: Living entities exhibit resilience and adaptability in the face of adversity. Similarly, successful organizations and industries are resilient, capable of recovering from setbacks and adapting their strategies to changing conditions. Industries follow organizations' suit and emulate their behavior as they are made up of them.
- *Interdependence*: Living entities often rely on each other for mutual benefits, creating interdependence. In the same way, organizations and industries are interconnected and interdependent. Within an organization,

skill teams and business units collaborate cross-functionally to achieve the organization's objectives. Similarly, suppliers and customers in an industry rely on each other's success.

■ ***Emergence of New Entities***: Living systems can give rise to new organisms through reproduction or evolution. Similarly, successful organizations may spawn new ventures, subsidiaries, or spin-offs. Industries may experience the emergence of new sectors or sub-industries driven by innovation.

■ ***Capacity for Change***: Living entities can change over time. Similarly, organizations and industries must be adaptable and open to change. Those that resist change or fail to innovate risk becoming obsolete.

When we understand the industry life cycle, we become able to anticipate future trends, an ability that prepares us for the challenges and opportunities that lie ahead. In a way, the industry life cycle phase becomes the backdrop that informs our frameworks for strategic decision-making, resource allocation, and market positioning. By aligning our strategies with the life cycle phase of the industry we compete in, we increase the likelihood of business survival and enable our organizations to thrive in an ever-changing business landscape.

A Precursor for Macroenvironment, Complexity Differential, Organization as CAS, and the Industry Life Cycle: To fully grasp the significance of aligning strategies with the industry life cycle, it is important to examine several key concepts including the macroenvironment, complexity differential, the organization as a CAS, and the industry life cycle. These concepts lay the foundation for understanding the dynamic nature of strategy and its interaction with the industry environment.

The Macroenvironment: Embracing the External Influences

The macroenvironment refers to the set of external factors that influence an organization's operations and strategic decisions. It encompasses a wide range of elements including social and cultural trends, economic conditions, technological advancements, political and regulatory forces, and ecological factors. The macroenvironment provides an implicating context in which organizations operate and must be considered when developing strategies. Understanding the macroenvironment allows organizations to identify opportunities, anticipate threats, and adapt their strategies accordingly.

The consensus among industry experts, academics, and academic practitioners is that understanding the macroenvironment is crucial for identifying emerging trends, anticipating shifts in customer preferences, and recognizing potential disruptions. By conducting thorough macroenvironmental assessments, organizations can gain insights into the forces at play and make informed strategic choices. This proactive approach enables organizations to align their strategies with the changing landscape and capitalize on emerging opportunities.

For example, the rapid adoption of digital technology has significantly impacted numerous industries. Companies like Amazon and Netflix recognized the shift in consumer behavior toward online shopping and digital media consumption, respectively. By aligning their strategies with these technological advancements and leveraging the opportunities presented, they achieved remarkable success in their respective industries.

Complexity Differential (The Sophisticated Way of Referring to "Reacting to Market Conditions")

If you imagine a CAS ("the organization") nested within its macroenvironment and recall how it reacts to changes in its surroundings, then complexity differential is nothing but the difference between the complexity of the organization and the complexity of its macroenvironment. What is in the complexity domain for both? Information, data, market signals, structures, etc.

Complexity in organizations plays a critical role in strategic planning. Its magnitude and scope vary from one organization to the other. Similarly, complexity differential could mean different things to different people, but for our purpose, we will borrow its definition from Lumann's Social Systems Theory: the inherent complexity and differentiation among different elements or components within a social system. Proposed by Niklas Luhmann, a German sociologist, social systems theory emphasizes the study of communication and how it forms the basis of all social interactions. According to Luhmann, society is composed of various interconnected subsystems, each exhibiting complexity and differentiation. The term "complexity differential" highlights that different subsystems within a society possess distinct characteristics, functions, and structures, leading to diversity and variety in their operations. These subsystems can range from organizations, institutions, and communities to more specific domains like the economy, education, and politics.

Luhmann's theory suggests that social systems maintain their complexity by managing the flow of information and communication effectively. The complexity differential arises from the intricate web of relationships, exchanges, and interdependencies among various subsystems, and how they process and interpret information differently, all of which are part of the macroenvironment. Sequentially, complexity differential becomes the medium between an organization and its macroenvironment. In a way, managing the complexity differential is about managing the signals and signs emitted from the macroenvironment. Understanding this complexity is crucial for comprehending how social systems operate and evolve over time.

COMPLEXITY DIFFERENTIAL—AT LENGTH

The strategic importance of tackling complexity has grown for organizations responding to the ever-evolving macro-environmental landscape. This strategic priority often involves the simplification of organizational structures and processes as a vital business objective for ensuring organizational survival. A wealth of research has demonstrated that organizations tend to increase their internal complexity in response to changes in environmental complexity. Effectively managing this complexity differential is crucial to prevent internal complexity from exceeding environmental complexity. However, the research focus has primarily been on how organizations increase their internal complexity, neglecting the drivers of this complexity or the mechanisms through which it hinders strategic change implementation. This paper aims to address this gap by utilizing strategic episodes as a social mechanism to examine the drivers of internal complexity.

Organizations, as social systems (Luhmann, 1973), are essentially networks of communications that emerge over time (Nassehi, 2005, p. 181). The concepts of "social systems" and "complexity" are interconnected, with the latter referring to the levels of elements that constitute the former. Therefore, the more elements that exist in a system (along with their interrelations), the higher the complexity (Luhmann, 1975). Social systems theory offers a sociological perspective based on complexity; it aims to explain how social systems (organizations) respond to environmental challenges. This theory suggests that a social system should ideally be less complex than its surrounding environment (Luhmann, 1995). This differential is necessary for the system to operate efficiently by selectively processing a subset of the information available in the surrounding environment. Therefore, for organizational survival, the complexity differential must be manageable, requiring ongoing adjustments to the system's complexity. In other words, if the environmental complexity increases (causing an increase in the complexity differential), the internal complexity must also increase in line with it to reduce the complexity differential down to a manageable level, ensuring that the system's complexity does not exceed the complexity of the surrounding environment.

Here, we distinguish between environmental and internal complexity, aligning with existing research. "Environmental complexity" refers to "the number of items or elements that must be dealt with simultaneously by an organization" (Scott, 1992, p. 230). This environmental complexity has a profound influence on how organizations respond to these elements. Early research in cybernetics (Ashby, 1956) laid the foundation for the assumption that organizations adapt to the increase in environmental complexity by adjusting their processes, structures, routines, and rules, a notion leveraged in several studies (Daft and Lengel, 1986; Galbraith, 1982; Galunic and Eisenhardt, 1994). This inquiry has been central to organizational research across many decades, from the 1960s (Burns and Stalker, 1966; Emery and Trist, 1965; Lawrence and Lorsch, 1967) to more recent work (Chandler, 2014; Child and Rodrigues, 2011; Faulconbridge and Muzio, 2015; Reus et al., 2009). Much of this research has examined organizational adaptation to environmental complexity at the individual level (Ghoshal and Nohria, 1989; Pache and Santos, 2010; Scott and Meyer, 1987; Siggelkow and Rivkin, 2005; Weick, 1976), primarily leveraging mathematical complexity theory to advance concepts such as unpredictability, chaos, and non-linearity (Anderson, 1999; Boisot and Child, 1999; Maguire et al., 2006; Tsoukas, 1998).

Conversely, "internal complexity" refers to the organization's internal processes (Daft and Lengel, 1986; Tushman and Nadler, 1978) and structures (Blau, 1970; Child and Mansfield, 1972; Hsu et al., 1983) and can be increased as a result of modifying organizational processes, functional specialization, or structural differentiation (Schneider et al., 2016). Recognizing the impact of internal complexity on organizational performance, additional research has been conducted to advance the development of complexity measurement systems using quantitative/mathematical and qualitative input. Among the early building blocks for this research was determining the degree of complexity of a critical path network, namely, complexity network coefficient (CNC), which has been defined as the "quotient of activities squared divided by events or proceeding work items squared divided by work items" (Kaimann, 1974, p. 172). The CNC and similar metrics have been instrumental in quantifying the complexity of organizational processes and structures, aiding in the analysis and management of internal complexity.

To further explain the modification of organizational processes as a driver of internal complexity (in response to environmental complexity), researchers suggest that an organization could increase communication density by increasing the number and diversity of internal stakeholders in communication. In other words, aligning the range of communication (increase in internal complexity) to the range of changing elements in their environment (increase in environmental complexity). More practically, increasing communication density pertains to increasing the frequency of meetings and discussions and increasing the number of participants in those activities (Daft and Lengel, 1986), an important notion to be argued in later sections. This highlights the interconnectedness of internal and external complexity, as organizations adapt their communication patterns and processes to better understand and respond to environmental demands.

To further explain functional specialization as a driver of internal complexity, researchers suggest that groups and individuals in organizations tend to focus on specialized activities within their functions (Child and Mansfield, 1972). This notation enables a targeted response to information in the environment (environmental complexity). In terms of structural differentiation, internal complexity can be modified through vertical and horizontal differentiation. While "vertical differentiation" refers to the number of managerial/hierarchical levels in an organization (Hsu et al., 1983), "horizontal differentiation" refers to the number of business units, groups, or divisions (Blau, 1970). Both tend to increase as internal complexity increases (Aldrich and Herker, 1977) in a way necessary to process information in a more targeted manner (Tushman and Nadler, 1978). This structural differentiation allows organizations to develop specialized expertise and respond more effectively to specific environmental challenges.

Along with the "magnitude" of change in internal complexity (manifested in the number of actions taken by the organization) as a response to changes in environmental complexity comes the notion of "variety" of change (referring to the range of activities taken), which was first introduced by Ashby (1956) as "requisite variety." Following this notion is that the larger the requisite variety, the greater the extent to which the system (organization) can adapt (or handle) its environmental complexity. In other words, the organization must have sufficient variety to respond to environmental complexity. Requisite variety emphasizes the importance of having a diverse range of responses available to address the diverse challenges posed by a complex environment.

For the increase of requisite variety (and therefore, reduction of complexity differential), organizations must be able to leverage their structures and processes to acquire and process information about their environment (Aguilar, 1967). Due to the common ambiguity and lack of clarity in the information available to the organization, it can be subject to broad interpretation (Daft and Mackintosh, 1981). This view informs the need for organizations to create mechanisms for processing information about market conditions, trends, competitive landscape, and technological development (Daft and Weick, 1984; Tushman and Nadler, 1978).

These mechanisms enable organizations to make sense of the vast and often ambiguous information in their environment and translate it into actionable insights.

Theoretical Foundation

The theoretical foundation of this paper is built upon two interconnected pillars derived from social systems theory: the concept of internal complexity and the concept of "episodes" as a social mechanism for driving strategic change. The following sections focus on these two pillars, establishing a link between internal complexity and strategic episodes and proposing that the latter can be utilized as a strategic tool to examine the former.

Internal Complexity within Strategic Episodes

To construct a robust theoretical foundation for this study, we begin by discussing the concept of internal complexity as posited by social systems theory. Subsequently, we review pertinent concepts from organizational complexity literature to elucidate how internal complexity influences strategy work. By employing this framework, internal complexity is grounded in strategic episodes to understand how episodes, over time, contribute to the formation and adaptation of requisite variety. According to social systems theory, internal complexity is contingent upon environmental complexity. As a result, a social system selectively processes information (aspects) from its environment and responds to them because they are perceived as relevant and essential for the organization's survival. Conversely, the system disregards other information deemed irrelevant and unnecessary for organizational survival (Schreyogg and Steinmann, 1987). Luhmann (1997) suggested that this ongoing selection process contributes to constructing specific organizational tasks, thereby maintaining operational efficiency. Due to the constant state of flux in the organizational environment, influenced by political, economic, socio-economic, technological, and physical forces, as suggested by Emery and Trist (1965) and Child and Rodrigues (2011), organizations must continuously adjust their internal complexity to ensure their survival.

Utilizing internal complexity, as positioned by social systems theory, serves as the first pillar for establishing the theoretical foundation of this study. While understanding how organizations increase their internal complexity in response to rising environmental complexity (as a means of maintaining manageable levels of complexity differential) is crucial, it is equally important to recognize the evolution of how organizations build internal complexity. In other words, drawing on insights from Schneider et al. (2016), examinations of extensive and "traditional" organizations from the 1960s and 1970s (Blau, 1970; Child, 1973) are likely to yield different observations in contemporary organizational contexts. For instance, the evolution of organizational structures along the centralization spectrum (from highly centralized to more decentralized) has created a gap in organizational literature concerning complexity measurement. This highlights the need for an evolved mechanism to measure complexity in social systems. Consequently, it is essential to re-examine the organizational structures and processes through which organizations build internal complexity.

Given the limited research focusing on the managerial perspective on internal complexity in highly complex organizations, there is a need to identify a practical mechanism to understand this perspective. Schneider et al. (2016, p. 20) suggest that researchers can utilize various concepts, ranging from mental models (Porac and Thomas, 1990) to cognitive categories (Barr, 1998; Kaplan, 2008) and attention (Ocasio, 2011), to make sense of managers' responses to complexity. Methods such as qualitative comparative analysis (Fiss, 2007) could help identify configurations of structures and processes that innovative organizations employ to represent their environments in a highly complex way. Such a practical mechanism can be derived from another tenet of social systems theory: the concept of an "episode," which forms the second pillar of the theoretical foundation of this study.

Episodes as a Social Mechanism for Strategic Change

Grounded in social systems theory, the fundamental element of all social systems is communication (Luhmann, 1986, 1995), encompassing any synthesis of written, verbal, visual, or physical information. As an interaction between at least two entities (or individuals), the effectiveness of communication, from a sociological perspective, is determined by the level of understanding achieved rather than the intention behind the utterance (von Foerster and Pörksen, 1998). Social systems theory posits that social systems are inherently systems of communication. Because communication is the product of the communication process itself, social change can be explained through the logic of the communication system.

Furthermore, Luhmann's theory proposes an evolutionary model of social change, serving as the mechanism that facilitates communication in societies and organizations. According to this model, the communicative system produces mutations, some of which are selected for change.

This applies to both first-order change (incremental) and second-order change (reflexive). Second-order change refers to the social system's (or organization's) ability to question its structure. The mechanism through which such reflective discourse can be pursued is introduced as an "episode," a concept denoting a communication event (or sequence of events) with a defined beginning and end.

A unique aspect of the "episode" concept is that it can take place without disrupting the system, often manifesting as a typical business meeting with a designated start and end time. In this context, a goal-oriented episode is one where the communication event is focused on a specific objective; thus, achieving the goal marks the conclusion of the episode. Time constraints, aligned with standard practice (e.g., the allotted time for a business meeting), can also terminate an episode. Additionally, an episode (like a business meeting) can be concluded regardless of goal attainment and can be established spontaneously (a one-off meeting) or as a recurring cadence based on business needs. The end of an episode also signifies the end of restrictions associated with it.

Through a series or sequence of episodes, the system can temporarily modify its structure for the duration of each episode (Luhmann, 1990). However, it is crucial to clarify that the episode itself does not dictate the change in structure, nor does it offer insight into the relationship between internal and external structures. When episodes are employed to drive strategic change, it is important to recognize the shift in communication context and differentiate between strategic and operational conversations (Roos and von Krogh, 1996). Since this shift can be observed in episodes, strategizing episodes can be understood as temporal junctures for the shift in communication. Notably, during this switching via episodes, the existing structures are merely suspended, not damaged or destroyed. This raises questions about what and how structures typically change at the onset of an episode.

Returning to strategizing episodes, Roos and von Krogh (1996) emphasize that the outcome of the strategy process hinges on communication characteristics such as "who talks to whom, why they talk, what they talk about, and when these conversations take place" (p. 55). A central question posed by Hendry et al. (2003) revolves around how structures for strategic episodes are determined, acknowledging that the organization does not have complete control over this determination. This inquiry is valid because organizations are rarely closed systems. Strategic change is often associated with changes in the organization's environment, including the appointment of a new CEO, particularly if hired from outside the organization (Grinyer et al., 1988; Johnson, 1992). Other triggers for strategic change include seeking counsel from external consultants or industry experts (Mezias et al., 2001; Pettigrew, 1985). In such cases, it is common for discursive structures to be introduced into the organization (Pettigrew, 1985; Weber, 1998). This aligns with the core of what an episode strives to achieve: a space where structures are temporarily suspended to enable strategic change to unfold.

Building upon the summarized reflections on Luhmann's theory of strategic episodes by Hendry et al. (2003), this paper draws on three key insights regarding strategic episodes: (1) they are an integral and recurring part of organizational life, (2) they can serve as a mechanism to confirm, sustain, and reinforce change, and (3) they represent focused, routine strategic practice. Applying Luhmann's framework for episodes suggests an emphasis on three aspects: initiation, termination, and conduction of the episode. In other words, following guidance from this framework, a systematic study can be conducted to examine how strategic episodes are set up, how they are concluded, and how they are carried out.

Leveraging Strategic Episodes as a Mechanism to Examine Internal Complexity

An essential function of social systems is to interpret environmental complexity, which involves detecting events, technological trends, and other factors in the task environment that impact the organization and its strategic focus. This interpretive function, referred to as requisite variety, allows social systems to develop internal structures and processes for producing information to scan the environment and create a certain degree of internal (i.e., organizational) complexity. This process occurs because organizations tend to reduce the complexity differential between the environment and their internal activities to achieve their organizational goals. In essence, requisite variety is about how a social system, through episodes, interprets environmental complexity and, consequently, how it develops a certain degree of internal complexity.

Episodes, according to social systems theory, are the very social mechanisms that enable reflexivity within organizations. To instigate reflexivity, these mechanisms need to be temporarily "suspended" from regular organizational routines. Thus, episodes can be seen as lapses in organizational life where individuals deliberately, either in planned or impromptu ways, dedicate time and effort to address and reflect on strategic matters. Building on Luhmann's concept of episodes, Hendry et al. (2003) theorized the role of strategic episodes in enabling strategic change as a recurring and essential part of organizational life. During the temporary suspension of organizational structures throughout an episode, the organization "distances itself from itself in such a way as to allow it to observe itself and from that position initiate a change of its structures" (Hendry et al., 2003).

Case Study and Data Description

In the pursuit of a case study that would yield particularly enlightening insights (Eisenhardt and Graebner, 2007), the aim was to select an organization that met two key criteria: (1) undergoing a strategic change triggered by changes in the organizational environment (e.g., the appointment of a new CEO), and (2) actively addressing complexity as a key topic on its strategic agenda. SAC (a pseudonym used to protect the organization's identity), a major corporation in the automotive industry, fulfilled these criteria. SAC is a large, globally operating organization with numerous managerial levels and a highly complex decision-making process. Recognizing the adverse impact of internal complexity on operational efficiency and business performance, the newly appointed CEO spearheaded a series of strategic changes aimed at tackling internal complexity, with a particular focus on simplifying business processes. Consequently, complexity reduction emerged as a strategic business initiative, featuring prominently in senior leadership forums and cascaded throughout the organization as a critical strategic priority.

Framework for Analysis: Episodes and Participants

To structure the analysis framework for this case study, two fundamental questions were posed to identify the relevant episodes and participants, providing a baseline for the research. The first question was, "How are episodes happening?" Answering this question required aligning on the need for these episodes to be easily identifiable and naturally occurring as part of the strategic change process. Therefore, executive forums, formal meetings, and workshops centered on the topic of complexity were selected for study. The episodes included in this case consisted of:

> Workshops with subject matter experts (SMEs): These workshops involved asking SMEs to perform specific activities in support of the defined strategic initiative (complexity reduction) or reflect upon it. These interactions aimed to generate substantial debate, conversations, buy-ins, and consensus.

Formal Meetings: These meetings were held to discuss progress on complexity reduction, address necessary amendments, and allocate resources to support the workshops.

Executive Report Outs: These forums were used to communicate awareness of the complexity reduction initiative and obtain strategic direction from executives when required, fostering dialog and ensuring alignment.

The design of diverse episodes aimed to ensure diversified communication among participants. The second question was, "Who are the participants?" The participants included members of the top management team (TMT) championing the complexity reduction initiative, mid-level management, and SMEs, who were often instrumental in deep-dive sessions due to their specialized knowledge and expertise.

Grounding the Case in Social Systems Theory

To firmly ground the case study in social systems theory, a set of preliminaries were clearly defined to guide the research:

Organization as a Social System: An organization is viewed as a social system, primarily a system of communications rather than actions.

Reflexive Communication: Communication within social systems is reflexive, prompting participants to reflect on and question organizational structures and processes for strategic purposes.

Change Generation: Reflexive communication among organizational participants generates changes that enable the organization to pursue its strategic objectives.

Episodes as Loci of Reflection: Strategic episodes serve as the primary loci for reflection and discourse, where changes are initiated and implemented.

Data Collection and Triangulation

The primary dataset consisted of recent materials spanning from 2020 to 2022, informed by the new strategic direction. These materials included strategy documents (19 items), transcribed town hall meetings (9 items), and meeting minutes (31 items). To gain a comprehensive understanding of SAC, publicly available material, including annual reports and published media, was also reviewed. The objective was to focus on SAC's perspective on the evolution of internal complexity. To triangulate the data and ensure the validity of findings, 29 interviews were conducted with various participants in the strategic episodes, ranging from TMT members to

SMEs. The interview protocol consisted of seven open-ended questions revolving around complexity drivers, designed to (1) define context to establish the organizational context and the nature of the strategic change initiative; (2) expound complexity issues to explore the specific complexity issues faced by the organization; (3) explore sentiment on internal complexity drivers to uncover participants' sentiments and perceptions regarding the drivers of internal complexity; and (4) explore reflexiveness to investigate the extent to which reflexive communication occurred during strategic episodes.

The rationale for each question was provided to ensure clarity and focus. Interviews were conducted in a semi-structured format, allowing for flexibility and probing, and notes were meticulously captured as part of the data analysis process.

Data Analysis

In alignment with the conceptualization of internal complexity within social systems theory, the data analysis centered around strategic episodes to explore the drivers of internal complexity within SAC. The research employed a four-step process based on inductive case analysis in conjunction with diverse data sources.

Document Review: Internal and external corporate strategy/complexity documents, including publications and meeting minutes, were reviewed over a two-year period. This review aimed to establish a baseline narrative of the organizational perception of internal complexity and its role in strategic planning. Principles of qualitative content analysis (Silverman, 2001) were applied to extract themes related to internal complexity and their emergence throughout the study.

- ■ Artifact Collation: Corresponding artifacts were gathered to further examine the structure and intended messaging of the documents, shedding light on the evolving correlation between strategy and complexity throughout the study. Specifically, strategy and complexity documents (publications and meeting minutes) were reviewed in pairs to gain insights into how internal complexity influenced strategic planning at SAC over the two-year period.
- ■ Interview Analysis: Responses from interviews (both written and transcribed) were analyzed to identify recurring themes and synthesize information. These responses were then reflected upon in the

context of corresponding documents to contextualize findings and validate consistency in the organizational evolution centered on internal complexity. This approach aimed to understand the perceptions of TMT members and SMEs regarding internal complexity and its drivers in strategic planning by comparing and contrasting related documents over the study period.

■ Strategic Episode Coding: Strategic episodes, encompassing workshops, meetings, and executive forums where topics related to strategy planning and internal complexity were discussed, were coded. These episodes were coded by quarter over two years, aligning with SAC's newly implemented quarterly performance review cadence. This coding aimed to compare participants' sentiments and assessments of what drove internal complexity over eight quarters, triggered by the announcement of complexity reduction as a strategic priority for the organization.

It is important to clarify that this approach does not imply that SAC did not contemplate complexity before the new CEO's arrival. Rather, it highlights the prioritization of complexity reduction as a key business objective under the new leadership. The significance of quarterly coding lies in its alignment with the routine quarterly goal-setting and performance review process at SAC. This coding approach was adopted to uncover any potential links between internal complexity and organizational goal-setting processes. The review of responses from strategic episodes alongside strategy documentation aimed to understand how the content was "acknowledged, mobilized, or foregrounded in the context of language use" (Schoeneborn et al., 2014, p. 308) when discussing strategic planning and internal complexity topics (or raising related issues). Comparing and contrasting coded episodes and correlating them to documents and interviews was crucial. This structured approach facilitated the transition between theory and data (Alvesson and Kärreman, 2007), employing conceptual constructs from the literature as an analytical lens (Alasuutari, 1996).

Contemplating Competing Priorities in Strategic Episodes

The initial section of this paper has illuminated how the lack of clarity surrounding organizational goals can impede the progress of discussions aimed at achieving strategic objectives. As more stakeholders become involved in the strategic process, the emergence of competing goals (or priorities) presents an additional layer of complexity. The longitudinal data utilized in this study have facilitated an examination of this recurring process over a span of two years, enabling a deeper understanding of how the recursive nature of strategic processes contributes to internal complexity within organizations.

This section focuses on the complexities arising from competing strategic priorities among various stakeholders and their impact on internal complexity at SAC. Recalling the association between strategic goal-setting and the top management team (TMT) discussed earlier, a senior executive aptly summarizes this phenomenon by stating, "Objective setting is getting leaders to agree, and that is a lot." This statement underscores the inherent challenges in aligning the diverse perspectives and interests of top-level executives when defining organizational goals.

To further explore this issue, participants were asked, "In what way do you see these complexity drivers preventing the organization from achieving the corporate strategic objectives?" Their responses highlighted strategic competing priorities, which often lead to competition for resources, and the necessity of aligning various stakeholders, resulting in a need for multiple approvals to proceed with strategic initiatives. These competing priorities and the associated alignment challenges can significantly hinder the organization's ability to efficiently and effectively implement strategic changes.

To gain deeper insights into these dynamics, participants were asked to recall "a couple of episodes where one was easy (clear/straightforward) to define the complexity drivers while the other was hard." Their responses consistently converged on a central theme: the influence of stakeholder dynamics and the need to consider numerous competing priorities. Participants noted that "easy" episodes were often characterized by the relative absence of stakeholder interactions, such as instances where teams focused on technical aspects of IT/automated systems or followed established structured processes. In contrast, "hard" episodes typically arose when participants had to navigate the complexities of multiple stakeholders with diverse and often conflicting strategic priorities. This unprompted distinction between "easy" and "hard" episodes emphasizes the significant impact of grappling with competing priorities on internal complexity.

The strategy-as-practice literature, which views strategy as a situated and socially accomplished activity, offers valuable insights into these dynamics. Jarzabkowski et al. (2007) examined strategy meetings as ongoing social practices, highlighting their implications for the flow of strategic activity through stabilization or destabilization within organizations. In this perspective, strategy unfolds as an interaction between broader social practices and the micro-level actions, interactions, and negotiations in which participants (actors) engage to construct strategic activity (Johnson et al., 2003; Whittington, 2006; Jarzabkowski et al., 2007). This dynamic was evident in the observed meetings within SAC, where participants utilized micro-practices to advance strategic actions, demonstrating the link between strategy meetings and consequential strategic outcomes. The presence of competing priorities and the need for negotiation and compromise among stakeholders can significantly influence the trajectory of strategic activity and the resulting outcomes.

An interesting concept that emerged from the data was the need to "grease the tracks" to overcome the friction caused by competing priorities and advance discussions during strategic episodes. Participants emphasized that recognizing the multitude of competing priorities and the associated need for various decisions and approvals often requires significant resources to facilitate and navigate the complexities involved in achieving organizational goals. This "greasing the tracks" phenomenon can involve activities such as building coalitions, managing conflict, and securing buy-in from key stakeholders. It is a crucial aspect of navigating the complexities of competing priorities and ensuring the successful implementation of strategic initiatives.

Additionally, the concept of "cooperation" emerged as another reaction to competing priorities. Participants highlighted the importance of teams being cooperative and flexible in reacting to multiple and competing agendas, especially when facing changes in direction from senior leadership. This cooperative approach is essential for managing the tensions and conflicts that can arise when different stakeholders have different priorities. By fostering a culture of cooperation and collaboration, organizations can create a more conducive environment for addressing competing priorities and achieving strategic goals.

The findings of this study also underscore the influence of shifting strategic direction and the clarity (or lack thereof) of cascaded objectives on internal complexity within SAC. When strategic direction changes, it can lead to confusion and misalignment among stakeholders, as they try to interpret and adjust their priorities accordingly. This can result in a proliferation of competing priorities and a lack of clarity regarding the most important goals to pursue. To mitigate this issue, it is crucial for organizations to communicate strategic changes clearly and consistently to all stakeholders, ensuring that everyone understands the new direction and how it impacts their individual and team goals.

Returning to goal-setting theory, this section focuses on the concept of "bottom-line outcomes" as a key element in understanding competing priorities. Locke and Latham (1990) suggest that focusing on bottom-line outcomes can serve as a unifying goal for employees to strive toward. While the term "bottom line" is often used in financial contexts, it can also refer to the most important factor or consideration in any given situation. In the context of organizations, the bottom line can be interpreted as the ultimate objective or goal that the organization is trying to achieve.

The concept of bottom-line mentality (BLM) refers to a phenomenon where employees prioritize the bottom line above all else (Greenbaum et al., 2012). While subscribing to the BLM model can have positive effects on organizational profitability (Brenner and Molander, 1977; Treviño et al., 2006, 2014) and has been linked to employee rewards (Crotts et al., 2005; Drucker, 1963; Latham and Locke, 2007; Pringle and Longenecker, 1982), it can also have negative consequences (Wolfe, 1988). The issue with BLM is that employees' singular focus on bottom-line outcomes can lead to the neglect of other organizational priorities, diminishing their attention to the dynamics among actions needed to achieve multiple goals. This can create a situation where different departments or teams within the organization are working toward different goals, potentially leading to conflict and hindering the organization's overall performance.

McGrath (2001) also offers insights into goal difficulty, highlighting how challenging goals can demand significant attention from employees, impacting their perception and thinking about other workplace priorities (Kanfer and Ackerman, 1989; Locke and Latham, 1984; Locke et al., 1981). Practically speaking, striving to achieve challenging goals consumes cognitive resources, limiting the mental capacity available for other organizational goals. This suggests that when employees are focused on achieving a particularly challenging goal, they may be less able to consider and address other important priorities, potentially leading to a neglect of those priorities and an increase in internal complexity.

Therefore, both the number of goals (competing priorities) and the difficulty of individual goals can contribute to internal complexity. Both factors require employees to contemplate and prioritize, further adding to the complexity of the situation. In the context of strategic episodes, this can manifest as conflicting viewpoints, disagreements about priorities, and difficulties in reaching consensus. To effectively manage internal complexity in strategic episodes, it is crucial for organizations to establish clear priorities, foster a culture of cooperation and collaboration, and provide adequate resources and support to help employees navigate the complexities involved in achieving multiple goals.

Organization as a CAS: Embracing Adaptability and Emergence

Viewing organizations as CASs highlights their inherently complex and dynamic nature. Why? Because CASs are collections of interacting elements that exhibit emergent behavior, adaptability to changing surroundings, and self-organization. These CASs respond to internal and external stimuli (complexity differential) in the macroenvironment. They learn from their experiences and adapt their behaviors accordingly; much like organizations.

Embracing the CAS perspective emphasizes the importance of adaptability in strategy development and deployment (also known as formulation and execution). Organizations need to foster a culture that encourages emergent behavior and supports experimentation. This enables organizations to respond effectively to changes in the business environment and seize opportunities that emerge.

Google, an organization known for its dynamic and innovative culture, encourages employees to utilize a significant portion of their time on independent projects; an approach that fosters a spirit of experimentation and drives innovation. It enables the company to adapt swiftly to changing market dynamics.

The Industry Life Cycle: Navigating Phases for Strategic Success

The conceptual framing of the industry life cycle facilitates an understanding of the evolutionary path of industries (clusters of organizations) over time. Just as living organisms go through different stages of birth, growth, maturity, and decline, industries also exhibit similar phases. The framework helps organizations recognize the unique challenges and opportunities associated with each phase. Therefore, it allows them to tailor their strategies accordingly. Once aligned, these strategies enable organizations to position themselves advantageously and respond effectively to industry dynamics.

In the embryonic phase, organizations must focus on disruption and innovation to establish a strong position in the market. A prime example of an effective strategy during this phase is Uber's entry into the transportation industry with its ride-hailing platform. They disrupted the traditional taxi industry by understanding customer needs and leveraging technology.

As the industry enters the growth phase, organizations must differentiate themselves or become cost leaders to capture market share. For example, Southwest Airlines' strategy of offering low-cost, no-frills (where non-essential services have been removed to keep the cost down) air travel positioned them as a cost leader in the highly competitive airline industry during the growth phase.

During the shakeout phase, organizations must adapt their strategies to survive and remain relevant. For example, Netflix's strategic pivot from a DVD rental company to a leading streaming service exemplifies effective strategy during this phase. They recognized the shift toward digital media consumption and adjusted their strategy accordingly.

In the maturity phase, organizations must sustain and expand their market share. For example, Apple's entry into the smartphone market with the iPhone is a prime demonstration of an effective strategy during this phase. By creating a blue ocean of untapped market space, they disrupted the existing market and maintained a competitive edge.

Finally, in the decline phase, organizations must decide whether to exit the market, pivot to new industries, or reinvent themselves. When an organization fails to make a decision, then its destiny is likely to be like Kodak's (failing to adapt to the digital revolution causing a devastating loss in market share and position). On the other hand, when it makes an informed decision, it can navigate the transition successfully, much like Nokia. The company transitioned from being a leading mobile phone manufacturer to a prominent player in the telecommunications infrastructure market. In other words, by exiting the mobile phone market, Nokia decided to end its old game and play another one, demonstrating an effective strategy during the decline phase.

When organizations align their strategies with the industry life cycle they can capitalize on the inherent characteristics and dynamics of each phase, enhancing their competitive position and long-term success.

By integrating the concepts of the macroenvironment, complexity differential, organization as CAS, and the industry life cycle, we develop a comprehensive approach to strategy that embraces adaptability, resilience, and long-term value creation. This holistic perspective empowers organizations to navigate the complexities of the business landscape and drive sustainable success in an ever-changing world. Approaching strategy in an insolation of the industry life cycle in which the organization competes renders the guidance misleading.

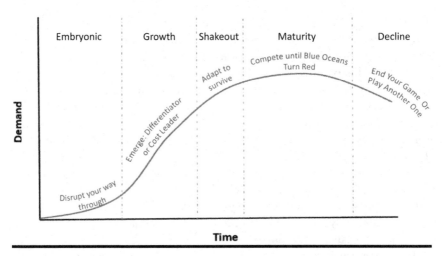

Figure 1.1 **Navigating strategy framework: harnessing industry dynamics for success.**

Navigating Strategy Framework: Harnessing Industry Dynamics for Success

Figure 1.1 visualizes the industry life cycle phases—embryonic, growth, shake-out, maturity, and decline. Organizations of various sizes and maturity levels must respond to their relative macroenvironment as they progress through these phases. Each phase presents unique challenges and opportunities, requiring specific strategic approaches. For example, in the embryonic phase, the focus might be on innovation and market penetration, while in the maturity phase, efficiency and cost leadership could become more critical.

The outcomes and impact of strategic decisions are depicted in the diagram. This includes representations of competitive advantage, sustainable success, and organizational resilience. These elements symbolize the organization's position within the industry, its ability to outperform competitors, its capacity to adapt to evolving circumstances, and its long-term viability.

By observing this visual framework, we can better understand the interconnected nature of the organization as a CAS, the influence of the macroenvironment, the complexity dynamics, the progression through industry life cycle phases, and the importance of strategy alignment. It provides a holistic perspective on how organizations can navigate the complexities of their business environment and develop strategies that drive sustainable success.

In the subsequent chapters of this book, we will dig deeper into each of these concepts, exploring their implications for strategy across the industry life cycle.

First, we define the strategy as either disruptive, competitive, or otherwise, depending on the specific needs and goals of the organization within the context of its ecosystem and industry life cycle. For instance, in the embryonic stage of the industry life cycle, a disruptive strategy might be most appropriate to establish a strong market presence. As the industry evolves through growth, shakeout, maturity, and decline stages, the strategic focus might shift toward competitive differentiation, adaptation, or even strategic withdrawal. By aligning the strategy with the current stage of the industry life cycle and the broader ecosystem, we ensure that the strategic direction is relevant and timely.

Second, we stratify the strategy using the magnifying lens concept, which involves viewing the strategy through corporate-level, business-level, and functional-level perspectives. This approach ensures that each level of the organization understands and aligns with the overall strategic objectives, creating a clear and workable cascade. By zooming in and out through these lenses, we can ensure that the strategy is detailed and specific at every level, while remaining coherent and aligned with the overarching goals.

Finally, the implementation phase, or the "doing" of the strategy, involves approaching it as a negotiation, where continuous dialogue and alignment among stakeholders are crucial to adapt and refine the strategy as needed, ensuring successful execution and achieving desired outcomes. Much like a monarch butterfly navigating its multi-thousand-mile journey, our strategy must adapt and transform at each stage to thrive in its ever-changing environment, ensuring resilience and success over the long haul.

Through examples, case studies, and strategic frameworks, we will build a solid understanding of how organizations can leverage these concepts to formulate and implement effective strategies. By integrating these precursor concepts with the industry life cycle, we can develop a comprehensive approach to strategy that embraces complexity, adaptability, and sustainable growth.

On Strategy Tiers as Magnifying Lenses: Unlocking Strategic Direction

In the realm of strategy development, organizations operate across multiple levels to align their efforts and achieve their goals. These levels (or tiers) are essentially what we consider as magnifying lenses. Their sole purpose is to provide drill-down perspectives and insights into the strategic direction of the organization. In other words, they serve as top-down guidance to help the organization make its trade-offs while staying strategically aligned. Rather than considering these tiers as separate strategies, which many organizations regrettably do, they should be seen as complementary and interconnected components along the same strategic direction. To help illustrate this conceptual framing, let's explore each tier in a bit more detail and uncover how it helps the organization zoom in on its direction starting at the top, from corporate-level to functional (or tactical)-level. An informed senior leadership team at any organization should leverage the tiers to zoom in and out to ensure strategic alignment as broader (or even aspirational) objectives translate into more tactical ones.

Corporate-Level Strategy: Setting the Direction with Growth and a Business Model

At the highest level, corporate strategy encompasses the overarching direction and growth ambitions of the organization. It focuses on fundamental questions such as which markets to enter or exit, which business models to adopt, and how to allocate resources effectively. Corporate strategy serves as the guiding framework that sets the tone for subsequent tiers. But it is not some abstract conceptualizing of what the future may hold, it is an actual strategy. It is a broad perspective informed by organizational choices and anchored in the realities of the business. Therefore, it makes sense that it sets the strategic direction for the entire organization.

The corporate-level of strategy development acts as a magnifying lens by zooming out to see the bigger picture. It enables leaders to assess the organization's portfolio of businesses, explore growth opportunities, and make decisions that shape the overall trajectory of the company. By analyzing market dynamics, competitive forces, and internal capabilities, corporate strategy determines the strategic choices and priorities for the entire organization.

Business-Level Strategy: Differentiation or Cost Leadership

Theoretically, once the growth of the organization has been envisioned along with a business model (though conceptual) that could enable that growth, it is time to understand what that means at a business-level. So, moving down to the business-level, the focus gets a bit more sharpened to translate the corporate-level strategy into business decisions of differentiation vs. cost leadership (or perhaps, a deliberate intention to be somewhere in between). And so, the organization is essentially now zooming in on the next level. The sole purpose of the "zooming" in and out is to ensure strategic alignment. In other words, your organization can't grow like Rolex with Walmart's cost leadership. Or I guess you could try, but that won't be smart. Would it? I mean, this is exactly how many companies lost their way. They confused themselves before confusing their customers and so, both were lost. In more practical terms, at this level, business-level examination of business segmentation, resources, capabilities, product lines, etc. all informed by the growth and business model envisioned earlier, should yield a strategic decision to differentiate one's organization from competition or assume a position of cost leadership within the market in which it competes.

Clearly, a thorough understanding of what each means entails, and a comprehensive understanding of the implications is a pre-requirement. A business-level strategy is not one where the organization just rolls the dice for a hit or miss. As much as strategy should be perceived as a dynamic and ongoing process, it is not random. The criticality of business-level strategy resides in its channeling mission (serving as a conduit) to connect corporate-level to functional-level strategies. So, what does each mean?

Differentiation strategy entails creating unique value propositions and offerings that set the organization apart from rivals. There are several bases for this differentiation spanning from innovation to customer experience. In other words, this could involve innovative products, exceptional customer experiences, or specialized market segments. On the other hand, cost leadership (or low-cost) strategy centers around achieving operational efficiencies and hence, translating these efficiencies to lower prices on products and services to customers.

So again, while corporate-level strategy informs the destination (not to be mistaken with vision), the business-level strategy forges the path. It acts as a magnifying lens that zooms in to understand which direction leads to that destination, in a bit more practical terms. It allows for a more focused examination of competitive dynamics, customer needs, and opportunities for differentiation or cost optimization. By leveraging the organization's core competencies and aligning business-level strategies with the corporate strategy, the organization can achieve a sustainable competitive advantage. If you imagine that path forged in rocks, then functional-level strategy defines the building blocks needed (you guessed it right, building blocks for sustained competitive advantages....or even transient ones).

Sears—A Tale of Strategic Misalignment

Sears, Roebuck & Co., founded in 1892, was once a titan of the American retail industry. It dominated the market with its innovative catalog sales and expansive department stores. At its peak in the 1960s, Sears was the largest retailer in the world, accounting for 1% of the U.S. GDP and employing over 350,000 people. However, as the retail landscape evolved, Sears found itself struggling to keep pace with emerging competitors like Walmart and Amazon. The company's downfall provides a poignant example of what happens when there is a lack of alignment across different strategy tiers.

At the corporate-level, Sears attempted to diversify its portfolio by acquiring a range of unrelated businesses, including Kmart in 2004 and Lands' End in 2002. The goal was to build a retail conglomerate that could compete on multiple fronts. However, these acquisitions were not part of a coherent strategic vision. Instead of focusing on strengthening its core competencies, Sears diluted its brand and stretched its resources thin.

Moving to the business-level, Sears struggled to define a clear competitive strategy. The company was caught between trying to be a low-cost leader like Walmart and a differentiator like Nordstrom. This indecisiveness led to confusion both internally and externally. Customers were unsure what Sears stood for, and employees lacked clear direction on what to prioritize. For instance, Sears invested over $1 billion in remodeling stores to create a more upscale shopping experience. Simultaneously, they attempted to compete on price with deep discounting strategies. This conflicting approach meant that Sears was unable to achieve the efficiencies required for cost leadership or the customer experience needed for differentiation. As a result, the brand's identity became muddled, and customer loyalty waned.

At the functional-level, Sears' various departments operated without a unified strategic direction. Marketing campaigns were inconsistent, alternating between promotions for luxury goods and deep discounts. The supply chain was inefficient, unable to support either a high-volume low-cost model or a premium service model effectively. Innovation was stifled as resources were spread too thin across diverse initiatives without a clear focus.

For example, while the technology department attempted to roll out e-commerce solutions to compete with Amazon, the in-store experience deteriorated due to lack of investment. The human resources department faced challenges in training and retaining staff who were unclear about the company's direction and their role in it.

The strategic misalignment across Sears' corporate, business, and functional-levels ultimately led to its decline. From 2005 to 2017, Sears' revenue dropped from $49.1 billion to $16.7 billion, and its stock price plummeted from over $140 per share in 2007 to under $1 in 2017. The lack of a cohesive strategy meant that Sears could not compete effectively in any segment of the market. The company filed for bankruptcy in 2018, serving as a stark reminder of the importance of strategic alignment and focus.

Functional Strategy: Building Blocks of Sustained Competitive Advantages

At the functional (or tactical) level, the strategy focuses on attaining competitive advantages via the four known building blocks: innovation, quality, efficiency, and/or customer responsiveness. You could argue that the name "functional" comes from focusing on the respective functions within the organization in which the building block(s) is to be built. You won't be wrong. You could also argue that the term implies a practical lens, you won't be wrong either. Here, the emphasis is on leveraging and enhancing the organization's capabilities and performance within specific areas to build those blocks that would yield the respective competitive advantages. The functional strategy contributes to the overall strategic direction by addressing the building blocks of sustained competitive advantages: innovation, quality, efficiency, and/or customer responsiveness.

So, for an organization, what does this mean? It means an organization needs to decide on which competitive advantages to attain and therefore, should understand which blocks to build. For example, Toyota's attains a sustained competitive advantage from the quality building block. So, at the functional (or tactical) level, it has leveraged/transferred/shared its resources and capabilities to strengthen its quality muscle. In other words, we can say that one source for Toyota's sustained competitive advantage over its rivals is the quality of its products.

Similar narrative can be told about Apple's innovation or Walmart's efficiency. The intent here is not to suggest a singular selection of building blocks to attain those competitive advantages. In fact, many successful organizations could deploy their resources to build more than one and hence, attain more than one competitive advantage. But the key word is "deploy," because this is in reality what organizations do to build those blocks. Resources are required to build the blocks… all kinds of resources: human, financial, etc. Because resources are effectively scarce, not one successful organization operates on the assumption of unlimited resources. Hence, a careful selection of which building blocks(s) to focus on becomes critical, otherwise, resources are depleted.

Many organizations seem not to understand exactly how these components are interconnected and so, they seem to arbitrarily select to focus on some or none in an epic mix-and-match saga between modes of growth, business models, competitive advantages building blocks without a structured approach, or even an attempt to be strategic about it. This may sound harsh, but it is the reality of some organizations manifested in failures and market exists.

Innovation aims to foster a culture of creativity and continuous improvement, driving the development of new products, processes, or business models. Quality centers on delivering products or services that meet or exceed customer expectations, ensuring superior value and satisfaction. Efficiency aims to optimize operations, streamline processes, and achieve cost-effectiveness in the organization's activities. Customer responsiveness focuses on understanding and meeting customer needs promptly, building strong relationships and loyalty.

So back to connecting the dots, the functional-level strategy acts as a magnifying lens that zooms in even further, focusing on specific functions and their contribution to the organization's competitive advantage. Each functional-level strategy complements and supports the overarching corporate and business-level strategies to ensure strategic alignment and amplify impact.

Magnifying Lenses: A Unified Approach to Strategy

Rather than viewing these strategy tiers as separate and distinct strategies, it is crucial to recognize them as interconnected magnifying lenses that provide different perspectives on the same strategic direction. The corporate-level strategy establishes the foundation and guides the overall direction, while the business and functional-level strategies further refine and operationalize that direction. Imagine the analogy of the forged path we used earlier. Corporate-level strategy defines a destination (this is not the same as the vision, which is likely to be an aspiration or a dream), business-level strategy forges a path to the destination, and functional-level strategy paves the path with building blocks.

The metaphor of magnifying lenses is appropriate because each tier brings its own focus and emphasis, allowing senior leaders to zoom in and examine specific aspects of the strategy in greater detail and more practicality. They complement one another, with the corporate-level strategy providing the context and broad perspective, the business-level strategy zooming in on market positioning in terms of differentiation or cost leadership, and the functional-level strategies addressing the core capabilities that sustain the organization's competitive advantage using the appropriate building block(s).

The essence of the unified approach to strategy, employing magnifying lenses across different tiers, lies in its ability to bring strategic coherence and alignment throughout the organization. By viewing the strategy tiers as interconnected and complementary components (never in conflict with one another), executives and senior leaders can ensure that each level contributes to the overall strategic direction in a streamlined fashion. This unification enhances strategic effectiveness and enables the organization to navigate complexities, make informed decisions, and achieve sustainable success.

> ***Procter & Gamble (P&G)***: P&G is a prime example of an organization that has effectively employed the unified approach of magnifying lenses in its strategy development. At the corporate-level, P&G's strategy focuses on driving growth through product innovation and expanding into new markets. The company has a strong corporate vision and clear growth objectives that guide its overall direction. For instance, P&G's corporate strategy of "touching and improving more consumers' lives in more parts of the world more completely" sets the broad framework for the organization.

Moving to the business unit level, P&G develops specific strategies for each of its product categories, such as fabric care, beauty, and grooming. These business unit strategies align with the corporate strategy while addressing the unique market dynamics and consumer demands within each category. For example, P&G's business unit strategy for its fabric care category includes differentiating its products through superior performance, innovation, and sustainability.

At the functional-level, P&G's strategy focuses on building core capabilities and competitive advantages. Each functional area, such as marketing, research and development, and supply chain, has its own specific strategies that support the overall corporate and business unit strategies. For instance, P&G's marketing strategy emphasizes customer-centricity and creating emotional connections with consumers to drive brand loyalty.

P&G's unified approach to strategy ensures that the corporate, business unit, and functional strategies are interconnected and aligned. It enables P&G to leverage its core competencies and resources effectively, drive innovation, and deliver value to customers in a consistent manner.

Amazon: Amazon is another notable example of employing a unified approach to strategy using magnifying lenses. At the corporate-level, Amazon's strategy is centered around customer obsession, continuous innovation, and long-term value creation. The company's corporate strategy focuses on expanding its customer base, offering a wide range of products and services, and leveraging technology to enhance customer experiences. Amazon's commitment to customer-centricity guides its overall direction and decision-making.

Moving to the business unit level, Amazon develops strategies tailored to each of its business segments, such as e-commerce, cloud computing, and digital content. For example, within its e-commerce business, Amazon has implemented strategies for different market segments, including its Prime membership program, which aims to enhance customer loyalty and drive repeat purchases. These business unit strategies align with the corporate strategy while addressing the specific needs and opportunities within each segment.

At the functional-level, Amazon's strategies in areas such as operations, logistics, and technology enable the company to drive efficiency, scalability, and innovation. For instance, Amazon's focus on operational excellence and continuous process improvement allows the company to deliver products to customers quickly and reliably. The functional strategies support the overall corporate and business unit strategies, ensuring seamless execution and superior customer experiences (Amazon, n.d.).

Amazon's unified approach to strategy empowers the organization to adapt to evolving market dynamics, maintain a customer-centric focus, and drive continuous innovation. The alignment across strategy tiers enables Amazon to respond effectively to changing customer needs and market trends, while leveraging its strengths and resources to maintain a competitive advantage.

Importance of the Unified Approach

The unified approach of magnifying lenses in strategy development is of paramount importance for several reasons, including:

1. *Strategic Alignment*: The unified approach ensures that the strategies at different levels align with each other and with the organization's overall direction. This alignment facilitates coherent decision-making and resource allocation, reducing potential conflicts and enhancing the organization's ability to execute its strategic goals effectively.

2. *Synergy and Resource Optimization*: By considering the interdependencies and interactions between strategy tiers, organizations can leverage synergies and optimize resource allocation. The integrated approach allows the organization to harness the collective capabilities and expertise across different levels, maximizing the overall strategic impact.

3. *Agility and Adaptability*: The unified approach promotes agility and adaptability in a rapidly changing business environment. By monitoring and adjusting strategies across different tiers, organizations can quickly respond to market shifts, emerging trends, and competitive threats. This flexibility allows them to seize new opportunities and navigate challenges effectively.

4. *Consistency and Brand Cohesion*: A unified approach ensures consistency in the organization's strategic messaging, brand identity, and customer experiences. It fosters a cohesive and aligned organizational culture, enabling employees to work toward shared goals and deliver a unified brand promise to customers.

By embracing the unified approach of magnifying lenses, organizations can enhance their strategic effectiveness, foster strategic coherence, and achieve sustainable success in today's complex and dynamic business landscape.

On Strategy as a Negotiation

In the context of strategy development, the role of a strategist goes beyond traditional planning and decision-making. It involves navigating a complex landscape of choices, trade-offs, and conflicting commitments. The strategist acts as a negotiator, engaging in a process of give-and-take with various stakeholders within the organization. This makes sense for the following two reasons: (1) the essence of a strategy resides in making trade-offs, and (2) the reality of business when it comes to limited resources.

Understanding Strategy as a Negotiation

In this section, we examine the concept of strategy through a negotiation lens and explore its significance in the organizational context. Strategy, at its core, involves making choices and trade-offs to allocate limited resources effectively. These choices require engaging in a negotiation process with various stakeholders within the organization, typically senior leaders. This might not sound readily intuitive in a business environment where the underlying assumption is that robust financial forecasting, competitive benchmarking, and market analyses (among other tools and mechanisms, just think Drucker and Kotter) breed effective strategy. In other words, if business alternatives are carefully identified and supported by viable business cases, what is there to negotiate and...why?

In theory, after all, everyone in the organization should be marching to the same beat...not really. At a minimum, not always.

In reality, many organizations (including those mature ones competing in mature industries) make irrational decisions based on aspirational measures (not business targets) and are influenced by leadership styles.

Therefore, the strategist must wear a negotiator hat because there will likely be several compelling business cases to evaluate and prioritize. At the end of the day, one CEO is likely to have several VPs, each of which is trying to secure resources to deliver on annual objectives. Perhaps our strategist negotiator here is not Detective Keith Frazier but certainly, there are some common threads.

The strategist acts as a negotiator, facilitating discussions, seeking alignment, and resolving conflicts to arrive at strategic decisions. Within the organizational environment, the strategist navigates business alternatives and strategic priorities. Any senior business professional in the organization tasked with exerting influence to inform business strategies is likely to navigate diverse business goals and interests, priorities of stakeholders, and potential modes of growth. By engaging in negotiation, the strategist aims to find common ground, establish shared goals, and align the organization's efforts toward a coherent strategic direction.

One of the key reasons why strategy can be seen as a negotiation process is the need to reconcile different perspectives and priorities. So, what does that mean?

Within an organization, there are often competing interests and divergent viewpoints that need to be considered, regardless to the existence of a unified vision (although this might be practically less than common). At a minimum, different executives and business units would have different interpretations when it comes to the articulation of the vision.

Take for example an enterprise priority to "grow the business" (believe it or not, the broadness of the direction doesn't make CEOs of some multi-billion organizations blink, the VPs will figure it out). So, what exactly is this growth? Where will it come from? How?....Well, VPs will figure it out. The problem comes when each VP (or leading executive) turns themselves into micro CEO over their own business unit and cascade that type of behavior down....bringing rise to the epic silos! And if you think silos bring autonomy, think again. Within our adaptive complex systems (aka organizations), hardly anything good comes out of silos. Silos breed competing commitments and strategic misalignment. For example, this "growth" to the CMO means an aggressive market expansion to capture new customers, independent of implications on product development, or manufacturing. To the COO, it might mean streamlining processes to reduce cost. In the spirit of growth, this may get translated into freed up capital to pursue new prospects (on top, of course, to the improved profitability). Regardless, the strategist must navigate these conflicting viewpoints, seeking to strike a balance that aligns with the overall strategic objectives of the organization.

In addition to managing conflicting interests, the negotiation aspect of strategy also arises from the dynamic nature of the business environment. External factors, such as market trends, technological advancements, and competitive forces, constantly evolve and present new challenges and opportunities. Because strategy is the guiding compass through uncertainties and ever-increasing complexities of the business environment, it must be approached through a lens of negotiation to enable effective navigation and adaptation to trends and changing market dynamic, externally, and to competing and conflicting commitments, internally.

Negotiating Competing and Conflicting Commitments

In this section, we focus a bit on competing and conflicting commitments and explore how strategy as a negotiation implicates that space of contention within the organization.

Competing and conflicting commitments arise from opposing views, diverse interests, goals, and priorities of key stakeholders (likely to be executives and business unit heads). To develop and deploy an enterprise strategy, careful navigation of these conflicts is critical to identify synergies and compromises that align with the overall strategic objectives.

Competing and conflicting commitments can manifest in various ways within an organization. Different departments or business units may have distinct strategic priorities, each with its own set of objectives and targets. For example, the sales department may prioritize revenue growth and market share expansion, while the human resources department may focus on talent retention and development. At a tactical level, this is not likely to be an issue, in fact, it is expected especially in complex organizations. Research even acknowledges productive conflict as means to invigorate innovation and new perspectives. However, this is likely to be an issue at the top of the organizations where mega decisions on resource allocation, technology investment, manufacturing and IT infrastructure are made. At the corporate-level, misalignment can be detrimental to the company.

Even at a business unit level where strategy development is still needed, competing and conflicting commitments can also arise for similar reason, but now at a lower level. Individual team members may have different perspectives, preferences, or interpretations of the strategic goals. The strategist must facilitate dialogue and negotiation among team members to align their commitments and foster a sense of shared purpose.

Negotiating conflicting commitments requires effective communication, active listening, and the ability to manage diverse perspectives. The strategist must encourage open dialogue, create a safe space for stakeholders to express their viewpoints, and promote empathy and understanding among the parties involved. By understanding the underlying motivations and interests of different stakeholders, the strategist can seek common ground and explore win-win solutions that address multiple priorities.

Addressing competing and conflicting commitments is not about compromising the strategic direction but finding synergies and trade-offs that maximize the value for the organization. It involves making tough decisions, evaluating the potential risks and rewards, and ensuring that the strategic choices align with the organization's long-term vision and purpose.

By effectively negotiating conflicting commitments, the strategist can build consensus, drive stakeholder engagement, and increase the likelihood of successful strategy execution. It requires the strategist to balance the art of persuasion, rational analysis, and emotional intelligence to navigate the complexities and challenges inherent in strategic decision-making.

IDEA IN BRIEF: Understanding strategy as a negotiation process is crucial for strategists to navigate conflicting commitments and align stakeholders toward a common strategic direction. The negotiation aspect of strategy allows the organization to integrate diverse perspectives, manage conflicts, and make strategic choices that optimize resource allocation and support long-term value creation. By embracing the role of negotiator, the strategist can effectively drive the implementation of the chosen strategic direction while fostering collaboration, engagement, and stakeholder alignment.

Challenges and Strategies for Negotiating Competing and Conflicting Commitments

Perhaps negotiating a strategy is not very different than negotiating in general and so, it has challenges. Competing and conflicting commitments can lead to disagreements, power struggles, and resistance to change within the organization. The strategist must employ effective communication, negotiation skills, and conflict resolution techniques to navigate these challenges. By employing these strategies, the strategist can effectively negotiate conflicting commitments, build consensus, and drive the implementation of the chosen strategic direction. Negotiating strategy requires not only analytical thinking and strategic acumen but also effective communication, empathy, and conflict resolution skills. By embracing the art of negotiating strategy, organizations can achieve strategic coherence, enhance stakeholder alignment, and unlock the full potential of their strategic initiatives.

To negotiate conflicting commitments successfully, the strategist should:

- Foster open dialogue and create a safe space for stakeholders to express their perspectives and concerns.
- Seek to understand the underlying motivations and interests of different stakeholders, promoting empathy and building trust.
- Encourage collaboration and joint problem-solving, seeking win-win outcomes that address multiple priorities.
- Use data, evidence, and strategic analysis to inform and support negotiation discussions, bringing objectivity and rationale to the decision-making process.
- Continuously engage in ongoing communication and feedback loops to ensure that commitments remain aligned and can be adapted as needed.

How Is This Book Structured

In Part I of this book, We lay the groundwork for understanding strategy in the context of the dynamic business ecosystem. Together, we explore the evolving nature of strategy and its interaction with various factors that shape organizational success.

- ■ *Chapter 1: What Strategy Is and Is Not*
  We begin by examining the essence of strategy and dispelling common misconceptions. Strategy is not merely a static plan; it has evolved into a dynamic and adaptive process that propels organizations toward success. At its core, strategy involves making deliberate choices and trade-offs to achieve specific objectives. Strategy is a compass. It goes beyond goal setting and extends into decision-making that shapes the competitive position and future prospects of the organization.

  To gain insights into different perspectives on strategy, we draw from a comparative analysis of renowned strategy books such as *Playing to Win* by A.G. Lafley and Roger L. Martin, *Blue Ocean Strategy* by W. Chan Kim and Renée Mauborgne, and *Good to Great* by Jim Collins. These books provide valuable insights into strategic thinking and offer practical guidance for organizations in various industries.

  In this book, we will be perceiving strategy as an ongoing and adaptive process, responsive to the external environment and the organization's unique context. And so, we will explore how strategy needs to be aligned with the industry life cycle, which acts as a living concept mirroring the phases of birth, growth, maturity, and decline observed in living organisms. By understanding the industry life cycle, organizations can adapt their strategies to the specific phase, leveraging opportunities and mitigating risks.

- ■ *Chapter 2: Macroenvironment and the Complexity Differential*
  In this chapter, we dive into the macroenvironment and its influence on strategy. The macroenvironment encompasses external factors such as economic conditions, technological advancements, political and regulatory forces, social and cultural trends, and ecological considerations. These factors create both opportunities and threats that organizations must navigate.

  Recognizing the complexity differential among industries is crucial as it influences the strategic choices organizations should adopt. Some industries are characterized by high levels of complexity, such as rapidly changing technology or intense competition, while others exhibit more stable and predictable dynamics. By understanding the complexity differential, organizations can tailor their strategies to effectively navigate the challenges and capitalize on the opportunities within their specific industry.

■ *Chapter 3: The Organization as a CAS*
Building upon the understanding of the macroenvironment and complexity differential, we explore the organization as a CAS. This perspective recognizes that organizations are living entities that exhibit emergent behavior, adaptability, and self-organization. Like living organisms, organizations respond to internal and external stimuli, learn from their experiences, and adapt their behaviors accordingly.

Understanding the CAS perspective is crucial for strategy formulation. It emphasizes the need for organizations to be agile, innovative, and responsive to changing circumstances. By embracing adaptability and emergent behavior, organizations can effectively respond to complex and uncertain environments. We will showcase real-world examples where companies like Google and Apple have embraced the CAS perspective to drive innovation and maintain a competitive edge.

■ *Chapter 4: The Industry Is Alive, and It Has a Life Cycle*
In this chapter, we revisit the concept of the industry life cycle with a fresh perspective. The industry life cycle provides a framework for understanding the evolutionary path of industries over time. It mirrors the stages of birth, growth, maturity, and decline observed in living organisms.

By aligning strategies with the specific phase of the industry life cycle, We argue that organizations can position themselves advantageously. In the embryonic phase, disruptive strategies and innovation are key to establishing a strong foothold. requires differentiation or cost leadership to capture market share. The shakeout phase demands adaptation and survival strategies. The maturity phase necessitates strategies for sustaining and expanding market share. Lastly, the decline phase requires decisions regarding exiting the market, exploring new opportunities, or reinventing the organization.

Throughout this chapter, we illustrate how organizations like Uber, Southwest Airlines, Netflix, and Apple have effectively aligned their strategies with the respective phases of the industry life cycle, enabling them to thrive and maintain a competitive advantage.

■ *Chapter 5: Organizations and Industries Are Alive, So Should Strategy*
In the final chapter of Part I, we synthesize the concepts discussed thus far, emphasizing that strategy is a dynamic and proactive process that aligns with the organization's industry life cycle phase. We highlight the importance of adaptability and responsiveness in strategy formulation and execution.

Strategies should not be seen as rigid plans but as living and evolving approaches that enable organizations to navigate the complexities and uncertainties of the business landscape. We continue to showcase examples where companies have demonstrated strategic agility, embracing change and leveraging emerging opportunities.

By understanding strategy within the context of the dynamic business ecosystem, organizations can position themselves for sustainable success. This holistic approach, integrating the macroenvironment, complexity differential, organization as CAS, and the industry life cycle, sets the stage for the subsequent chapters in this book. We will examine specific strategies across the industry life cycle, explore leadership considerations, and examine the intersection of academia and practice.

In Part II of this book, we examine strategies across the industry life cycle, offering insights and frameworks to guide organizations through each phase. By aligning strategies with the specific characteristics and challenges of each phase, organizations can navigate the complexities and capitalize on opportunities for growth and success.

- ■ *Chapter 6: Embryonic: Disrupt Your Way Through*
  In the embryonic phase of the industry life cycle, organizations face a unique set of challenges and opportunities. This chapter explores strategies for disruption and innovation, providing real-world examples of companies that have successfully navigated this phase. By embracing a disruptive mindset and capitalizing on early-mover advantages, organizations can establish a strong foothold and gain a competitive edge.
- ■ *Chapter 7: Growth: Emerge as a Differentiator or Cost Leader*
  As industries transition into the growth phase, organizations must focus on differentiation or cost leadership to capture market share. This chapter examines strategies for sustaining growth, showcasing examples of companies that have emerged as leaders in their respective industries. By effectively differentiating their offerings or implementing efficient cost strategies, organizations can position themselves for continued success.
- ■ *Chapter 8: Shakeout: Adapt to Survive*
  The shakeout phase presents challenges as market competition intensifies and consolidation occurs. In this chapter, we explore strategies for adaptation and survival, highlighting examples of companies that have successfully navigated this phase. By being agile, responsive, and strategic in their decision-making, organizations can weather the shakeout phase and emerge stronger.
- ■ *Chapter 9: Maturity: Compete Until Blue Oceans Turn Red*
  In the maturity phase, competition intensifies and organizations must continually innovate and find new sources of differentiation. This chapter examines strategies for sustaining and expanding market share in mature industries, drawing on real-world examples of companies that have successfully competed in this phase. By embracing continuous improvement, customer-centricity, and strategic partnerships, organizations can prolong their success in mature markets.

■ *Chapter 10: Decline: End Your Game or Play Another One*
In the decline phase, industries face diminishing demand and declining growth prospects. Organizations must make critical decisions regarding their future, whether to exit the market, explore new opportunities, or reinvent themselves. This chapter explores strategies for managing decline and showcases examples of companies that have effectively responded to declining industries. By adapting their business models, diversifying into new markets, or undertaking strategic transformations, organizations can navigate the decline phase and find new avenues for growth.

In Part III of this book, we focus on leadership considerations and practical aspects of strategy implementation. Effective leadership is vital for translating strategic vision into action and driving organizational success.

■ *Chapter 11: Strategy Tiers: The Magnifying Lenses*
This chapter introduces the concept of strategy tiers, which act as magnifying lenses that focus on different aspects of strategy. We explore the three tiers of strategy: corporate-level strategy, business-level strategy, and functional-level strategy. By understanding and aligning these tiers, organizations can enhance strategic coherence and drive effective execution.

■ *Chapter 12: Negotiating Your Strategy*
Negotiation plays a critical role in strategy development, as organizations must navigate competing interests and conflicting commitments. This chapter explores the art of negotiating strategy, providing practical insights and strategies for aligning diverse perspectives and driving consensus.

■ *Chapter 13: Strategy Imperative: Thought Leadership, Blue Ocean, and Innovation*
Thought leadership, blue ocean strategy, and innovation are critical components of successful strategies. This chapter examines the strategy imperative, emphasizing the need for organizations to become thought leaders, create uncontested market space, and foster a culture of innovation.

■ *Chapter 14: Leadership Considerations: Ambidexterity*
In this chapter, we explore leadership considerations for strategy implementation. We discuss the concept of ambidexterity, which involves balancing exploration and exploitation, and how it contributes to organizational agility and adaptability. Additionally, we also examine strategic episodes, identifying key moments in an organization's journey where leadership plays a critical role in shaping outcomes.

By following the structure outlined in this book, the aim is to provide a comprehensive understanding of strategy across the industry life cycle. Finally, we will explore leadership considerations as we provide valuable insights to senior executive leaders in implementing effective strategies in today's rapidly changing business landscape.

Chapter 2

Macroenvironment and the Complexity Differential

Set-the-Stage Mini Case

Pfizer's Strategic Response to the COVID-19 Pandemic

As the COVID-19 pandemic emerged in early 2020, Pfizer faced an unprecedented macroenvironmental challenge. The company needed to navigate a rapidly evolving landscape characterized by political pressure, economic instability, technological demands, and social upheaval. Despite these obstacles, Pfizer's ability to quickly adapt and strategically respond positioned it as a crucial player in the global fight against the pandemic. This case highlights how understanding and responding to macroenvironmental factors can significantly impact an organization's strategic direction and success.

To effectively respond to the pandemic, Pfizer entered into an unprecedented partnership with BioNTech, a German biotechnology firm, to develop one of the first mRNA-based COVID-19 vaccines. This strategic collaboration leveraged Pfizer's extensive experience in vaccine development and BioNTech's innovative mRNA technology. The urgency of the situation required rapid decision-making, agile project management, and an accelerated regulatory approval process. Pfizer's leadership played a critical role in navigating the political and

DOI: 10.4324/9781003564133-3

regulatory landscape, securing emergency-use authorizations from multiple countries, and scaling up manufacturing capabilities to meet global demand. The company's ability to mobilize resources, streamline operations, and engage in strategic partnerships exemplifies how organizations can adapt to macroenvironmental challenges to achieve significant breakthroughs and deliver impactful solutions in times of crisis.

Defining the Term: Macroenvironment

In today's dynamic and rapidly changing business landscape, organizations face a multitude of external forces that significantly impact their strategic decision-making. To navigate this complex environment effectively, it is essential to understand the macroenvironment and manage the complexity differential. Here, we will be examining these critical aspects, exploring their implications, and offering practical insights on how organizations can align their strategies with these external factors.

In today's fast-paced and interconnected business landscape, organizations operate within a dynamic and ever-changing ecosystem. To effectively navigate this complex terrain, it is important to view organizations not as static entities but as complex adaptive systems (CAS—an interconnected network of agents that continually adapt and self-organize in response to their environment, much like living organisms).

In this context, strategy becomes an essential tool for organizations to thrive and succeed. It is no longer sufficient to view strategy as a static plan but rather as a dynamic and adaptive process. However, we have to bear in mind that adaptive does not mean random. Strategy in the realm of a CAS involves making deliberate choices and trade-offs to achieve specific objectives, taking into account the intricate interplay of internal and external factors.

Through the CAS lens, the organization is a living entity that interacts with its environment, responds to stimuli, and evolves over time. This makes sense because the essence of organizations is people. So, just as a living organism adapts to changes in its ecosystem to survive and thrive, organizations must continually assess their surroundings, anticipate shifts, and make strategic choices accordingly. This perspective on strategy acknowledges the inherent complexity and uncertainty of the business environment, requiring organizations to be agile and responsive. Another aspect we also have to bear in mind here is that responsiveness must be selective. In other words, for example, as the organization receives market signals, responding to those signals must be selective and in line with the strategic priorities, otherwise we end up with an organization that loses its way and over-diversifies to the point of brand dilution and complete loss of customer focus.

The idea is that the CAS lens aligns closely with the industry life cycle reflecting the natural progression and evolution of industries over time. Each phase of the industry life cycle presents unique challenges and opportunities, and organizations must adapt their strategies to effectively navigate these stages. The CAS perspective recognizes that the external environment plays a pivotal role in shaping an organization's strategic choices and outcomes.

By embracing this lens, organizations can leverage the inherent adaptability and self-organizing nature of complex systems. They can foster a culture of learning, experimentation, and innovation, allowing them to respond to market dynamics and seize emerging opportunities. Strategy, then, becomes a dynamic and iterative process that aligns the organization's purpose, values, and desired outcomes with the ever-changing external landscape.

Navigating External Forces for Strategic Success

The macroenvironment represents the broader external context in which an organization operates. It encompasses a multitude of interconnected factors that influence the organization's strategic decisions, performance, and long-term viability. In this section, we will examine the components of the macroenvironment, its significance to organizations, and its profound impact on strategic management.

The macroenvironment comprises several key components, each exerting its influence on the organization. These components include political, economic, sociocultural, technological, environmental, and legal dimensions:

- Political Factors: The political dimension encompasses the influence of government policies, regulations, and political stability on organizations. It includes factors such as trade agreements, taxation policies, political ideologies, and labor laws. Political shifts can significantly impact an organization's strategic decisions, market access, and competitive landscape. For instance, changes in government regulations regarding data privacy can necessitate adjustments to an organization's data management and marketing strategies; similarly, this also happens with NHTSA's mandate proposal for vehicle-to-vehicle communication.
- Economic Factors: Economic factors encompass the state of the economy, including GDP growth, interest rates, exchange rates, inflammation rates, and consumer purchasing power. Economic conditions directly affect organizations' revenue, profitability, and market demand. For example, during the 2008 economic downturn, organizations needed to adapt their strategies to address changes in consumer spending habits and market dynamics.

They focused on cost optimization, product diversification, and targeting new customer segments to maintain their competitiveness.

■ Sociocultural Factors: Sociocultural factors represent the societal values, attitudes, beliefs, and behaviors that shape market trends and consumer preferences. These factors include cultural norms, demographics, social values, lifestyle choices, and consumer attitudes toward health, sustainability, and social responsibility. Organizations must understand societal shifts and adapt their strategies accordingly. For instance, increasing consumer demand for sustainable products has prompted many organizations to integrate environmental considerations into their product development and marketing strategies from sustainable sourcing to utilizing recycled material for packaging.

■ Technological Factors: Technological factors encompass the advancements and innovations that impact industries and organizations. This category includes factors such as the rate of technological change, digital transformation, research and development activities, and disruptive technologies. Organizations need to stay at the forefront of technological developments to identify opportunities for innovation, process optimization, and competitive advantages (both sustained and transient). For instance, organizations embracing digitalization and leveraging emerging technologies like artificial intelligence (AI) or blockchain can gain a significant competitive edge in the market.

■ Environmental Factors: Environmental factors refer to the ecological and environmental aspects that influence organizations. Increasing environmental concerns and the need for sustainable practices have shaped consumer expectations and regulatory frameworks. Organizations must consider environmental factors such as climate change, resource scarcity, carbon footprint, waste management, and sustainable sourcing. Integrating environmental considerations into the strategy can enhance an organization's reputation, attract environmentally conscious customers, and ensure long-term sustainability.

■ Legal Factors: Legal factors encompass the laws, regulations, and legal frameworks that govern business operations. This includes industry-specific regulations, intellectual property protection, labor laws, health and safety regulations, and consumer protection laws. Organizations must comply with legal requirements and consider their implications when formulating strategies. Failure to adhere to legal obligations can result in legal consequences, reputational damage, or loss of market share.

Understanding the macroenvironment is critical for organizations for several reasons. First, it helps organizations identify opportunities and threats in the external environment. This is essentially the "signals" we mentioned earlier. By analyzing the political, economic, sociocultural, technological, environmental, and legal dimensions, organizations can uncover emerging trends, customer preferences, and potential risks that may impact their strategic decisions.

Second, it provides insights into the competitive landscape. By monitoring industry dynamics, regulatory changes, and market trends, organizations can assess their competitive position and identify areas for differentiation. For instance, an organization that anticipates shifts in consumer preferences toward eco-friendly products can proactively develop sustainable alternatives to gain a competitive advantage.

Third, it influences the organization's strategic direction. Organizations must adapt their strategies to align with the external forces at play. By assessing the macroenvironment, organizations can make informed choices regarding market entry, product development, resource allocation, and strategic partnerships.

The impact of the macroenvironment on organizations can be observed in numerous real-world examples. For instance, the emergence of ride-sharing platforms such as Uber and Lyft has been shaped by the confluence of technological advancements, sociocultural shifts toward convenience and cost-effectiveness, and regulatory challenges. These companies have had to navigate the macroenvironment to address changing customer expectations, comply with transportation regulations, and manage the impact of disruptive technologies.

IDEA IN BRIEF: The macroenvironment encompasses various dimensions, including political, economic, sociocultural, technological, environmental, and legal factors. Understanding and analyzing these components is crucial for organizations to navigate the complexities of the external environment. By monitoring and responding to the macroenvironment, organizations can identify opportunities, mitigate risks, and develop strategies that align with market trends, consumer preferences, and regulatory requirements.

Macroenvironmental Implications on Strategy

Macroenvironmental Implications on Strategy: Navigating the External Landscape. The macroenvironment, with its various components, exerts a profound influence on strategy development and deployment within organizations. In this section, we will explore how macroenvironmental factors impact strategic decision-making and shape the choices organizations make to navigate the external landscape. By understanding these implications, organizations can better align their strategies with the prevailing market conditions and position themselves for success.

- ■ Political Implications: Government policies, regulations, and political stability can create opportunities or present challenges for organizations. For example, changes in trade policies can impact supply chain strategies and market access for organizations operating internationally. Additionally, shifts in political ideologies can influence strategic decisions related to corporate social responsibility and sustainability initiatives.
- ■ Economic Implications: Economic conditions, such as GDP growth, inflation rates, and consumer purchasing power, shape market demand and influence an organization's revenue and profitability. Organizations need to analyze economic indicators to understand market trends and adjust their strategies accordingly. For instance, during an economic downturn, organizations may need to focus on cost optimization, explore new markets, or introduce affordable product lines to maintain their competitiveness.
- ■ Sociocultural Implications: Changing demographics, cultural norms, and societal values shape consumer preferences and demand. Organizations need to align their strategies with these sociocultural shifts to stay relevant and meet customer expectations. For example, organizations catering to health-conscious consumers need to offer healthier product alternatives and transparent labeling to address changing consumer preferences.
- ■ Technological Implications: Technological factors have transformative effects on strategy development and deployment. Rapid technological advancements and digital disruption create both opportunities and challenges for organizations. Organizations must monitor and embrace emerging technologies to remain competitive and drive innovation. For instance, the rise of e-commerce and the shift toward online shopping have prompted traditional retailers to adopt omnichannel strategies and invest in digital platforms to reach and engage customers effectively.
- ■ Environmental Implications: Environmental factors have become increasingly important in strategic decision-making. Organizations need to consider environmental sustainability and integrate it into their strategies. Factors such as climate change, resource scarcity, and environmental regulations influence the choice of products, production processes, and supply chain management strategies. Organizations that proactively address environmental implications can enhance their reputation, attract environmentally conscious customers, and gain a competitive advantage.

IDEA IN BRIEF: Understanding the macroenvironmental implications on strategy is crucial for organizations to make informed choices. By analyzing the political, economic, sociocultural, technological, and environmental factors, organizations can develop strategies that align with market dynamics and leverage opportunities.

Tesla: Tesla's strategic choices are deeply influenced by macroenvironmental factors. The company's focus on electric vehicles aligns with the growing sociocultural emphasis on sustainability and environmental consciousness. Additionally, Tesla's strategy is shaped by the political landscape, with governments around the world implementing regulations and incentives to promote the adoption of electric vehicles. Tesla's strategic decisions are informed by an understanding of the macroenvironmental factors that shape the automotive industry.

Airbnb: Airbnb's success can be attributed to its ability to leverage technological advancements and sociocultural shifts. The company recognized the changing preferences of travelers who sought unique and personalized accommodation experiences. By capitalizing on the sharing economy enabled by technology, Airbnb created a platform that aligned with the sociocultural desire for authentic and cost-effective travel experiences. The company's strategy was informed by the macroenvironmental factors of technology and sociocultural shifts.

What you might read about macroenvironment

1. "The Five Competitive Forces That Shape Strategy" by Michael E. Porter (*Harvard Business Review*, 2008)—This seminal article explores the competitive forces within an industry, including macroenvironmental factors, and their influence on strategy development.
2. "Marketing Myopia" by Theodore Levitt (*Harvard Business Review*, 1960)—While not specifically focused on macroenvironmental factors, this article emphasizes the importance of understanding customer needs and external market dynamics when formulating strategy.
3. *Blue Ocean Strategy* by W. Chan Kim and Renée Mauborgne—This book introduces the concept of creating uncontested market space by exploring new market segments and customer value propositions, considering macroenvironmental factors to identify blue ocean opportunities.
4. *The Innovator's Dilemma* by Clayton M. Christensen—This book explores how disruptive technologies can reshape industries and the macroenvironment, challenging established companies to adapt their strategies to the changing landscape.

5. *Competitive Strategy: Techniques for Analyzing Industries and Competitors* by Michael E. Porter—In this book, Porter provides a framework for analyzing the macroenvironment, industry structure, and competitive forces to develop effective strategies.

6. *The Lean Startup: How Today's Entrepreneurs Use Continuous Innovation to Create Radically Successful Businesses* by Eric Ries—This book emphasizes the importance of considering macroenvironmental factors, such as customer feedback and market trends, in the iterative and agile development of startup strategies.

7. *The Art of Strategy: A Game Theorist's Guide to Success in Business and Life* by Avinash K. Dixit and Barry J. Nalebuff—This book explores strategic decision-making in various contexts, including macroenvironmental factors, and introduces game theory as a tool for strategic analysis.

8. *Strategy Safari: A Guided Tour Through the Wilds of Strategic Management* by Henry Mintzberg, Bruce Ahlstrand, and Joseph Lampel—This book provides an overview of various strategic management perspectives, including the analysis of macroenvironmental factors, to understand different approaches to strategy formulation.

9. *Environmental Scanning and Sustainable Development: An Introduction to the Theory* by Fergus Anderson—This article examines the concept of environmental scanning, which involves analyzing macroenvironmental factors to identify threats and opportunities for sustainable development.

10. *Globalization and the Environment: Determinants of Firm Self-regulation in China* by Richard M. Locke, Fei Qin, and Alberto Brause (Management Science, 2007)—This academic article explores the influence of macroenvironmental factors, including regulatory frameworks and market pressures, on firm self-regulation and environmental sustainability efforts in China.

Defining the Term: Complexity Differential

In today's dynamic and interconnected business environment, organizations are constantly bombarded with a vast array of signals from their macroenvironment. These signals come in various forms, such as market trends, customer feedback, technological advancements, regulatory changes, and competitive moves. Effectively managing these signals and distinguishing the ones that require a response from the noise is a crucial aspect of strategic decision-making.

The concept of complexity differential refers to the challenge organizations face in navigating the complex and often ambiguous signals emanating from their macroenvironment. It involves the ability to identify and understand the signals that are relevant to the organization's strategic goals and respond to them appropriately. The complexity differential arises due to the increasing complexity and interconnectedness of the business landscape, making it difficult for organizations to discern meaningful patterns and make well-informed decisions.

One of the key factors in managing complexity differential is effective communication within the organization. Communication serves as the vital link that connects the external signals from the macroenvironment with the internal decision-making processes. It involves the flow of information, ideas, and knowledge across different levels and functions of the organization, enabling a shared understanding of the external environment and facilitating coordinated responses.

To manage complexity differential effectively, organizations need to establish robust communication mechanisms that facilitate the exchange of relevant information and insights. This includes creating channels for capturing and disseminating external signals, such as market research, customer feedback systems, industry reports, and competitive intelligence. It also involves fostering a culture of open communication and collaboration, where employees are encouraged to share their observations, insights, and ideas related to the macroenvironment.

Furthermore, organizations need to develop processes for filtering, analyzing, and interpreting the signals they receive from the macroenvironment. This involves employing data analytics, trend analysis, scenario planning, and other strategic tools to make sense of the complex and diverse information streams. By leveraging these tools, organizations can identify patterns, spot emerging trends, and assess the implications of the signals on their strategic direction.

To illustrate the importance of managing complexity differential, let's consider a hypothetical example of a global consumer goods company; we will call it XYZ. The company operates in a highly competitive and rapidly changing market, with numerous macroenvironmental factors influencing its business. These factors include shifting consumer preferences, technological advancements, regulatory changes, and evolving market dynamics.

To stay ahead in this complex environment, XYZ recognizes the need to effectively manage complexity differential. So what do they do? They established a dedicated market intelligence team responsible for monitoring and analyzing the signals from the macroenvironment. The data and analytics team at XYZ collects data on consumer trends, competitor activities, and market insights. The information and insights are then disseminated to relevant departments within the organization leveraging XYZ's internal communication channels and business processes.

Thus, when the marketing department receives updates on changing consumer preferences and emerging market trends, this information helps them develop targeted marketing campaigns, launch new products that align with consumer needs, and adapt their messaging to stay relevant in the market. All of this must be in line with the strategic priorities at XYZ, and therefore, only act on the market signals that advance the company's business agenda. The product development team, on the other hand, uses the signals from the macroenvironment to identify opportunities for innovation and develop products that address emerging customer demands.

By effectively managing complexity differential through robust communication and information-sharing processes, XYZ can make informed strategic decisions and respond to the changing macroenvironment. This enables them to seize opportunities, mitigate risks, and maintain a competitive edge in their industry.

In reality, there is an urge in poorly led organizations to overreact to macroenvironmental signals, and hence, these organizations feel obligated to respond.... so they do, and they do it often. How? Via new product announcements, commitment to regulatory conditions (regardless of the applicability)...; think of the current trends relevant to AI and electrification. There are certain signals in the market, regulatory domains, etc. So instead of taking a calculated look at these signals, many organizations focusing on finding a "use case" for AI, for example, to demonstrate their awareness and level of advancement.

IDEA IN BRIEF: Complexity differential poses a challenge for organizations in navigating the signals from their macroenvironment. Effective communication and information management play a critical role in managing this complexity. By establishing robust communication mechanisms, filtering and interpreting signals, and fostering a culture of collaboration, organizations can enhance their ability to respond to the relevant signals from the macroenvironment and make well-informed strategic decisions.

Complexity Differential Implications on Strategy

The concept of complexity differential recognizes that not all signals are equally important or actionable for an organization. It emphasizes the need for strategic decision-makers to differentiate between noise and valuable insights, enabling them to make informed choices and trade-offs. Organizations cannot afford to respond to every signal they receive, as resources are limited, and not all signals will have a significant impact on their strategic direction.

To illustrate the implications of complexity differential on strategy, let's consider our earlier example; but this time, XYZ is a technology company in the automotive industry. In recent years, XYZ observed a surge in signals related to "Big Data," "connected vehicles," and AI technologies. These signals suggest potential opportunities for innovation and disruption in their industry. However, responding to every signal without strategic discernment would be inefficient and ineffective.

Aware of the complexity differential, XYZ recognizes the importance of selectively choosing the signals they respond to. They conducted a thorough analysis of the macroenvironmental signals related to Big Data, connected vehicles, and AI technologies. This analysis involved assessing the potential market size, customer needs, competitive landscape, technological feasibility, and alignment with their overall strategic objectives.

Through this analysis, XYZ identified while Big Data presents significant opportunities for data-driven decision-making and customer insights, connected vehicles offer possibilities for new revenue streams and enhanced customer experiences. Additionally, AI technologies hold the potential for process automation and improved operational efficiency. These signals align with the company's strategic focus on innovation, customer-centricity, and operational excellence.

However, XYZ also recognizes that not all signals are equally relevant or feasible for their organization. For instance, they may identify signals related to blockchain technology, virtual reality, or quantum computing. While these signals may be disruptive and attract attention in the broader market, XYZ determines that they do not align with its strategic priorities or core competencies at present. Thus, they choose to focus their resources on the signals that have a higher potential for impact and value creation.

By strategically selecting and responding to the signals that are most relevant to its strategic direction, XYZ can effectively allocate its resources, prioritize its initiatives, and seize the opportunities that align with its competitive advantage. This approach allows them to maintain focus, streamline their innovation efforts, and achieve a higher likelihood of success in their strategic endeavors.

Selecting from the signals received from the macroenvironment is of utmost importance for organizations as it directly influences their strategic decisions. So, why is this selective process actually important? Well, for several reasons:

■ Resource Allocation: Organizations have limited resources, including financial capital, human capital, and time. By selecting signals that align with their strategic objectives, organizations can allocate their resources efficiently and effectively. This ensures that resources are directed toward initiatives that have a higher potential for success and value creation. For example, if an organization's strategic focus is on technological innovation, it may prioritize signals related to emerging technologies and invest resources in research and development, talent acquisition, and infrastructure to support innovation efforts.

■ Competitive Advantage: Strategic choices made based on the selected signals can contribute to an organization's competitive advantage. By analyzing and responding to signals that align with their unique capabilities, organizations can differentiate themselves from competitors. For instance, if a signal suggests a market opportunity that leverages the organization's core competencies, the organization can develop tailored strategies to capitalize on that opportunity, creating a competitive edge.

■ Market Alignment: Selecting signals that are relevant to the organization's target market and customer needs is crucial for market alignment. By understanding customer preferences and market trends, organizations can develop products, services, and value propositions that resonate with their target audience. This customer-centric approach enables organizations to deliver superior customer experiences, increase customer satisfaction, and build long-term customer loyalty.

■ Risk Mitigation: Not all signals may carry equal levels of risk for an organization. By carefully selecting signals, organizations can manage and mitigate risks effectively. They can assess the potential risks associated with each signal, such as market volatility, regulatory changes, or technological uncertainties. This enables organizations to make informed decisions and develop risk mitigation strategies to minimize potential negative impacts on their operations and performance.

■ Agility and Adaptation: The process of selecting signals and making strategic choices fosters organizational agility and adaptability. In today's dynamic business environment, organizations must be responsive to changes and seize emerging opportunities swiftly. By continuously evaluating and selecting signals, organizations can adapt their strategies to evolving market conditions, emerging technologies, and customer preferences. This agility allows organizations to stay ahead of the competition and navigate disruptions effectively.

What you might read about complexity differential

1. "Sensemaking in Organizations" by Karl E. Weick (1995)—This influential article explores how organizations make sense of complex and ambiguous situations and highlights the importance of interpreting and selecting signals in the decision-making process.

2. *Strategic Management: Concepts and Cases* by Fred R. David and Forest R. David (2020)—This comprehensive textbook covers various aspects of strategic management, including the analysis of complex environments and the process of selecting signals to inform strategic decisions.

3. *The Signal and the Noise: Why So Many Predictions Fail—But Some Don't* by Nate Silver (2012)—While not specifically focused on business strategy, this book explores the challenges of distinguishing meaningful signals from noise in various domains, providing insights applicable to decision-making in organizations.

4. *Competing on Analytics: The New Science of Winning* by Thomas H. Davenport and Jeanne G. Harris (2007)—This book emphasizes the importance of effectively analyzing and interpreting data signals to drive strategic decision-making and gain a competitive advantage.
5. *The Strategist: Be the Leader Your Business Needs* by Cynthia Montgomery (2012)—Montgomery highlights the role of leaders in selecting and interpreting signals to make strategic choices that align with the organization's purpose and values.
6. *The Innovator's Dilemma: When New Technologies Cause Great Firms to Fail* by Clayton M. Christensen (1997)—This book explores the challenges organizations face in navigating disruptive technologies and the need to carefully select signals to respond to in order to stay competitive in changing markets.
7. *Competitive Strategy: Techniques for Analyzing Industries and Competitors* by Michael E. Porter (1980)—Porter's classic book provides frameworks for analyzing industry dynamics and highlights the importance of selecting signals that align with an organization's competitive position and strategic goals.
8. *Good Strategy/Bad Strategy: The Difference and Why It Matters* by Richard P. Rumelt (2011)—Rumelt discusses the importance of selecting distinctive strategic moves and focusing on areas that provide a competitive advantage, rather than pursuing generic strategies that fail to differentiate.

Chapter 3

The Organization as a Complex Adaptative System

Set-the-Stage Mini Case

Hilton's Adaptation to Digital Transformation

Hilton Worldwide, a leading player in the global hospitality industry, faced the challenge of integrating digital innovation to enhance guest experiences and streamline operations. Recognizing the rapid shift towards digital technology and the evolving expectations of tech-savvy travelers, Hilton embarked on a comprehensive digital transformation strategy. This strategy included the introduction of the Hilton Honors app, which allowed guests to check in, select their room, and use their smartphones as room keys. The app also enabled guests to make requests for amenities and services, thereby enhancing convenience and personalizing the guest experience.

In addition to improving guest interactions, Hilton leveraged data analytics and artificial intelligence to optimize its operations. By analyzing data from its vast network of properties, Hilton could predict occupancy trends, manage inventory more effectively, and tailor marketing efforts to individual customer preferences. This digital shift not only improved operational efficiency but also allowed Hilton to provide a more personalized and seamless experience for its

DOI: 10.4324/9781003564133-4

guests. By embracing digital transformation, Hilton demonstrated the principles of a complex adaptive system, continuously evolving and adapting to external technological advancements and internal operational needs. This strategic approach positioned Hilton as a forward-thinking leader in the hospitality industry, capable of meeting the demands of modern travelers while maintaining a competitive edge.

Complex Adaptive System: The Concept

CAS provides a valuable lens through which we can understand organizations in a dynamic and interconnected world. Just like the human body, organizations are complex and adaptive entities, composed of interconnected parts that work together to achieve collective goals. The concept of CAS stems from complexity theory, which recognizes that organizations, much like living organisms, exhibit emergent properties and nonlinear behaviors that cannot be fully understood by examining their components in isolation.

In the context of the macroenvironment, organizations face a multitude of interconnected and dynamic factors that influence their operations and outcomes. These factors can include market trends, technological advancements, regulatory changes, customer preferences, and competitive forces. The macroenvironment acts as a complex and ever-evolving system that shapes the context in which organizations operate. Just as the human body must adapt to changes in the external environment, organizations must also adapt to these external influences to survive and thrive.

The complexity of organizations arises from their intricate network of relationships, both internal and external. Within the organization, there are numerous interconnected departments, teams, and individuals, each with their own goals, expertise, and perspectives. These components interact and influence one another, creating a web of relationships that can give rise to emergent behaviors and outcomes. This complexity can be seen in the way organizations respond to external stimuli and navigate through various challenges and opportunities.

The adaptive nature of organizations is rooted in their ability to sense and respond to changes in the environment. Just as our bodies respond to external stimuli through our senses and nervous system, organizations employ various mechanisms to gather information, interpret signals, and make decisions. This adaptability allows organizations to adjust their strategies, structures, processes, and resources to align with the changing dynamics of their environment.

By recognizing organizations as CASs, we gain a deeper understanding of their dynamic nature and the challenges they face. This recognition also highlights the importance of embracing complexity and uncertainty and the need for organizations to be agile, responsive, and innovative in their approach. Just as the human body constantly adapts and evolves to maintain equilibrium and health, organizations must continuously adapt and evolve to remain competitive and sustainable.

For instance, consider how companies in the technology industry, such as Google or Apple, continuously adapt their strategies and product offerings to keep up with rapidly changing customer needs and advancements in technology. These organizations operate in a highly dynamic and competitive environment, where they must navigate complex market trends, emerging technologies, and evolving consumer preferences.

Furthermore, organizations that operate in regulated industries, such as healthcare or finance, must adapt to changing regulatory frameworks and compliance requirements. They must navigate complex legal and ethical considerations while ensuring the delivery of high-quality services to their customers.

IDEA IN BRIEF: Organizations can be best understood as CASs, exhibiting properties of complexity and adaptability like living organisms. This perspective highlights the interconnectedness of various factors in the macroenvironment, the complexity of internal relationships within organizations, and the need for adaptability to navigate through uncertainty and change. Embracing the notion of organizations as CAS allows us to appreciate the challenges and opportunities they face and provides insights into effective strategies for managing complexity and fostering adaptability.

CAS Implications on Strategy

The notion of CAS has significant implications for strategy development and deployment in organizations. CAS recognizes that organizations exist within a complex and dynamic ecosystem, influenced by a multitude of factors in their macroenvironment. This complexity extends to the internal structure of the organization itself, creating a web of interconnected relationships and dependencies. Understanding and embracing CAS principles can inform strategic choices and enable organizations to navigate the challenges and opportunities presented by their ever-changing environment.

Strategy development in CAS recognizes that organizations operate in a dynamic and uncertain landscape. Traditional approaches to strategy often assume a stable and predictable environment, which is no longer the reality for many organizations. CAS thinking acknowledges the complexity and dynamism of the macroenvironment, which includes market trends, technological advancements, regulatory changes, customer preferences, and competitive forces. These factors continuously evolve, creating a need for a dynamic and adaptive approach to strategy.

Through the CAS lens, strategy is not a one-time, static plan, but an ongoing process of sense-making, adaptation, and learning. Organizations must continuously gather information, monitor signals from the macroenvironment, and adjust their strategies accordingly. This requires a keen awareness of the interconnections between the organization and its environment, as well as the ability to quickly sense and respond to emerging opportunities and threats.

The microenvironment, or the internal structure of the organization, is also influenced by CAS perspective. Just as the macroenvironment is complex and dynamic, so too is the internal network of relationships within an organization. Departments, teams, and individuals are interconnected and interdependent, with information and resources flowing through various channels. This complexity within the organization affects decision-making, communication, and coordination, all of which are essential elements of effective strategy development and deployment.

The industry life cycle further emphasizes the importance of CAS thinking in strategy. As industries evolve through different phases of the life cycle, from embryonic to decline, the dynamics and challenges faced by organizations change. A CAS perspective recognizes that effective strategies during one phase may not be suitable for another (kind of similar to how our clothing style changes as we transition from childhood to teenage and then to adulthood). Organizations must adapt their strategies based on the unique characteristics of each phase, including market growth, competition, customer preferences, and technological advancements.

Netflix: Started as a DVD-by-mail rental service, Netflix was later transformed into a leading streaming platform. It recognized the changing dynamics of the macroenvironment, including the shift in customer preferences toward digital content consumption. They adapted their strategy by embracing streaming technology and investing in original content, positioning themselves as a dominant player in the industry. This strategic adaptation was driven by an understanding of the CAS dynamics at play, both in the macroenvironment and within the organization itself.

Amazon: It is a company that continuously adjusts its strategies based on market trends, customer demands, and technological advancements. Amazon's success lies in its ability to sense emerging opportunities, such as the growing demand for e-commerce, cloud computing, and voice-assisted technology. By employing a CAS perspective, Amazon strategically positions itself at the forefront of innovation and disrupts traditional business models.

> **IDEA IN BRIEF**: CAS has profound implications for strategy development and deployment in organizations. It recognizes the complex and dynamic nature of the macroenvironment and the interconnectedness within the organization itself. CAS thinking informs strategic choices by acknowledging the need for a dynamic and adaptive approach to strategy, based on an understanding of the industry life cycle, market dynamics, and internal relationships. Embracing CAS principles enables organizations to navigate the complexities of their environment, seize opportunities, and stay competitive in a rapidly changing world.

What you might read about CAS

1. *Complexity: The Emerging Science at the Edge of Order and Chaos* by M. Mitchell Waldrop
2. *The Black Swan: The Impact of the Highly Improbable* by Nassim Nicholas Taleb
3. *Antifragile: Things That Gain from Disorder* by Nassim Nicholas Taleb
4. *Thinking in Systems: A Primer* by Donella H. Meadows
5. *Linked: How Everything Is Connected to Everything Else and What It Means for Business, Science, and Everyday Life* by Albert-László Barabási
6. *The Tipping Point: How Little Things Can Make a Big Difference* by Malcolm Gladwell
7. *The Innovator's Dilemma: When New Technologies Cause Great Firms to Fail* by Clayton M. Christensen
8. *Outliers: The Story of Success* by Malcolm Gladwell
9. *The Wisdom of Crowds: Why the Many Are Smarter Than the Few and How Collective Wisdom Shapes Business, Economies, Societies, and Nations* by James Surowiecki
10. *Thinking, Fast and Slow* by Daniel Kahneman

Chapter 4

The Industry Is Alive, and It Has a Life Cycle

Set-the-Stage Mini Case

John Deere's Evolution in Precision Agriculture

John Deere, a titan in the agricultural machinery industry, has consistently evolved to meet the changing demands of modern farming. Recognizing the transformative potential of technology in agriculture, John Deere has embraced precision agriculture, a farming management concept that uses GPS, IoT, and data analytics to optimize field-level management regarding crop farming. This strategic shift was driven by the need to enhance productivity, reduce costs, and promote sustainable farming practices.

In its journey through the industry life cycle, John Deere moved from simply manufacturing agricultural equipment to becoming a leader in agricultural technology. By integrating advanced sensors and data analytics into its machinery, John Deere enables farmers to collect real-time data on soil conditions, crop health, and equipment performance. This data-driven approach allows farmers to make informed decisions, optimize resource use, and increase crop yields. John Deere's precision agriculture solutions, such as the John Deere Operations Center and the ExactEmerge planting system, exemplify how the company has navigated the industry's growth stage by leveraging technological advancements to differentiate itself and

DOI: 10.4324/9781003564133-5

provide greater value to its customers. This evolution reflects John Deere's strategic adaptation to the industry's life cycle, ensuring it remains competitive and relevant in a rapidly advancing agricultural landscape.

In this chapter, we will revisit the concept of the *industry life cycle* from a new perspective. We will examine the implications of the industry life cycle on strategy development and explore how this understanding forms the foundation of this book's approach to strategy.

Throughout the chapter, we will highlight the genesis of this book's approach to strategy, which is rooted in the deep appreciation of the industry life cycle and its impact on strategic decision-making.

Defining the Industry Life Cycle—A New Perspective

At the heart of this book's approach to strategy lies a fresh perspective on the industry life cycle, which recognizes the dynamic nature of industries and their close resemblance to living organisms. To fully grasp the significance of the industry life cycle, it is important to understand the concept of the life cycle itself.

In its simplest form, a life cycle refers to the progression of stages that an entity undergoes from birth to maturity, and eventually to decline or renewal. Just as living organisms have life cycles characterized by different stages of growth, so do industries. The industry life cycle concept recognizes that industries, comprising clusters of organizations that perform similar tasks, exhibit patterns of evolution and transformation over time.

This notion of the industry life cycle as a reflection of the life cycle of living organisms is a fundamental aspect of this book's perspective on strategy. By viewing industries as living entities, we can draw parallels between the challenges and opportunities faced by organizations and the natural processes observed in the world around us.

The embryonic stage of an industry is analogous to the birth of a new organism. New firms enter the market, innovation is thriving, and the potential for disruption is high. This stage represents the early growth and development phase, where organizations are establishing their presence and competing for market share. Examples of industries in the embryonic stage include the electric vehicle industry in its early days, with companies like Tesla paving the way for the adoption of electric vehicles.

As an industry progresses into the growth stage, it experiences a period of rapid expansion and increasing competition. This stage is analogous to the adolescence of a living organism, where growth spurts and experimentation are common. Organizations in this stage focus on differentiating themselves from competitors or achieving cost leadership to gain a competitive edge. A notable example is the ride-sharing industry, with companies like Uber and Lyft emerging as dominant players through innovative business models and technological advancements.

The next stage in the industry life cycle is the shakeout phase, which can be compared to the adulthood of a living organism. This stage is characterized by intense competition and market consolidation, as weaker players are weeded out and only the strongest survive. Organizations must adapt and evolve to remain competitive in this challenging phase. The smartphone industry provides an illustrative example, with fierce competition between major players like Apple, Samsung, and Google, leading to market consolidation and the exit of several smaller players.

Maturity represents the next stage in the industry life cycle, mirroring the stability and maturity observed in the later stages of a living organism's life cycle. In this phase, competition may become more focused on market share and profitability, and innovation may take a backseat. Established industries like the airline industry, with well-established players such as Delta, United, and American Airlines, operate in the maturity stage, where the emphasis is on efficiency and customer service.

The last state, the decline stage of an industry's life cycle, parallels the decline and eventual demise observed in aging organisms. Industries in this stage experience shrinking markets, declining demand, and obsolescence. Organizations must confront the reality of a declining industry and make strategic decisions, such as diversification or exiting the market. The traditional print media industry serves as a pertinent example, as it grapples with the challenges of digital disruption and shifting consumer preferences.

By recognizing the parallels between the life cycles of organizations and industries, we underscore the importance of understanding the industry life cycle as a strategic lens. We are provided with a framework for organizations to navigate the challenges and capitalize on the opportunities that arise at each stage of the industry's evolution.

Industry Life Cycle Implications on Strategy— The Genesis of This Book

In viewing industries as living entities with life cycles, it becomes evident that organizations operating within these industries are intricately connected to the dynamics of their respective life cycles. By recognizing the parallels between the life cycles of organizations and industries, we can gain valuable insights into the strategic implications of the industry life cycle.

One of the key reasons for understanding the industry life cycle as a strategic lens is the ability to anticipate and adapt to the changing dynamics within an industry. Just as individuals go through various life stages with unique characteristics and challenges, organizations also experience different stages as they navigate the industry landscape. By recognizing the similarities, organizations can proactively shape their strategies to align with the prevailing stage of the industry life cycle.

Let's consider the example of the personal computer industry to illustrate this point. In the embryonic stage of the industry, companies like Apple and IBM entered the market with innovative products. They recognized the potential of personal computers to revolutionize the way people work and communicate. By understanding the embryonic stage of the industry life cycle, these companies were able to make strategic choices that focused on product innovation, market penetration, and establishing a strong brand presence. This early mover advantage propelled them to become industry leaders.

As the personal computer industry transitioned to the growth stage, characterized by increased competition and market expansion, organizations such as Dell and HP emerged as prominent players. These companies recognized the importance of cost-efficiency and operational excellence in capturing market share. By understanding the growth stage of the industry life cycle, they strategically positioned themselves as providers of affordable and customizable computers, catering to the evolving needs of consumers.

In the subsequent shakeout stage, marked by industry consolidation and heightened competition, organizations like Lenovo and Acer successfully navigated the challenges. They recognized the need for strategic partnerships, acquisitions, and a focus on cost leadership to survive in a fiercely competitive environment. By understanding the shakeout stage of the industry life cycle, these companies were able to adapt their strategies and consolidate their market positions.

Moving to the maturity stage, companies like Microsoft and Intel understood the changing dynamics of the personal computer industry. They recognized the need to shift their focus from pure hardware to software and integrated solutions. By anticipating the maturity stage of the industry life cycle, they strategically positioned themselves as providers of operating systems, software applications, and microprocessors, ensuring their relevance in the evolving market.

Lastly, as the personal computer industry entered the decline stage with the advent of mobile devices and cloud computing, organizations like Dell and HP had to reassess their strategies. They recognized the need to diversify their product offerings, invest in emerging technologies, and explore new business models. By understanding the decline stage of the industry life cycle, these companies made strategic decisions to transform their business and adapt to the changing market landscape.

Strategic Implications of the Industry Life Cycle

By understanding the industry life cycle as a strategic lens and recognizing the parallels between the life cycles of organizations and industries, leaders gain a powerful tool for making informed strategic choices, adapting to market dynamics, and positioning their organizations for long-term success. This understanding becomes particularly crucial when we consider the iterative and dynamic nature of the strategy development and deployment process.

In the process of developing and deploying strategies, organizations must continually gather information, assess market conditions, and make decisions based on the signals they receive from the macroenvironment. These signals provide valuable insights into industry trends, customer preferences, technological advancements, regulatory changes, and competitive forces. By paying close attention to these signals and aligning their strategies with the prevailing stage of the industry life cycle, leaders can proactively respond to market shifts and gain a competitive advantage.

The strategy development process is not a one-time, linear exercise but rather a dynamic and iterative feedback loop. It involves continuous scanning of the macroenvironment, evaluating the organization's internal capabilities, setting strategic objectives, formulating action plans, implementing initiatives, and monitoring performance. At each stage of this process, the organization relies on the signals from the macroenvironment to inform its strategic choices and make necessary adjustments to achieve its objectives.

In the early stages of the industry life cycle, organizations may need to focus on innovation, market penetration, and building brand presence. The signals from the macroenvironment guide leaders in identifying emerging customer needs, technological disruptions, and competitive threats. By understanding these signals and integrating them into their strategy development process, leaders can allocate resources to research and development, invest in new technologies, and develop unique value propositions that capture market share and establish a competitive position.

As the industry progresses to the growth stage, leaders must be attuned to changing customer preferences, shifts in market demand, and the emergence of new competitors. The signals from the macroenvironment inform leaders about evolving market dynamics, demographic trends, and technological advancements. Organizations can respond by differentiating their products and services, expanding into new markets, and optimizing their operational efficiencies. By aligning their strategies with these signals, leaders can capitalize on growth opportunities, penetrate new segments, and strengthen their market position.

During the maturity stage of the industry life cycle, leaders must navigate intense competition, market saturation, and the need for product diversification.

The signals from the macroenvironment guide leaders in identifying emerging customer preferences, disruptive technologies, and regulatory changes. Organizations can respond by investing in product innovation, enhancing customer experiences, and exploring strategic partnerships. By leveraging these signals in their strategy development process, leaders can sustain growth, adapt to market shifts, and maintain a competitive edge in the industry.

Finally, in the decline stage of the industry life cycle, leaders must be vigilant in detecting signals of market obsolescence, shifting consumer behaviors, and emerging industry disruptors. The signals from the macroenvironment inform leaders about changing market dynamics, technological advancements, and shifts in customer needs. Organizations can respond by diversifying their product portfolio, exploring new business models, and strategically exiting declining segments. By recognizing and interpreting these signals in their strategy development process, leaders can navigate the decline phase and position their organizations for new opportunities in other industries or emerging markets.

The dynamic nature of the strategy development process, combined with the understanding of the industry life cycle as a strategic lens, enables leaders to make informed choices, adapt to market dynamics, and position their organizations for long-term success. By embracing this perspective, leaders can proactively respond to industry shifts, leverage emerging opportunities, and effectively manage risks. This holistic approach to strategy development ensures that organizations remain agile, resilient, and competitive in an ever-changing business landscape.

The process of strategy development and deployment involves a strategic cascade that aligns the organization's objectives, choices, and actions. This cascade, as described in "Playing to Win" by A.G. Lafley and Roger L. Martin, provides a framework for translating high-level strategic intent into actionable plans at different levels of the organization.

At the highest level, leaders define the organization's overall strategic intent, which encompasses its purpose, vision, and desired outcomes. This strategic intent serves as a guiding star that informs the subsequent levels of strategy development. It provides a clear direction and sets the context for making choices and trade-offs.

The strategy cascade then moves to the business-level, where leaders formulate strategies that enable the organization to achieve its strategic intent. This involves making choices between differentiation and cost leadership, as well as identifying the core capabilities and value propositions that will drive the organization's competitive advantage. The signals from the macroenvironment, such as emerging market trends, customer preferences, and competitive dynamics, inform these strategic choices. For example, if the macroenvironment signals a shift toward sustainability and environmental consciousness, leaders may choose to develop a differentiation strategy centered around eco-friendly products and practices.

Moving further down the cascade, the strategy development process extends to the functional-level, where leaders translate the high-level strategies into specific action plans for each functional area of the organization. This includes marketing, operations, finance, human resources, and other key functions. At this level, the complexity differential and signals from the macroenvironment become even more critical. Leaders must select and prioritize the signals that are most relevant to their functional area and align their strategies accordingly. For instance, the marketing function may respond to signals of changing customer behaviors and preferences by developing targeted marketing campaigns and innovative customer experiences.

Throughout the strategy development and deployment process, there is a constant feedback loop between the different levels of the cascade. The choices and actions at the functional-level feed into the business-level strategies, which in turn align with the overall strategic intent. This iterative process ensures that the organization's strategies remain dynamic, adaptive, and responsive to the signals from the macroenvironment. By continuously monitoring the macroenvironmental factors and incorporating new information into the strategy cascade, leaders can make timely adjustments and keep the organization on track toward its strategic objectives.

A guideline for strategy development and deployment based on the concepts discussed:

1. Define the organization's strategic intent: Start by articulating the organization's purpose, vision, and desired outcomes. This strategic intent serves as a guiding star that informs subsequent strategic choices.
2. Conduct a thorough analysis of the macroenvironment: Understand the external factors that shape the industry landscape, including market trends, customer preferences, technological advancements, competitive forces, and regulatory factors. Identify the signals that are most relevant to your organization.
3. Make strategic choices at the business-level: Formulate high-level strategies that enable the organization to achieve its strategic intent. Consider the complexity differential and select the signals from the macroenvironment that will inform your strategic choices. Decide between differentiation and cost leadership and identify the core capabilities and value propositions that will drive your competitive advantage.
4. Cascade strategies to the functional-level: Translate the high-level strategies into specific action plans for each functional area of the organization. Align marketing, operations, finance, human resources, and other functions with the overall strategic direction. Ensure that the strategies within each function support the organization's differentiation or cost leadership approach.

5. Establish a feedback loop: Continuously monitor the macroenvironmental factors and incorporate new information into the strategy development process. Maintain an ongoing dialogue between different levels of the strategy cascade to ensure alignment and adaptability. Regularly review and adjust strategies as needed.

6. Communicate and align: Effectively communicate the strategic objectives and plans to all levels of the organization. Ensure that every employee understands their role in achieving the strategic objectives and how their work contributes to the overall strategy. Foster a culture of alignment, collaboration, and continuous improvement.

7. Monitor and evaluate: Implement a robust monitoring and evaluation system to track the progress of strategy implementation. Regularly assess the effectiveness of strategies, measure key performance indicators, and make data-driven decisions. Be open to feedback and adapt strategies based on lessons learned and changing market dynamics.

8. Foster a culture of agility and learning: Embrace the dynamic nature of strategy development and deployment. Encourage a mindset of agility, adaptability, and continuous learning throughout the organization. Emphasize the importance of staying responsive to the signals from the macroenvironment and making timely adjustments.

Remember, strategy development and deployment is an iterative process that requires ongoing assessment, adaptation, and alignment with the macroenvironmental factors. By following this guideline, organizations can navigate the complexities of the business landscape, make informed strategic choices, and position themselves for long-term success.

Strategy development and deployment process

1. Define strategic intent: Clarify the organization's purpose, vision, and desired outcomes.

2. Analyze the macroenvironment: Understand market trends, customer preferences, and competitive forces.

3. Make strategic choices: Select relevant signals, differentiate or pursue cost leadership, and identify core capabilities.

4. Cascade strategies: Translate high-level strategies into actionable plans for each functional area.

5. Establish a feedback loop: Continuously monitor and incorporate new information into the strategy development process.

6. Communicate and align: Ensure all employees understand their role in achieving strategic objectives.

7. Monitor and evaluate: Implement a robust system to track progress and make data-driven decisions.
8. Foster agility and learning: Embrace a culture of adaptability, responsiveness, and continuous improvement.

By following this guideline, organizations can develop and deploy effective strategies that align with their goals, respond to market dynamics, and drive long-term success.

What you might read about industry life cycle

1. Vernon, R. (1966). *The product life cycle and international trade.* Harvard University Press.
2. Sull, D. N., & Turconi, S. (2008). *Strategies for declining businesses.* Harvard Business Review.
3. Siegel, D. S., Shepherd, D. A., & DeTienne, D. J. (2012). Managing decline: The role of organizational structure. *Strategic Management Journal,* 33(8), 857–877.
4. Christensen, C. M. (1997). *The innovator's dilemma: When new technologies cause great firms to fail. Harvard Business Review Press.*
5. Brown, S. L., & Eisenhardt, K. M. (1998). Competing on the edge: Strategy as structured chaos. *Harvard Business Review.*
6. Kim, W. C., & Mauborgne, R. (2005). *Blue ocean strategy: How to create uncontested market space and make the competition irrelevant. Harvard Business Review Press.*
7. Baghai, M., Coley, S., & White, D. (2000). *The alchemy of growth: Practical insights for building the enduring enterprise.* Perseus Books Group.
8. Hartford, T. (2008). *Adaptive strategy: Profit from uncertainty.* MIT Sloan Management Review.
9. Holcomb, T. R., Sullivan, M. L., & Harrison, J. S. (2009). The dynamics of industry self-organization: Evidence from the video game industry. *Journal of Management Studies,* 46(7), 1197–1222.
10. Elkington, J., & Hartigan, P. (2008). *The power of unreasonable people: How social entrepreneurs create markets that change the world.* Harvard Business School Press.
11. Porter, M. E. (1996). *Competitive strategy: Techniques for analyzing industries and competitors.* Free Press.
12. Kotler, P., & Keller, K. L. (2012). *Marketing management.* Pearson.
13. Hamel, G., & Prahalad, C. K. (1994). *Competing for the future. Harvard Business Review Press.*

14. Mintzberg, H., Ahlstrand, B., & Lampel, J. (2009). *Strategy safari: A guided tour through the wilds of strategic management.* Free Press.
15. Collins, J. C. (2001). Good to great: Why some companies make the leap… and others don't. Harper Business.
16. Kim, W. C., & Mauborgne, R. (2005). *Blue ocean strategy: How to create uncontested market space and make the competition irrelevant. Harvard Business Review Press.*
17. Christensen, C. M. (1997). *The innovator's dilemma: When new technologies cause great firms to fail. Harvard Business Review Press.*
18. Grant, R. M. (2019). *Contemporary strategy analysis: Text and cases.* Wiley.

Chapter 5

Organizations and Industries Are Alive, So Should Strategy

Set-the-Stage Mini Case

Spotify's Adaptive Strategy in the Music Streaming Industry

Spotify's journey in the music streaming industry exemplifies a strategic approach that aligns with the dynamic nature of both the industry and the organization itself. Launched in 2008, Spotify entered the market during a period of significant disruption caused by the decline of physical media sales and the rise of digital piracy. Recognizing an opportunity in the embryonic phase of the music streaming industry, Spotify developed a unique value proposition centered around accessibility, convenience, and a vast library of music. Spotify's initial strategy focused on offering a freemium model, which allowed users to access a large catalog of music for free with ads, or opt for a premium subscription for an ad-free experience and additional features. This model effectively addressed the market's need for a legal and user-friendly alternative to piracy. By lowering entry barriers and providing an attractive value proposition, Spotify rapidly grew its user base and established itself as a key player in the industry.

As the industry evolved, so did Spotify's strategy. The company continuously invested in technology to enhance its platform,

DOI: 10.4324/9781003564133-6

focusing on personalized user experiences through sophisticated algorithms and data analytics. Spotify's Discover Weekly and Release Radar playlists, for instance, leverage user data to provide tailored music recommendations, increasing user engagement and retention. This data-driven approach not only improved the user experience but also created a competitive edge by differentiating Spotify from other streaming services. Moreover, Spotify expanded its strategic focus by integrating podcasts into its platform, recognizing the growing demand for diverse audio content. Acquisitions of podcast companies like Gimlet Media and Anchor, along with exclusive deals with popular podcasters, have positioned Spotify as a comprehensive audio platform, catering to a wide range of consumer preferences. Spotify's adaptive strategy is a testament to its ability to navigate the complexities of the macroenvironment, respond to market signals, and leverage its capabilities as a Complex Adaptive System (CAS).

In this brief and recap chapter, we bring together the notion of a living entity for organizations (CAS) and industries (life cycle) and propose that strategy should also be perceived as such. As we explored the dynamic nature of strategy and its close relationship with the industry life cycle and organizations that operate within those industries, it becomes necessary to extend this notion to strategy as well. We have seen how organizations actively shape and respond to their industry's evolutionary path, positioning themselves for success. And so, strategy is not a static plan but a living and adaptive process that aligns with the changing dynamics of the industry. The backdrop, however, for any strategy work should be by the phase in which the respective industry is in.

So far in this book, I have emphasized the parallelism between organizations and living organisms. Just as living organisms adapt and evolve in response to their environment, organizations must also be agile and responsive to the changing dynamics of their industry. Strategy, in this context, becomes a dynamic and ongoing process that involves proactive actions and reactive adjustments.

And so, organizations must constantly evaluate their industry's current phase and position themselves accordingly. In the embryonic phase, they may need to disrupt existing norms and establish a strong foothold. During the growth phase, they must emerge as differentiators or cost leaders to capture market share. In the shakeout phase, they need to adapt and survive amidst fierce competition. In the maturity phase, they must compete effectively while navigating the challenges of a crowded market. And in the decline phase, they face the decision to either exit or reinvent themselves.

Each phase requires a unique strategic approach that aligns with the industry's characteristics and the organization's capabilities. It involves a deep understanding of the market, customer needs, competitive landscape, and emerging trends. Strategy becomes a dynamic dance, as organizations continually reassess and refine their direction based on market feedback, technological advancements, and competitive dynamics.

As we dig deeper into the subsequent chapters, we will explore each phase of the industry life cycle in detail, providing practical frameworks, real-world examples, and insightful strategies for success. Strategy comes alive as organizations actively navigate their industry's evolutionary path, leveraging their capabilities, and making strategic choices that shape their destiny.

Unfortunately, many organizations large and small across a multitude of industries approach strategy differently. Many times, strategy (especially coined concepts like Blue Ocean and Disruptive Innovation (although one can argue that is not a strategy per se) is treated as a flavor of the month or influenced by what's buzzing in the business world; regardless of the implications of the industry phase in which the organization competes.

And so, what we end up with is just a "strategy exercise" that does not have any bearing on the strategic direction or produce value for the organization. Many of these "strategy exercises" end up being pet projects for executives in the company.

In the context of this book, we have already established grounds for the strategy being a dynamic and adaptive process (as opposed to a static plan) that organizations engage in as they compete in their industries. The strategy then becomes a reflection of the organization's proactive and reactive actions to navigate the challenges and opportunities presented by the evolving market dynamics. Strategy is the guiding force that shapes the organization's direction and enables it to thrive in a complex and ever-changing business environment.

The industry life cycle provides a framework for understanding the evolution of an industry over time. It consists of distinct phases, including embryonic, growth, shakeout, maturity, and decline. Each phase is characterized by unique challenges, market conditions, and competitive dynamics. By recognizing and responding to the industry life cycle phase, organizations can tailor their strategies to capitalize on emerging opportunities and mitigate risks.

In the embryonic phase, organizations are at the early stages of an industry's development. The market is still nascent, and there is high uncertainty and experimentation. It is during this phase that innovative companies have the opportunity to disrupt the existing market and establish a strong foothold. One example is Tesla, a company that entered the embryonic phase of the electric vehicle industry and revolutionized the market with its cutting-edge technology and sustainable transportation vision.

As the industry transitions into the growth phase, organizations experience rapid expansion and increased competition. This is the phase where market demand for products or services rises, attracting new entrants and intensifying rivalry. Companies need to differentiate themselves or focus on cost leadership to gain a competitive advantage. Amazon exemplifies this approach as it emerged as a dominant player in the e-commerce industry during the growth phase by offering a vast selection of products, competitive prices, and superior customer service.

In the shakeout phase, the industry becomes more mature and competition intensifies. Companies face increased pressure to adapt and survive amidst market consolidation. Strategic alliances, mergers, and acquisitions become common as organizations seek to strengthen their position and streamline operations. Nokia, once a leader in the mobile phone industry, faced challenges during the shakeout phase as it struggled to adapt to the emergence of smartphones and the changing market dynamics.

The maturity phase is characterized by market saturation and intense competition. Organizations need to focus on maintaining market share and sustaining customer loyalty. They invest in product innovation, customer experience, and operational efficiency. Procter & Gamble (P&G) is an example of a company that successfully navigated the maturity phase by continuously innovating its product portfolio, expanding into new markets, and enhancing customer engagement through strategic marketing campaigns.

Lastly, in the decline phase, organizations face declining market demand and shrinking opportunities. Some companies choose to exit the market gracefully, while others reinvent themselves by exploring new avenues for growth. IBM provides an example of a company that transformed itself during the decline phase of the mainframe computer industry. By shifting its focus to enterprise software and services, IBM successfully navigated the decline phase and established itself as a leader in the new era of technology.

Throughout the industry life cycle, strategy is what organizations do to position themselves strategically and respond to the changing market dynamics. It is not a one-size-fits-all approach but a dynamic process that requires continuous evaluation, adaptation, and innovation. By proactively identifying emerging trends, understanding customer needs, and leveraging their core competencies, organizations can make strategic choices that align with the industry life cycle phase.

Strategy in the context of the industry life cycle is a dynamic interplay between proactive and reactive actions. Organizations must be proactive in anticipating and capitalizing on emerging opportunities, such as technological advancements, shifts in customer preferences, or changes in regulatory landscapes. At the same time, they must be reactive to market feedback, competitive moves, and macroenvironmental shifts.

This dynamic nature of strategy requires organizations to be agile, flexible, and adaptive. They must constantly monitor the macroenvironment, analyze industry trends, and gather insights from customers, competitors, and other stakeholders. By staying attuned to the pulse of the industry, organizations can make informed strategic choices that maximize their chances of success.

IDEA IN BRIEF: Strategy is what organizations do to position themselves competitively within their respective industry life cycle phase. It is a dynamic and adaptive process that enables organizations to navigate the evolving market dynamics and position themselves strategically. By recognizing the parallels between the life cycles of organizations and industries, leaders can make informed strategic choices, adapt to market dynamics, and position their organizations for long-term success. Through proactive and reactive actions, organizations can leverage their capabilities, capitalize on emerging opportunities, and navigate the challenges of a dynamic business environment.

STRATEGY ACROSS THE INDUSTRY LIFE CYCLE

Chapter 6

Embryonic: Disrupt Your Way Through

Set-the-Stage Mini Case

Netflix: notable example of a company that implemented a disruptive strategy is Netflix. Netflix started as a DVD rental-by-mail service, challenging the traditional brick-and-mortar video rental stores like Blockbuster. Their disruptive approach completely transformed the home entertainment industry.

In the early 2000s, Netflix recognized the changing landscape of media consumption and the potential of digital streaming. They shifted their focus from physical DVDs to an online streaming platform, offering customers the convenience of instantly accessing a vast library of movies and TV shows from their devices.

Netflix disrupted the industry by introducing a subscription-based model that allowed unlimited streaming for a monthly fee, eliminating the need for physical rentals and late fees. This innovative approach resonated with consumers who sought convenience and flexibility in their entertainment choices.

To support its disruptive strategy, Netflix heavily invested in technology infrastructure, content acquisition, and algorithmic recommendations. They used customer data and preferences to personalize the streaming experience, enhancing customer satisfaction and retention.

By continuously adapting its strategy, Netflix expanded into original content production, disrupting the traditional television

DOI: 10.4324/9781003564133-8

industry and becoming a major player in the streaming space. Their hit original series like "House of Cards," "Stranger Things," and "The Crown" have attracted a large and loyal subscriber base.

The disruptive strategy employed by Netflix fundamentally changed the dynamics of the home entertainment industry. It forced traditional video rental stores like Blockbuster to become obsolete, unable to compete with the convenience and breadth of content offered by Netflix's streaming platform. Today, Netflix is a global leader in the streaming industry, serving millions of subscribers worldwide.

Uber: Another notable example of a company that implemented a disruptive strategy is Uber. Uber revolutionized the transportation industry by introducing a platform that connects riders with drivers using a smartphone app. Their disruptive approach transformed the traditional taxi and transportation services.

Before Uber, hailing a taxi or arranging transportation often involved challenges such as limited availability, uncertain pricing, and lack of convenience. Uber saw an opportunity to address these pain points by leveraging technology and the sharing economy concept.

Uber disrupted the industry by offering a seamless and convenient ride-hailing experience. Through their app, users can request a ride, track the driver's location, and make cashless payments. This approach revolutionized the transportation experience by providing greater transparency, shorter wait times, and competitive pricing.

By leveraging the power of their platform, Uber created a network of independent drivers who could use their own vehicles to provide transportation services. This decentralized model allowed for scalability and flexibility, enabling Uber to rapidly expand its services to cities around the world.

Uber's disruptive strategy faced resistance from established taxi services and regulatory challenges. However, their focus on providing a superior customer experience and leveraging technology to optimize operations allowed them to gain a significant market share.

Uber's success prompted traditional taxi companies to adapt and invest in their own mobile app-based platforms to compete. The introduction of ride-hailing services by other companies further transformed the transportation industry and highlighted the impact of disruptive strategies.

Airbnb: a company that disrupted the hospitality industry. Airbnb created a platform that allows individuals to rent out their properties or spare rooms to travelers, offering an alternative to traditional hotels and accommodations.

Before Airbnb, travelers typically had limited options when it came to finding accommodations, and hotels dominated the industry. Airbnb saw an opportunity to tap into the sharing economy and provide a more personalized and unique lodging experience for travelers.

By leveraging their platform, Airbnb enabled property owners to list their spaces for short-term rentals, giving travelers access to a wide range of accommodations at various price points. This disrupted the traditional hotel industry by offering more affordable options, greater flexibility, and a more local and authentic experience.

Airbnb's disruptive strategy not only provided value to travelers but also empowered homeowners and individuals to monetize their properties. It opened up a new revenue stream for homeowners and allowed them to leverage their assets in a way that was not possible before.

The impact of Airbnb's disruption was significant, challenging the dominance of traditional hotels and prompting the industry to adapt. Many hotels responded by diversifying their offerings, enhancing their digital presence, and embracing new technologies to compete with the growing popularity of Airbnb.

The success of Airbnb's disruptive strategy can be attributed to its ability to create a trusted platform, facilitate seamless transactions, and offer a unique value proposition to both hosts and guests. By focusing on building a community-driven marketplace, Airbnb fostered a sense of trust and authenticity that resonated with travelers seeking more personalized experiences.

Defining the Embryonic Phase

The embryonic phase of the industry life cycle represents the earliest stage of development for an industry or market. At this stage, the industry is characterized by low market penetration, limited product offerings, and a small customer base. The embryonic phase is often marked by high levels of uncertainty and experimentation as companies seek to establish themselves and define the industry's trajectory.

One key aspect of this phase is the relative instability of the industry. Market dynamics and customer preferences are still being shaped, and there may not be a clear dominant business model or industry structure. Companies entering this phase face the challenge of understanding the market potential and identifying the most effective strategies for growth.

The regulatory environment during the embryonic phase can vary depending on the industry. In some cases, regulations may be minimal or non-existent, allowing for more flexibility and innovation. However, in other industries, there may be significant regulatory hurdles that companies must navigate. Regulatory factors can impact market entry, product development, and business operations, making it crucial for companies to understand and comply with relevant regulations.

The competitive landscape in this phase is often characterized by a limited number of rivals. As the industry is still nascent, there may be few established players, providing opportunities for new entrants to make an impact. However, competition can still exist, especially if multiple companies are vying to establish themselves as leaders in the emerging market. Competitive dynamics during this phase can shape the industry's direction and determine the future competitive landscape.

In terms of pricing and market offerings, those can vary significantly. Companies may experiment with different pricing models, trying to find the optimal balance between attracting customers and generating sufficient revenue. Product offerings may also be limited initially, with companies focusing on developing and refining their core offerings. As the industry evolves, companies may introduce new features, services, or variations to differentiate themselves and capture market share.

To illustrate an example of the embryonic phase, let's consider the emergence of electric vehicles (EVs). Over the past decade, the EV industry has transitioned from its embryonic phase to the growth phase. In the early stages, the industry had a limited number of players, such as Tesla, Nissan, and Chevrolet, offering a small range of EV models. The market penetration of EVs was low, and there were significant uncertainties surrounding consumer adoption, charging infrastructure, and government policies.

During the embryonic phase, the EV industry faced challenges related to the regulatory environment. Government policies and incentives played a crucial role in promoting EV adoption and supporting the development of charging infrastructure. For example, initiatives like tax credits, rebates, and grants encouraged consumers to purchase EVs and helped address concerns about range anxiety.

The competitive landscape in the embryonic phase of the EV industry was relatively small but growing. Tesla emerged as a prominent player, pioneering EVs with long ranges and innovative features. Other automakers, including Nissan and Chevrolet, introduced their own electric models to capitalize on the emerging market.

In terms of pricing and market offerings, early EVs were often positioned as premium products, reflecting the higher costs of battery technology and limited economies of scale. However, as the industry matured and technology advancements were made, prices began to decrease, making EVs more accessible to a broader range of consumers.

The embryonic phase is not limited to the EV industry. Other examples include the early days of the personal computer industry, where companies like Apple and IBM introduced their initial models, or the early stages of the internet industry, with the emergence of companies like Netscape and Yahoo.

THE EMBRYONIC PHASE IN BRIEF: This phase of the industry life cycle represents a period of low market penetration, limited product offerings, and high levels of uncertainty. The stability of the industry, regulatory environment, competitive landscape, pricing, and market offerings all play crucial roles in shaping the trajectory of the industry. Understanding the dynamics of the embryonic phase is essential for companies seeking to establish themselves in emerging markets and position themselves for long-term success.

Key Characteristics of This Phase

✓ *Low Market Penetration*: The market penetration of products or services within the industry is typically low. This is because the industry is still in its early stages, and customer adoption is limited. Companies entering this phase face the challenge of attracting customers and building market demand for their offerings.

✓ *Limited Product Offerings*: Small range of product offerings or variations. They focus on developing and refining their core offerings to meet the initial market needs. The product offerings may lack the diversity and sophistication seen in the later stages of the industry life cycle.

✓ *High Level of Uncertainty*: High level of uncertainty and ambiguity. Companies may face challenges in understanding market potential, customer preferences, and the overall industry landscape. Uncertainties may arise from technological advancements, regulatory changes, or the lack of established industry standards.

✓ *Experimentation and Innovation*: Companies engage in experimentation and innovation as they seek to define the industry's trajectory. They explore different business models, pricing strategies, and approaches to meet customer needs. This experimentation lays the foundation for future growth and differentiation.

✓ *Limited Industry Structure*: Not well-defined. There may not be a clear dominant player or established industry standards. The lack of a defined structure allows for more flexibility and innovation but also introduces challenges in terms of market positioning and competitive dynamics.

✓ *Regulatory Challenges*: Government policies, regulations, and standards may be in their early stages or subject to change. Companies must navigate these regulatory hurdles and adapt to the evolving regulatory landscape.

✓ *Emerging Competitive Landscape*: Limited number of competitors. While there may be a few pioneering companies, the overall competitive landscape is still emerging. This provides opportunities for new entrants to establish themselves and gain market share. Competition may be intense as companies vie for early-mover advantage.

✓ *Pricing Flexibility*: Pricing strategies vary as companies seek to attract customers and establish their market presence. Pricing may reflect the costs associated with new technologies or limited economies of scale. Companies may experiment with different pricing models to find the right balance between attracting customers and generating sufficient revenue.

The Recommended Approach to Strategy During This Phase and Why

During the embryonic phase of the industry life cycle, organizations are advised to adopt a disruptive strategy as a recommended approach. Disruptive innovation, a concept introduced by Clayton Christensen, refers to the process by which new technologies, products, or services enter the market and disrupt the existing industry landscape. It often starts by targeting overlooked or underserved customer segments with simpler, more affordable, or more accessible alternatives. As organizations navigate the uncertainties and challenges of the embryonic phase, a disruptive strategy offers several advantages.

■ Exploiting White Spaces: Disruption allows organizations to identify and exploit the white spaces or gaps in the market that established players have overlooked. By focusing on underserved customer segments or unmet needs, disruptive companies can gain a foothold and establish themselves as market leaders.

■ Lowering Entry Barriers: Disruptive strategies often leverage new technologies or innovative business models to lower the entry barriers into the industry. This enables new entrants to compete effectively against established players who may be burdened by legacy systems, high-cost structures, or resistance to change. By embracing innovation, organizations can disrupt the status quo and gain a competitive advantage.

■ Navigating Uncertainty: The embryonic phase is characterized by a high level of uncertainty, making it challenging to predict market dynamics and customer preferences. Disruptive strategies allow organizations to remain agile and adapt to evolving circumstances. By focusing on experimentation and iteration, disruptive companies can quickly learn from feedback and make necessary adjustments to their offerings.

■ Capitalizing on Flexibility: Disruption capitalizes on the flexibility and adaptability of organizations as CASs. These organizations can respond to changing market conditions, customer needs, and technological advancements. By embracing a disruptive mindset, organizations can proactively shape the industry landscape rather than being passive observers.

One of the key reasons why a disruptive strategy is recommended in the embryonic phase is the potential for significant market share capture. As established players are still grappling with defining the market and its dynamics, disruptive organizations can enter the scene and establish themselves as pioneers in their respective domains. By targeting underserved customer segments or unmet needs, disruptive companies can gain an early advantage and build a loyal customer base.

In the context of organizations as CASs, a disruptive strategy aligns with their ability to adapt, learn, and evolve. It allows organizations to explore new possibilities, experiment with different approaches, and respond to signals from the macroenvironment, selectively. By embracing disruption, organizations can leverage their inherent capabilities to drive innovation, challenge the status quo, and position themselves as industry leaders.

As disruptors, organizations become able to seize opportunities, gain market share, and establish a strong foundation for growth. By embracing a disruptive strategy, companies can effectively navigate the complexities of the macroenvironment, leverage their capabilities as CASs, and position themselves for long-term success in the evolving industry landscape.

A disruptive strategy allows organizations to challenge the traditional incumbents and their business models. By introducing innovative products, services, or business models, disruptors can offer customers a unique value proposition that the existing players fail to deliver. This ability to offer something new, different, and compelling positions the disruptor as an attractive alternative, leading to customer acquisition and market share growth.

Moreover, embracing disruption enables organizations to capitalize on emerging trends, technologies, and market shifts. Disruptors have the flexibility to adopt and leverage new technologies, business models, or distribution channels that align with the evolving preferences of customers. By keeping a pulse on the macroenvironment and spotting signals of change, organizations can proactively shape their strategies and offerings to stay ahead of the curve.

An essential aspect of disruptive strategies is the focus on innovation and experimentation. Disruptors are not bound by the legacy systems or rigid structures that often hinder established players. They have the freedom to challenge conventions, take risks, and explore novel approaches to solving customer problems. This mindset of continuous innovation and iteration allows disruptors to learn quickly, adapt to feedback, and refine their offerings to better meet customer needs.

Real-world examples demonstrate the effectiveness of disruptive strategies in the embryonic phase. For instance, Uber disrupted the transportation industry by introducing a ride-hailing platform that revolutionized the way people travel. By leveraging technology, Uber offered a convenient, cost-effective alternative to traditional taxis, fundamentally reshaping the industry. Similarly, Spotify disrupted the music industry by providing a streaming platform that transformed how people consume music, challenging the dominance of physical CDs and traditional distribution models.

Embracing a disruptive strategy requires a deep understanding of the macroenvironment, industry dynamics, and customer preferences. Organizations must conduct thorough market research, identify gaps or inefficiencies, and envision innovative solutions that address those gaps. This understanding of the external landscape allows disruptors to position themselves strategically and exploit untapped opportunities.

To successfully navigate the embryonic phase, organizations should foster a culture of innovation and agility. This involves empowering employees to think creatively, encouraging collaboration and experimentation, and embracing a growth mindset. By fostering an environment that supports disruptive thinking, organizations can harness the collective intelligence and creativity of their workforce to drive innovation and shape their industry's future.

THE RECOMMENDED APPROACH IN BRIEF: Disrupt your way through. This enables your organization to seize opportunities, gain market share, and establish a strong foundation for growth. By embracing a disruptive strategy, organizations can effectively navigate the complexities of the macroenvironment, leverage their capabilities as CASs, and position themselves for long-term success in the evolving industry landscape. Through innovation, agility, and a customer-centric focus, disruptors can reshape industries, challenge incumbents, and create value in ways that were previously unimaginable.

Assess: is your organization competing during an embryonic phase

✓ Market Size and Growth Potential: Evaluate the overall market size and its growth potential. Look for indications of a relatively small market size with significant growth prospects. Assess market trends, consumer preferences, and emerging technologies that suggest the potential for disruptive innovation and market entry.

✓ Market Fragmentation and Disruption: Identify signs of market fragmentation with multiple small players or emerging startups entering the industry. Look for disruptive technologies, business models, or new market entrants that challenge traditional players and create opportunities for market transformation.

✓ Regulatory Environment: Examine the regulatory landscape to identify the absence or limited presence of specific regulations or industry standards. Look for regulatory frameworks that are still in development or are yet to be established, indicating a relatively unregulated environment.

✓ Competitive Landscape: Assess the level of competition in the industry. Look for a limited number of established players and a low degree of market concentration. Identify signs of intense rivalry, including aggressive pricing strategies, frequent product launches, and high marketing expenditure by competitors.

✓ Innovation and Technological Advancements: Evaluate the level of innovation and technological advancements in the industry. Look for indications of emerging technologies, disruptive business models, or novel approaches that have the potential to reshape the industry landscape.

✓ Customer Adoption and Awareness: Analyze customer behavior and adoption patterns. Look for early signs of customer interest, willingness to try new products or services, and a desire for innovative solutions. Identify customer segments that are receptive to new offerings and demonstrate an affinity for early adoption.

✓ Resource Availability and Investment Climate: Assess the availability of resources, including financial capital, skilled talent, and technological infrastructure, that support industry growth and innovation. Evaluate the investment climate, including venture capital funding, government initiatives, and support for startups or new entrants.

✓ Industry Networking and Collaboration: Explore industry associations, conferences, and collaborations that promote knowledge sharing, networking, and collaboration among industry participants. Look for indications of collaborative efforts to address common challenges, explore new opportunities, or develop industry-wide standards.

By considering these key factors and evaluating the industry landscape through the lens of organizations as CASs, business leaders can gain insights into whether their industry is in the embryonic phase. This assessment will help inform strategic decision-making, resource allocation, innovation priorities, and the adoption of a disruptive strategy that aligns with the characteristics of this phase. It is essential to regularly reassess the industry landscape to adapt strategies as the industry evolves and progresses through subsequent life cycle phases.

Tesla

Let's consider the example of Tesla, a company that disrupted the automotive industry with its EVs and sustainable energy solutions. Tesla recognized the need for a shift toward sustainable transportation and set out to redefine the automotive industry with its innovative approach. While traditional automakers were primarily focused on internal combustion engine (ICE) vehicles, Tesla bet on electric powertrains and renewable energy technologies.

By introducing high-performance EVs with cutting-edge technology, Tesla challenged the notion that EVs were impractical or had limited range. The company's flagship models, such as the Tesla Model S and Model 3, showcased the potential of EVs, offering impressive range, acceleration, and advanced features. Tesla also disrupted the traditional dealership model by selling directly to consumers, bypassing the traditional dealer network. This direct-to-consumer approach allowed Tesla to control the customer experience, gather valuable data, and iterate quickly based on customer feedback.

Furthermore, Tesla invested in building a proprietary charging infrastructure, known as the Supercharger network, which addressed one of the key concerns associated with EVs—charging convenience. By strategically expanding the Supercharger network globally, Tesla alleviated "range anxiety" and made long-distance travel feasible for EV owners. The impact of Tesla's disruption reverberated across the automotive industry. It compelled traditional automakers to shift their focus toward electric mobility, accelerate their EV development efforts, and invest in charging infrastructure. Tesla's success also catalyzed the development of new EV startups, fostering competition and innovation in the industry.

The disruptive strategy of Tesla was underpinned by a relentless focus on technological innovation, sustainable transportation, and creating a brand synonymous with cutting-edge EVs. By challenging the status quo and offering a compelling alternative to conventional ICE vehicles, Tesla reshaped the automotive industry and paved the way for the broader adoption of electric mobility.

Develop the Strategy for This Phase

1. Embrace Disruptive Thinking: Recognize the instability and lack of established norms in the industry. Encourage a culture of innovation and open-mindedness to challenge existing assumptions. Foster a mindset that welcomes experimentation, risk-taking, and learning from failure.

2. Identify Underserved Customer Segments: Conduct thorough market research to identify unmet customer needs and pain points. Seek opportunities to serve niche markets or overlooked customer segments. Develop a deep understanding of customers' preferences, behaviors, and aspirations.

3. Create a Unique Value Proposition: Leverage disruptive technologies, business models, or distribution channels to differentiate from incumbents. Focus on delivering a compelling value proposition that addresses customers' pain points or offers a new solution. Communicate the unique benefits and advantages of your offering to attract early adopters.

4. Prioritize Rapid Market Entry: Move quickly to establish a presence in the market and gain first-mover advantage. Develop minimum viable products (MVPs) or prototypes to test and validate your value proposition. Iterate and refine your offerings based on customer feedback and market insights.

5. Build Strategic Partnerships: Form alliances or partnerships with complementary organizations to enhance capabilities and market reach. Collaborate with technology providers, suppliers, or distribution channels to leverage their expertise and resources. Create ecosystems that foster innovation, knowledge sharing, and mutual growth.

6. Monitor and Respond to Industry Signals: Stay attuned to changes in customer preferences, technological advancements, and emerging trends. Continuously scan the macroenvironment for signals that may impact your industry or disrupt existing business models. Be agile and responsive in adapting your strategies and offerings to align with evolving market dynamics.

7. Foster a Learning Organization: Encourage a culture of continuous learning and improvement. Emphasize data-driven decision-making and leverage analytics to gain insights into customer behavior and market trends. Encourage cross-functional collaboration and knowledge sharing to harness collective intelligence.

Practical Implications for Strategy development

Embracing disruption requires a mindset shift and a willingness to challenge the status quo. Leaders must create an environment that encourages experimentation, rewards innovative thinking, and supports calculated risk-taking.

A. Strategic planning should be flexible and adaptable, focusing on short-term goals while remaining aligned with a long-term vision. Regular strategy reviews and adjustments are crucial to capitalize on emerging opportunities or address unexpected challenges.

    B. Continuous market research and customer feedback are essential to understand changing customer needs and preferences. Organizations should invest in gathering and analyzing data to make informed decisions and drive strategy development.

    C. Collaborative partnerships and ecosystem thinking can provide access to resources, capabilities, and market reach that accelerate growth and increase competitive advantage.

    D. Developing a learning organization culture fosters resilience and adaptability. Organizations should promote a growth mindset, encourage learning from failures, and provide opportunities for professional development and knowledge sharing.

Deploy the Strategy for This Phase

Agile Resource Allocation: Allocate resources flexibly based on evolving priorities and emerging opportunities. Prioritize investments in research and development to drive innovation and product/service refinement. Continuously evaluate and adjust resource allocation to support growth and competitive advantage.

1. Rapid Prototyping and Testing: Implement an iterative approach to product or service development, focusing on speed and experimentation. Create prototypes or MVPs to gather customer feedback and validate market demand. Incorporate insights from testing and iterate quickly to improve products or services.

2. Strategic Pricing: Determine pricing strategies that reflect the value proposition and market dynamics. Consider pricing models that encourage early adoption or create a competitive advantage. Monitor competitor pricing and adjust pricing strategies as needed to capture market share.

3. Market Penetration Strategies: Deploy aggressive marketing and promotional campaigns to raise awareness and attract early adopters. Leverage digital marketing channels and social media to reach target customers effectively. Identify key influencers and partnerships to amplify the visibility and credibility of your offerings.

4. Build a Scalable Infrastructure: Develop an adaptable and scalable infrastructure to support growth. Invest in technology systems that can handle increasing customer demand and transaction volumes. Establish strategic partnerships with logistics providers or distribution channels to ensure efficient delivery.

5. Customer-Centric Focus: Continuously gather customer feedback and integrate it into the product or service development process. Personalize

customer experiences and engage in proactive communication to build loyalty. Implement customer service processes that address customer needs and resolve issues promptly.

6. Foster a Culture of Innovation: Encourage employee creativity and entrepreneurial thinking. Implement mechanisms for capturing and evaluating employee ideas. Recognize and reward innovation to motivate and sustain a culture of continuous improvement.

Practical Implications for Strategy Deployment

Strategy deployment in the embryonic phase requires a high level of agility, adaptability, and experimentation. Organizations should embrace an iterative and flexible approach, focusing on rapid prototyping, testing, and quick adjustments based on market feedback.

A. Pricing strategies should balance the need to capture market share with the need for revenue generation and profitability. Organizations should carefully consider the value proposition, competitive landscape, and target customer segment when determining pricing models.

B. Market penetration efforts should be focused and targeted, leveraging digital channels and strategic partnerships to maximize reach and impact.

C. Scalability is a critical consideration during strategy deployment. Organizations should anticipate growth and build infrastructure and systems that can support increased demand and customer volume.

D. Customer-centricity should be at the core of strategy implementation. Organizations should actively engage with customers, gather feedback, and tailor their offerings and services to meet customer needs and preferences.

E. Nurturing a culture of innovation and empowering employees to contribute ideas and experiment fosters creativity and resilience in strategy deployment.

Failing to Strategize Effectively During the Phase

Failing to strategize effectively during the embryonic phase can have significant implications and consequences for organizations.

■ Lack of Market Understanding: Reason for Failure: Insufficient research and understanding of customer needs, preferences, and market dynamics.

- Consequence: Organizations may develop products or services that do not resonate with the target market, resulting in low adoption rates and limited customer interest. This can lead to wasted resources and missed opportunities for market penetration.
  - Example: Juicero, a startup that developed a high-priced internet-connected juicing machine, failed to understand the market demand and customer willingness to pay for such a product. The lack of market understanding resulted in a lackluster response from consumers, leading to the company's eventual closure.
- Ineffective Differentiation: Reason for Failure: Failure to differentiate from existing offerings or address unmet customer needs.
  - Consequence: Organizations may struggle to gain a competitive advantage and attract customers. They become vulnerable to intense competition and pricing pressures, limiting their ability to establish a strong market presence.
    - Example: Quibi, a short-form streaming service, failed to effectively differentiate itself in a crowded market dominated by established players like Netflix and YouTube. The lack of a compelling value proposition and unique positioning resulted in limited user adoption, leading to the company's shutdown within a year of its launch.
- Inadequate Resource Allocation: Reason for Failure: Poor allocation of resources, including financial, human, and technological resources.
  - Consequence: Organizations may face constraints in product development, marketing, or operational capabilities, limiting their ability to execute their strategies effectively. This can result in delayed product launches, compromised quality, or ineffective market reach.
    - Example: Segway, the personal transportation device manufacturer, initially received significant media attention and investor interest. However, due to the high cost of production and limited market demand, the company struggled to generate sustainable revenues and ultimately faced financial challenges.
- Ignoring Competitive Dynamics: Reason for Failure: Failure to recognize and respond to competitive forces in the industry.
  - Consequence: Organizations may find themselves unable to withstand competitive pressures and market disruptions. This can lead to market share erosion, decreased profitability, and potential business decline.
    - Example: Kodak, once a dominant player in the photography industry, failed to adapt to the digital revolution and the rise of digital cameras and smartphones. The company's delayed response

to changing market dynamics resulted in a significant loss of market share and eventually bankruptcy.

■ Regulatory and Legal Challenges: Reason for Failure: Ignoring or underestimating the impact of regulatory requirements or legal constraints.
  – Consequence: Organizations may face legal battles, fines, reputational damage, or even forced closure if they fail to comply with regulatory frameworks or industry-specific regulations.
    • Example: Theranos, a health technology company, faced severe consequences when it failed to meet regulatory standards and provide accurate testing results. The company's non-compliance with industry regulations resulted in legal disputes, reputational damage, and a significant loss of trust from investors and customers.

Failing to strategize effectively during the embryonic phase can have detrimental consequences for organizations. Lack of market understanding, ineffective differentiation, inadequate resource allocation, ignoring competitive dynamics, and regulatory challenges are among the key reasons for failure. By examining real-world examples, we can learn valuable lessons about the importance of strategic planning, market research, resource allocation, competitive analysis, and compliance with regulations in ensuring the success of organizations in the embryonic phase.

Lesson from a leader

Jeff Bezos

Let's explore an example of a business leader who successfully led their organization through disruption: Amazon and its CEO, Jeff Bezos.

Jeff Bezos, the founder and former CEO of Amazon, is widely recognized for his visionary leadership and his role in transforming the retail industry. Under Bezos' guidance, Amazon disrupted the traditional brick-and-mortar retail model by leveraging e-commerce and pioneering new strategies to create a customer-centric experience.

One notable example of successful disruption by Amazon is the introduction of Amazon Prime. Recognizing the growing demand for faster and more convenient shipping options, Bezos launched Amazon Prime in 2005. This subscription-based service provided customers with free two-day shipping, unlimited streaming of movies and TV shows, and various other benefits.

Amazon Prime not only disrupted the retail industry but also altered consumer expectations for delivery speed and convenience. By offering a seamless shopping experience and expedited delivery, Amazon gained a competitive advantage and established a loyal customer base. This disruptive strategy allowed

Amazon to expand its market share and capture a significant portion of online retail sales.

Furthermore, Bezos demonstrated a relentless focus on innovation and investment in emerging technologies. Amazon invested heavily in developing its own infrastructure, such as fulfillment centers and logistics networks, to enhance its operational efficiency and enable faster delivery. Additionally, Amazon's foray into cloud computing with Amazon Web Services (AWS) disrupted the technology industry by providing scalable and cost-effective cloud solutions.

Bezos's strategic vision and willingness to take risks propelled Amazon to continually disrupt and reshape various industries. The company's relentless pursuit of customer-centricity, focus on long-term growth, and commitment to innovation have been key drivers of its success.

This example illustrates how a business leader, like Jeff Bezos, can lead their organization through successful disruption by anticipating market trends, leveraging technology, and relentlessly focusing on meeting evolving customer needs. Through strategic choices aligned with the industry life cycle and a deep understanding of the organization as a CAS, leaders can drive transformative change and position their companies for sustained success in dynamic and competitive markets.

Chapter 7

Growth: Emerge as a Differentiator or Cost Leader

Set-the-Stage Mini Case

Freshly is a meal delivery service that provides customers with freshly prepared, healthy, and plant-based meals delivered to their doorstep. The company was founded in 2015 and has rapidly gained popularity, especially among health-conscious consumers seeking convenient and nutritious meal options. The plant-based food industry, also known as the plant-based or plant-forward food sector, refers to the segment of the food market that produces and sells products primarily derived from plant sources. These products aim to replace or reduce animal-based ingredients traditionally found in the mainstream food industry. The growth of the plant-based food industry is driven by several factors, including shifting consumer preferences, environmental concerns, health consciousness, and ethical considerations. The most significant distinction between the plant-based food industry and the mainstream food industry lies in the ingredients used to create products. The plant-based foods are primarily composed of vegetables, fruits, grains, legumes, nuts, and seeds, while animal-based foods are derived from animals, such as meat, dairy, eggs, and seafood. In terms of target audience, the plant-based food industry targets a diverse range of consumers, including vegetarians, vegans, flexitarians, and health-conscious individuals seeking alternative and healthier food options. In contrast, the mainstream food

DOI: 10.4324/9781003564133-9

industry caters to a broader consumer base, which includes those who consume both animal-based and plant-based foods. This type of food industry places a strong emphasis on sustainability and environmental impact. Producing plant-based foods typically requires fewer natural resources, such as water and land, and generates fewer greenhouse gas emissions compared to raising animals for meat and dairy production. This focus on sustainability aligns with consumers' increasing awareness and concern about climate change and its relation to dietary choices.

Freshly succeeded during the growth phase of the plant-based food industry life cycle due to several key factors, including:

1. Unique Value Proposition: Freshly offered a unique value proposition in the plant-based meal delivery space. The company provides fully prepared, chef-cooked meals made with natural, high-quality ingredients. This set Freshly apart from traditional meal kit delivery services that required customers to cook the meals themselves. The convenience and high quality of Freshly's offerings attracted health-conscious consumers looking for time-saving, nutritious meal options.

2. Meeting Consumer Demand: During the growth phase, there was a rising demand for healthier and plant-based food options. Freshly tapped into this growing trend and positioned itself as a provider of nutritious and delicious plant-based meals. As more consumers sought healthier eating choices, Freshly's menu offerings aligned with the changing preferences and demands of the target market.

3. Scalable and Efficient Operations: Freshly's business model was designed for scalability and efficiency. By cooking meals to order and delivering them directly to customers, the company minimized waste and reduced overhead costs. This allowed Freshly to scale its operations rapidly and efficiently to meet the increasing demand for its services during the growth phase.

4. Customer-Centric Approach: Freshly maintained a customer-centric approach, actively seeking and incorporating customer feedback into its menu and service improvements. This strategy not only helped the company retain existing customers but also attracted new ones through positive word-of-mouth and referrals.

5. Strategic Partnerships and Nationwide Availability: During the growth phase, Freshly strategically partnered with major retailers and expanded its nationwide availability. These partnerships provided the company with access to a larger customer base and increased brand visibility, contributing to its success in the industry.

6. Adapting to Market Changes: Freshly demonstrated agility and adaptability in response to market changes and trends. As the plant-based food industry evolved, Freshly continuously updated its menu offerings, taking advantage of new ingredients and culinary innovations to keep its meals fresh and appealing to consumers.

7. Emphasis on Sustainability: The increasing awareness of environmental sustainability among consumers was another key aspect of Freshly's success during the growth phase. The company's commitment to eco-friendly packaging and sustainable practices resonated with environmentally conscious consumers, contributing to its positive brand image.

8. Leveraging Technology: Freshly leveraged technology to streamline its operations and enhance the customer experience. An efficient online platform allowed customers to easily customize their meal plans, manage subscriptions, and track deliveries, contributing to a seamless and user-friendly experience.

Defining the Growth Phase

The growth phase is marked by increasing market demand, rapid industry expansion, and the emergence of new players. During this phase, industries experience a surge in customer adoption, higher sales volumes, and a growing number of market participants. During the growth phase, organizations experience a higher level of industry stability compared to the embryonic phase. Market demand becomes more predictable, and customer preferences start to solidify. Established players gain market share, and the industry structure becomes more defined. In terms of the regulatory environment, this phase is also marked with some variation depending on the industry. In some cases, government regulations may become more stringent as the industry matures and its impact on society and the economy increases. Regulatory compliance and adherence to industry standards become essential considerations for companies operating in the growth phase.

The competitive landscape during this phase expands as the number of rivals increases, intensifying competition. New entrants and existing players vie for market share, driving innovation and differentiation. Competition may be fueled by factors such as product features, pricing strategies, marketing efforts, and customer service. As for pricing and market offerings, companies often focus on capturing market share and maximizing revenue. Pricing strategies may involve competitive pricing to attract customers, volume discounts, or bundled offerings. Market offerings may evolve to cater to different customer segments, with companies introducing new products or expanding their product lines to meet growing demand.

The Growth Phase in Brief: The growth phase of the industry life cycle signifies a period of rapid expansion, increased competition, and evolving market dynamics. Organizations must navigate this phase by leveraging their understanding of the industry's stability, regulatory environment, competitive landscape, pricing dynamics, and market offerings. By capitalizing on growth opportunities and effectively managing competitive pressures, companies can position themselves for continued success and sustainable growth in this phase of the industry life cycle.

Key Characteristics of This Phase

Here are the key characteristics of the growth phase in the industry life cycle:

✓ Market Expansion: The growth phase is characterized by a significant increase in market demand and customer adoption. Customers are more receptive to the industry's offerings, leading to higher sales volumes and revenue growth. Market expansion creates opportunities for companies to capture market share and expand their customer base.

✓ Increasing Competition: As the industry gains traction and attracts attention, competition intensifies. New players enter the market, seeking to capitalize on the growth potential. Existing competitors may also enhance their offerings and strategies to maintain or grow their market share. The competitive landscape becomes more crowded, requiring companies to differentiate themselves and stay ahead of the competition.

✓ Technological Advancements: The growth phase often witnesses rapid technological advancements. Innovation and new product development become crucial drivers of success. Companies invest in research and development to introduce new features, functionalities, and technologies to cater to evolving customer needs and preferences. Technological advancements can lead to breakthroughs and disruptions within the industry.

✓ Scalability and Expansion: With increasing demand, companies in the growth phase need to scale their operations to meet customer requirements. This may involve expanding production capacity, establishing new facilities or distribution networks, and enhancing supply chain capabilities. Scalability becomes essential to keep up with market growth and maintain competitiveness.

✓ Market Acceptance and Standardization: As the industry expands, its offerings become more widely accepted by customers. Standardization of products, processes, and industry practices may occur to meet customer expectations and facilitate interoperability. Standards and certifications may be established to ensure quality and safety across the industry.

✓ Pricing Strategies: In the growth phase, companies often adopt pricing strategies aimed at capturing market share and maximizing revenue. This may involve competitive pricing to attract customers, volume discounts, or promotional offers to drive adoption. Companies may also invest in marketing and advertising to increase brand visibility and customer awareness.

✓ Investment and Financing: The growth phase attracts increased investment and financing opportunities. Investors recognize the potential for high returns in rapidly growing industries. Companies may secure funding to support their expansion plans, product development, marketing efforts, and talent acquisition. Access to capital becomes crucial for sustaining growth and fueling further innovation.

✓ Market Segmentation: As the market expands, companies may identify and target specific customer segments to optimize their offerings and marketing strategies. Market segmentation allows organizations to tailor their products, services, and messaging to meet the diverse needs of different customer groups. This enables companies to achieve better customer satisfaction and gain a competitive advantage.

The Recommended Approach to Strategy During This Phase and Why

During the growth phase of the industry life cycle, organizations are advised to adopt a strategic approach that focuses on emergent strategy.

■ Emergent Strategy: In the dynamic and evolving nature of the growth phase, organizations often face uncertainties and changing market conditions. This calls for the adoption of an emergent strategy, as proposed by Clayton Christensen. Emergent strategy emphasizes the importance of continuously monitoring the market, experimenting, and adapting to emerging opportunities and challenges. It recognizes that strategies may evolve and emerge based on new information, customer feedback, and market dynamics.

By adopting an emergent strategy, organizations can be agile, responsive, and open to adjusting their course based on real-time insights. This flexibility allows companies to seize emerging opportunities, address market shifts, and stay ahead of the competition. In the growth phase, where market conditions are rapidly changing, emergent strategies can enable organizations to navigate uncertainties and make strategic decisions that align with evolving customer needs.

An example of an organization that embraced an emergent strategy during the growth phase is Amazon. Initially started as an online bookstore, Amazon continuously expanded its offerings and experimented with new business models, such as Amazon Prime, Amazon Web Services (AWS), and its own line of electronic devices. Through ongoing experimentation, Amazon identified emerging market trends, customer preferences, and technological advancements, which led to its transformation into a global e-commerce and technology giant.

By adopting an emergent strategy, organizations can seize emerging opportunities and quickly adapt to changes in the market. This requires a culture of experimentation, innovation, and a willingness to take calculated risks. Organizations that embrace emergent strategies are better equipped to respond to shifting customer preferences, disruptive technologies, and competitive threats.

A notable example of a company that has successfully utilized an emergent strategy during the growth phase is Google. Initially known for its search engine, Google continuously adapted its strategy to the evolving digital landscape. The company explored new business opportunities, expanded into various sectors such as advertising, cloud computing, and mobile operating systems, and made strategic acquisitions. Google's ability to adapt and leverage emerging opportunities has allowed it to maintain a leading position in the technology industry.

> **THE RECOMMENDED APPROACH IN BRIEF:** During the growth phase, the recommended approach is emergent strategy, which empowers organizations to thrive in the growth phase of the industry life cycle. This approach enables companies to differentiate themselves, gain market share, drive customer loyalty, and adapt to the changing market dynamics. By leveraging their capabilities as CAS and aligning their strategies with the unique characteristics of the growth phase, organizations can position themselves for sustainable success in the industry.

Assess: is your organization competing during this phase

- ✓ Analyze Market Demand and Customer Behavior: Conduct market research to assess the level of demand for your products or services. Monitor customer behavior, preferences, and trends to identify signs of increasing demand and market growth. Look for indications of expanding customer base, rising sales, and positive feedback from customers.
- ✓ Evaluate Market Size and Competition: Determine the size of the market and assess its potential for growth. Identify the number of competitors in the industry and evaluate their market share. Analyze the competitive

landscape to understand the level of competition and the strategies employed by key players.

✓ Assess Revenue and Profitability: Review financial data and performance metrics to evaluate revenue growth over time. Analyze profitability ratios to assess if the organization is experiencing increasing profit margins. Consider the overall financial health of the organization and its ability to generate sustained growth.

✓ Monitor Industry Trends and Technological Advancements: Stay updated on industry trends, innovations, and emerging technologies relevant to your sector. Assess how your organization is leveraging technological advancements to gain a competitive advantage. Look for signs of rapid technological changes, disruptive innovations, or new market entrants.

✓ Evaluate Customer Loyalty and Brand Recognition: Measure customer loyalty through metrics such as customer retention rates, repeat purchases, and customer satisfaction scores. Assess the strength of your brand and its recognition in the market. Determine if your organization has developed a loyal customer base and if customers perceive your brand as a leader in the industry.

✓ Consider Industry Regulations and Legal Environment: Evaluate the regulatory landscape specific to your industry. Assess the impact of existing regulations and potential changes in regulations on your organization's growth prospects. Consider the level of government intervention and its influence on market dynamics.

✓ Monitor Market Expansion Opportunities: Identify potential market expansion opportunities, such as entering new geographic regions or targeting new customer segments. Assess the feasibility of expanding product or service offerings to meet evolving customer needs. Evaluate the potential for strategic partnerships, mergers, or acquisitions to enhance market reach and drive growth.

✓ Foster a Culture of Innovation and Agility: Encourage innovation and creativity within the organization to capitalize on growth opportunities. Foster a culture of agility and adaptability to respond to market changes quickly. Promote cross-functional collaboration and knowledge sharing to facilitate innovation and continuous improvement.

Slack

Slack was launched in 2013 as an internal communication tool for a gaming company called Tiny Speck. The platform was initially designed to enhance team communication and collaboration within the company. However, the creators soon recognized the potential of their product to address broader market needs.

Slack, the cloud-based communication and collaboration platform, exemplifies the successful adoption of an emergent strategy during the growth phase of the team collaboration software industry. Slack's strategic approach showcases the importance of remaining agile and responsive to evolving market needs.

Adaptability to Market Needs: Slack's emergent strategy was highly effective during the growth phase because it demonstrated remarkable adaptability to evolving market needs. As the team collaboration software industry was experiencing rapid expansion, customer demands and preferences were constantly changing. Slack's ability to listen to user feedback and make iterative improvements to its platform allowed it to stay ahead of the competition and meet the dynamic demands of growing businesses.

Customer-Centric Approach: During the growth phase, the industry saw an influx of new players and products. Slack's customer-centric approach, driven by its emergent strategy, played a pivotal role in its success. By actively engaging with users and understanding their pain points, Slack was able to offer solutions that resonated with customers. This customer-centricity fueled the platform's growth and fostered a strong user community.

Differentiation and Value Proposition: Slack's emergent strategy enabled the platform to continuously differentiate itself from competitors, a crucial aspect of thriving in the growth phase. Through strategic integration partnerships and a focus on enhancing the user experience, Slack created a unique value proposition that set it apart from traditional communication tools. This differentiation allowed the platform to capture and retain a significant share of the growing market.

Expanding Market Reach: One of the key characteristics of the growth phase is the expansion of the market and the emergence of new customer segments. Slack's effective emergent strategy included expanding its target audience from small and medium-sized businesses to the enterprise market. By developing enterprise-grade features and security protocols, Slack tapped into a new and lucrative customer base, fueling its growth further.

Evolving Ecosystem: The growth phase often witnesses the development of an ecosystem around successful companies. Slack's emergent strategy of embracing a developer community was a masterstroke during this phase. It created an ecosystem of third-party apps and integrations that added value to the platform. This ecosystem not only enhanced Slack's capabilities but also solidified its position as a central hub for workplace communication and collaboration.

Continued Innovation: Emergent strategy drives innovation, and Slack's growth phase success was a testament to its commitment to continuous innovation. The platform regularly introduced new features and enhancements to cater to the diverse needs of its expanding user base. This innovation not only attracted new customers but also helped retain existing ones, contributing to sustained growth.

Competitive Advantage: Slack's effective emergent strategy allowed the company to gain a competitive advantage in the growing team collaboration software industry. By capitalizing on its adaptability, customer-centricity, differentiation, and innovation, Slack created a strong position for itself in the market. This advantage became a significant driver of its growth and success during the growth phase.

Develop the Strategy for This Phase

1. Leverage Differentiation: In the growth phase, organizations should focus on developing a differentiated value proposition that sets them apart from competitors. Identify unique features, product/service attributes, or customer experiences that can create a competitive advantage. Invest in research and development to continuously innovate and enhance your offerings to meet evolving customer needs.

2. Understand Customer Segments: Conduct thorough market research to identify target customer segments and their specific preferences and demands. Tailor your products, services, and marketing efforts to cater to these segments effectively. Gather customer feedback and use it to refine your offerings and better align with their evolving preferences.

3. Build Brand Equity: Invest in building a strong brand that resonates with your target customers. Develop a compelling brand identity and consistently deliver on your brand promise. Focus on building brand loyalty and customer trust through positive experiences and exceptional customer service.

4. Enhance Distribution Channels: Optimize your distribution channels to ensure the widespread availability of your products or services. Explore new channels and partnerships that can help you reach untapped markets and expand your customer base. Consider strategic alliances, online platforms, and partnerships with retailers or distributors to increase your market reach.

5. Develop Scalable Operations: As demand increases, it is crucial to develop scalable and efficient operations to support growth. Streamline internal processes, invest in technology and automation, and optimize your supply chain to meet growing customer demands while maintaining quality and cost-effectiveness.

6. Foster a Culture of Innovation: Encourage a culture of innovation within your organization to continually generate new ideas and stay ahead of the competition. Create channels for employees to contribute their insights and suggestions. Embrace experimentation, learn from failures, and reward entrepreneurial thinking.

7. Monitor Competitive Landscape: Stay vigilant about the evolving competitive landscape. Continuously monitor competitors' strategies, offerings, and

customer feedback. Identify emerging trends and potential disruptors that could impact your industry and adapt your strategy accordingly.

8. Nurture Strategic Partnerships: Explore strategic partnerships and collaborations that can accelerate your growth. Identify complementary businesses or industry players with whom you can collaborate to leverage synergies and expand your market presence. Joint ventures, licensing agreements, or strategic alliances can help you access new markets, technologies, or capabilities.

Practical Implications for Strategy Development

Agility and flexibility are key in the growth phase. Organizations must be willing to adapt their strategies based on market dynamics and changing customer preferences.

A. Continuous innovation and improvement are essential to sustain differentiation and meet evolving customer demands.

B. Effective communication and alignment within the organization are crucial to ensure everyone is working toward shared goals and understanding the strategic direction.

C. Strategic planning should involve regular evaluation and adjustments based on feedback from customers, competitors, and market trends.

D. It is important to allocate resources wisely and prioritize initiatives that align with your strategic objectives and offer the highest potential for growth and value creation.

Deploy the Strategy for This Phase

The following are the guidelines for strategy deployment in the growth phase:

1. Align Organizational Structure: Ensure that your organizational structure supports the execution of your growth strategy. Streamline decision-making processes, establish clear lines of communication, and empower employees to make decisions and take ownership of their areas of responsibility. Foster a collaborative and agile culture that encourages cross-functional collaboration and innovation.

2. Establish Key Performance Indicators (KPIs): Define relevant KPIs that align with your growth strategy. These may include metrics such as revenue growth, market share, customer acquisition and retention rates, product/service innovation, and customer satisfaction. Monitor these KPIs regularly to track progress and make informed adjustments to your strategy as needed.

3. Develop Action Plans: Create detailed action plans that outline the specific initiatives, projects, and activities required to execute your growth strategy. Assign responsibilities to teams or individuals, set clear timelines and milestones, and establish performance metrics for each initiative. Regularly review and update these action plans to ensure alignment with changing market conditions.

4. Invest in Talent Development: Recognize the importance of skilled and motivated employees in driving growth. Invest in training and development programs to enhance employees' skills and capabilities. Foster a learning culture that encourages continuous improvement and provides opportunities for career advancement. Identify and nurture high-potential individuals who can contribute to your organization's growth objectives.

5. Enhance Customer Experience: Focus on delivering an exceptional customer experience that exceeds expectations. Invest in customer service training, implement customer feedback mechanisms, and use customer insights to enhance your products, services, and processes. Leverage technology to streamline customer interactions and personalize experiences.

6. Leverage Technology and Data: Embrace technology solutions that can support your growth objectives. Implement robust systems for data collection, analysis, and reporting to gain insights into customer behavior, market trends, and competitive dynamics. Leverage data analytics to make data-driven decisions and optimize your operations.

7. Foster Strategic Alliances: Identify strategic partners or alliances that can help you accelerate growth. Collaborate with complementary businesses, suppliers, or distributors to access new markets, technologies, or resources. Joint marketing initiatives, co-branded offerings, or shared distribution channels can help expand your reach and increase market penetration.

8. Monitor and Adapt: Continuously monitor the market, customer preferences, and competitive landscape to identify emerging trends and opportunities. Regularly evaluate the effectiveness of your strategies and initiatives. Be prepared to make agile adjustments to your approach based on market feedback and changing circumstances.

Practical Implications for Strategy Deployment

Effective strategy deployment requires strong leadership, clear communication, and active engagement from all levels of the organization.

A. Foster a culture of accountability, where individuals and teams are responsible for delivering on their assigned goals and objectives.

B. Encourage cross-functional collaboration and knowledge sharing to foster innovation and ensure alignment across different departments and functions.
C. Regularly review and assess progress against the defined KPIs to measure the effectiveness of your strategy deployment efforts.
D. Stay agile and adaptable, willing to make necessary adjustments to your strategy and action plans based on market dynamics and customer feedback.

Failing to Strategize Effectively During the Growth Phase

Failing to strategize effectively during the growth phase can have significant implications for organizations, hindering their ability to capitalize on opportunities and sustain growth. Let's explore some common reasons for failure and the consequences they can have.

■ Lack of Differentiation: Organizations that fail to differentiate their products or services from competitors may struggle to attract and retain customers. Without a unique value proposition, they become susceptible to price wars and eroding profit margins.
  – Consequence: When organizations fail to differentiate their products or services from competitors, they risk blending into the crowded market and losing their unique value proposition. Without a compelling reason for customers to choose their offerings over competitors, price becomes a significant factor in decision-making. This can lead to price wars and eroding profit margins, as companies compete solely on price, resulting in a race to the bottom.
    • Example: Borders Group, a prominent bookseller, struggled to differentiate itself from the growing dominance of online retailers like Amazon. Borders' brick-and-mortar stores, while popular in the past, faced challenges in offering a unique experience or added value compared to the convenience of shopping online. As a result, Borders lost market share, faced declining sales, and eventually filed for bankruptcy in 2011.
■ Inadequate Scaling: Rapid growth can strain organizational resources and infrastructure. If an organization fails to scale its operations and processes to meet increasing demand, it may struggle to deliver products or services effectively. This can lead to customer dissatisfaction, quality issues, and missed market opportunities. A notable example is the electric vehicle

manufacturer Faraday Future, which faced challenges in scaling production capacity, resulting in delays and setbacks.

- Consequence: Rapid growth can put immense strain on organizational resources and infrastructure. When a company experiences a surge in demand but fails to scale its operations and processes accordingly, it may struggle to meet customer expectations and deliver products or services effectively. This can lead to customer dissatisfaction, quality issues, and missed market opportunities, hindering long-term growth prospects.
  - Example: Faraday Future, an ambitious electric vehicle manufacturer, faced challenges in scaling its production capacity to meet the high demand for its electric cars. As a result, the company encountered delays in delivering vehicles to customers, damaging its reputation and losing potential customers to competitors who could fulfill orders more efficiently.

■ Lack of Customer Focus: As organizations experience growth, there is a risk of losing sight of their customers' evolving needs and preferences. Failing to adapt and innovate based on customer feedback can result in declining customer satisfaction and market share. Nokia, once a dominant player in the mobile phone industry, failed to respond to the shift toward smartphones and the changing preferences of consumers, leading to a significant decline in market position.

- Consequence: Growing organizations may lose sight of their customers' evolving needs and preferences as they expand their operations. Failing to adapt and innovate based on customer feedback can result in declining customer satisfaction and a loss of market share to more customer-centric competitors.
  - Example: Nokia, a once-dominant player in the mobile phone industry, held a significant market share before the advent of smartphones. However, Nokia failed to recognize the shift in consumer preferences toward touch-screen devices and the emerging app ecosystem. The company's lack of customer focus and slow response to market changes led to a drastic decline in market position and ultimately contributed to Nokia's downfall.

■ Poor Management of Resources: Growth requires effective resource management. Organizations that fail to allocate resources appropriately may struggle to fund growth initiatives, invest in innovation, or maintain operational efficiency. This can limit their ability to seize market opportunities and sustain growth. One example is Blockbuster, which failed to adapt to the digital streaming era and neglected to invest in online platforms. As a result, the company lost its market dominance and eventually filed for bankruptcy.

– Consequence: Growth requires efficient resource management, and organizations that fail to allocate resources appropriately may struggle to fund growth initiatives, invest in innovation, or maintain operational efficiency. Inadequate resource allocation can lead to missed opportunities and hinder an organization's ability to capitalize on growth potential.

• Example: Blockbuster, a once-dominant video rental company, missed the opportunity to adapt to the digital streaming era. The company's management did not prioritize investment in online platforms and digital content distribution, despite the emerging trend. As a result, Blockbuster lost its market dominance, faced declining revenues, and eventually filed for bankruptcy.

■ Inability to Adapt to Market Changes: The growth phase is characterized by rapid market evolution. Organizations that are slow to respond to changing market dynamics risk becoming obsolete. BlackBerry, once a leader in the smartphone market, failed to adapt to the rise of touch-screen devices and the app ecosystem, resulting in a significant decline in market share.

– Consequence: The growth phase is characterized by rapid market evolution, and organizations that fail to keep pace with these changes risk becoming obsolete. When companies cannot adapt to shifts in consumer preferences, technology advancements, or new market entrants, they may lose market share and competitive advantage.

• Example: BlackBerry, a leading player in the smartphone market in the early 2000s, failed to adapt to the rise of touch-screen devices and the growing popularity of mobile apps. BlackBerry remained committed to its physical keyboard-centric design while its competitors embraced touch-screen interfaces and app ecosystems. The company's inability to adapt resulted in a significant decline in market share, impacting its long-term viability.

Lesson from a leader

Stewart Butterfield

Stewart Butterfield, the CEO and co-founder of Slack, demonstrated exceptional leadership in successfully implementing an emergent strategy that contributed to the company's remarkable growth and success. Stewart Butterfield's exceptional leadership played a pivotal role in successfully implementing the emergent strategy at Slack and driving the company's remarkable growth and success. His leadership style emphasized agility, innovation, and a strong customer-centric approach, which significantly influenced the overall strategy of the company.

Agile and Adaptive Leadership: Butterfield's leadership style can be described as agile and adaptive. He recognized that in a rapidly changing and competitive market, a rigid top-down approach to strategy would not suffice. Instead, he encouraged an environment that fostered creativity, experimentation, and quick decision-making. This allowed the team to respond rapidly to market shifts, customer feedback, and emerging opportunities.

Visionary and Purpose-Driven: As a visionary leader, Butterfield had a clear sense of purpose for Slack. He saw the potential for the platform to revolutionize workplace communication and collaboration. His unwavering belief in the product's potential and his ability to articulate the vision to his team and stakeholders inspired passion and dedication.

Customer-Centric Approach: Butterfield placed a strong emphasis on understanding and meeting customer needs. He encouraged a customer-centric culture within the organization, where teams were encouraged to engage directly with users and listen to their feedback. This approach allowed Slack to identify pain points, unmet needs, and emergent use cases that shaped the product's evolution. Encouraging Experimentation and Innovation: Butterfield fostered a culture of experimentation and innovation at Slack. He encouraged employees to think outside the box, take calculated risks, and explore new ideas. This allowed the company to stay ahead of the competition and continuously introduce innovative features and functionalities that resonated with users.

Embracing Emergent Opportunities: As Slack evolved from a gaming platform to a communication tool, Butterfield recognized the emergent opportunity and swiftly pivoted the company's focus. He showed a willingness to let go of the original plan and embrace the potential of a new direction. This adaptability was crucial in shaping Slack's emergent strategy and capitalizing on unforeseen opportunities.

Advocating Collaboration and Inclusion: Butterfield believed in the power of collaboration and inclusion. He promoted an open and inclusive work culture where diverse perspectives were valued. This approach not only led to a more innovative and creative workforce but also enabled Slack to better understand the diverse needs of its global user base.

Leading by Example: Butterfield led by example, embodying the values and principles he instilled in the organization. He actively engaged with employees, customers, and partners, fostering a sense of trust and transparency. His hands-on involvement in the product development process and close interaction with customers reinforced the importance of the emergent strategy's iterative nature.

CASE STUDY: DIFFERENTIATION AT JCI

Abstract

Using grounded theory as a methodological approach, this study explored the influence of the triple bottom line (TBL) as an emerging and substantially important phenomenon on strategic positioning through image differentiation. The research contributes to the sustainability scholarship (TBL as a subset of sustainability) and marketing scholarship by introducing and exploring the dynamics among TBL, strategic positioning, differentiation, and image. This is done by presenting the influence of TBL on strategic positioning framework, which illustrates how these four variables are connected. This work also contributes to strategic management, social investing, and human resource scholarship by suggesting the positive impact of the TBL Image (a term defined and introduced in this study) on developing long-term strategies, talent acquisition and retention, and business growth within a global organization.

Introduction

TBL is a sustainability-related construct coined by Elkington (1997). Driven by sustainability, TBL provides a framework for measuring the performance of the business and the success of the organization using the economic, social, and environmental lines. In essence, TBL expresses the expansion of the environmental agenda in a way that integrates the economic and social lines (Elkington, 1997). In his definition of TBL, Elkington used the terms profit, people, and the planet as the three lines. In this study, the economic, social, and environmental lines are referred to as profit, people, and planet, respectively. Similar to other sustainability-related constructs like sustainable development and corporate social responsibility (CSR), TBL has shown a positive impact on organizations (Goel, 2010).

Since marketing is necessary for a strong long-term performance of the organization (Lovette and MacDonald, 2005; Fahey, 1999), this study explored TBL from a marketing perspective. Given that prior research on TBL did not shed light on strategic positioning or differentiation (from the marketing domain), it became intriguing to investigate how TBL influenced strategic positioning through differentiation within a global organization. Further, Kotler (2000) noted five tools for differentiation: image, channel, personnel, services, and product. The image was selected as the differentiation tool, and the term TBL Image was introduced to refer to the image of the organization as a TBL-driven organization.

Literature Review

Research on Sustainability-Related Constructs

Among the terms most commonly interchanged with sustainability is sustainable development, which Brundtland (1987) defined as "the development in the economic and social areas that satisfy the needs of the existing generation without compromising the capability of the future generations to satisfy their own needs." Organizations need to understand the impact of sustainable development on their long-term survival, and the commitment of executive leadership is necessary for creating a sustainable development environment (Stavros and Sprangel, 2008).

An earlier construct that attracted the attention of organizations and is related to sustainable development is corporate social responsibility (CSR). Byus, Deis, and Ouyang (2010) defined CSR as the voluntary actions taken by an organization to improve environmental or social conditions. Although CSR is not the focus of the literature review, it was necessary to include it because of its close relation to sustainability and sustainable development constructs. To illustrate further, Ebner and Baumgartner (2008) conducted an extensive literature study on CSR and sustainable development. The objective of their study was to survey the relevant literature to understand the relationship between CSR and sustainable development. A key finding of the study showed a close relationship between the two constructs. In some research cases, sustainable development was used as a basis for CSR. In other cases, the two constructs were used interchangeably.

Despite the lack of significant research linking TBL to the performance of the organization, the literature contains many studies showing the benefits of other sustainability-related constructs and their positive impact on corporate performance (Husted and Salazar, 2006; Laszlo, 2008; Moneva and Ortas, 2010; Russo and Fouts, 1997; Waddock and Graves, 1997). Other studies focused on the relationship between corporate social performance and financial performance. For example, a study conducted by Waddock and Graves (1997) found corporate social performance to be positively related to the financial performance of the organization. Another study by Husted and Salazar (2006) showed that, if planned strategically, CSR can improve the profitability of the organization. As previously mentioned, the majority of research in the sustainability scholarship focuses on other sustainability-related constructs, and little significant research was found on TBL.

Marketing Constructs and Strategic Positioning

Strategic positioning and differentiation are essential aspects of marketing that contribute significantly to an organization's success. The literature contains numerous studies highlighting the positive impact of strategic positioning and differentiation on organizational performance (Banker, Hu, Pavlou, and Luftman, 2011; Mazzarol and Soutar, 2008). Additionally, image as a marketing construct has been shown to have a positive effect on an organization's performance, using different measures including shareholder value, stock returns, and profitability (Roberts and Dowling, 2002; Smaiziene, 2008; Wang, 2010).

The existing research showing the positive effect on TBL, strategic positioning, differentiation, and image forms an important basis for this research. It provides the initial evidence and theoretical platform necessary to explore the influence of TBL on strategic positioning through image differentiation. Although scholarship in the related fields discussed the relationship among strategic positioning, differentiation, and image to some extent, very little existed on the dynamics among all three specifically concerning TBL. In light of the limitations of prior research, this study makes several theoretical contributions. The first contribution is demonstrating the dynamics connecting TBL, strategic positioning, differentiation, and image within a global organization. The results show that strategic positioning is influenced by TBL through strategic priorities developed by the organization to ensure its long-term success. These strategic priorities manifest the three lines of TBL. The degree of business alignment between the TBL lines and the lines of business in the organization contributes to the influence of TBL on strategic positioning. For instance, in a business group where product lines are directly tied to the objectives of TBL (e.g., designing and selling highly efficient energy systems directly related to the environmental line of TBL), TBL is more deeply integrated into the strategic plans of that group.

This research makes a second theoretical contribution by suggesting that in TBL-driven organizations, the TBL approach is embedded in the strategic positioning of the organization. Results reveal that when TBL is manifested in the culture, DNA, fabric, and heritage of the organization, TBL is embedded in the strategic positioning. This research makes a third theoretical contribution by introducing the term TBL Image and shedding light on the business advantages of that image in terms of business development, human resources, and social investing.

Methods

The qualitative research approach for this study was justified by the exploratory purpose of the study in understanding TBL as an emerging phenomenon and in discovering its connection to strategic positioning. A qualitative approach is best suited when a phenomenon has not been explored yet, which demonstrates the value of qualitative research in enabling the researcher to develop constructs (Marshall and Rossman, 2006). This study used a grounded theory approach to gain a deeper understanding of how TBL influences strategic positioning through image differentiation within a global organization. The discovery of grounded theory as a strategy for qualitative research is credited to Glaser and Strauss (1967). Grounded in data, Glaser and Strauss suggested that "generating grounded theory is a way of arriving at theory suited to its supposed uses" (p. 3). Building on this position, grounded theory is derived from data through a multistep process. The process consists of iterations of inferring categories, reviewing the interferences against data, and then revisiting the inferred categories (Lee, 1999). This approach was applicable because the construct of using TBL in strategic positioning was still not well understood. The grounded theory process presented by Charmaz (2006) was followed in this study.

Unit of Analysis and Characteristics of Participants

The unit of analysis was Johnson Control, a Fortune 500 organization that adopted the TBL approach. Johnson Controls is a global leader and supplier of building efficiency, power solutions, and automotive experience. Utilizing the TBL approach, Johnson Controls promotes economic, social, and environmental practices that benefit the local communities, shareholders, customers, and employees. Research participants were identified using purposeful sampling. Participants (employees of the organization) were divided into groups based on the organizational rank, level of responsibility in strategic planning, and expertise in TBL and sustainability. Therefore, the list of participants included vice presidents of the three groups (building efficiency, automotive experience, and power solutions), directors of strategic planning, strategic planning managers, vice presidents and managers in sustainability, vice presidents and directors of public affairs and communications, and all members of the Global Environment and Sustainability Council (GESC).

Initially, purposeful sampling was used to allow for insightful inquiry. This helped the researcher to understand the phenomenon in-depth.

Key employees from GESC and strategic planning leadership at Johnson Controls were purposefully selected for the relevance of their expertise to the research topics. The initial list of participants included 54 employees. Due to workload, out of the 54 employees that were contacted, 20 were available to participate in the study at the end of purposeful sampling. Snowball sampling was used to locate information-rich key participants. Participants in the research were asked to recommend potential candidates that are suitable for the study. Snowball sampling identified one additional participant that was added to the list for a total of 21 at the end of snowball sampling.

Once the conceptual categories were constructed from the data, theoretical sampling was used to obtain further data for the purpose of explicating the categories. Theoretical sampling was used because it allows the researcher to discover the constructs that are relevant to this problem and population, because it allows the researcher to discover the constructs that are relevant to this problem and population, and allows the researchers to explore the constructs in-depth. Constructs related to talent acquisition and investors emerged from the analysis. In order to explore the constructs in-depth, theoretical sampling was used to add two more participants to the study.

Interview Guide

A total of 23 in-depth semi-structured interviews were conducted with individuals at Johnson Controls in strategic planning, public affairs, communications, and GESC functions. After an executive summary of the research was sent out to the participants, a sample of the interview guide followed via email. The interview questions were designed with the aim of answering the research questions. Interviews were conducted via conference calls. Each interview lasted from 30 to 60 minutes. Interview questions were designed in light of the research questions (main and sub-questions) and to ensure alignment between the two.

In addition to the in-depth interviews, data collection included document reviews. Collecting more data from other sources was necessary for documenting events and conflicts, simplifying the manipulation and categorization of the data, and quantifying the data as required for the statistical analysis. Documents included financial statements, annual financial reports, sustainability reports, and submissions to governmental agencies.

Data Analysis

Interviews were tape-recorded and transcribed. Transcription generated about 260 pages. The researcher reviewed notes from each interview and wrote a total of 27 memos. Different forms of data (written notes during the interviews, memos, and documents) were cross-referenced for patterns, relationships, and confirming and disconfirming data. The data were coded and grounded theory techniques were used to analyze them. The goal was to expand knowledge on TBL as an emerging phenomenon and to build a new theory around the influence of TBL on strategic positioning through image differentiation. At a point in the process, data analysis was done simultaneously with data collection. Data collection and coding continued until theoretical saturation was achieved. Theoretical saturation is the point in analysis when all categories are well developed in terms of properties, dimensions, and variations.

Continuously sorting the codes into several configurations and connecting categories enabled the researcher to gain a deeper understanding of the data. Guided by grounded theory, three types of coding were used in this study: open, axial, and selective coding. Open coding refers to the unrestricted identification of categories that are naturally occurring from the data. Initially, many codes were used to organize and assign the empirical data logically until a coherent structure was achieved. Open coding and axial coding went hand in hand. Although the data were broken apart to identify constructs (open coding), they were put back together by relating those constructs into categories (axial coding). Finally, categories were connected using selective coding. During selective coding, the categories were organized in terms of their potential to fit the data within them. Starting with the most powerful (important) categories, iterations of data fitting took place until all the data had been categorized. Selective coding was used to develop a story that connects the categories through integration.

Findings

The findings illustrate the interconnection of TBL, strategic positioning, differentiation, and image within a global organization. The research discovered that in a TBL-driven organization, TBL as an approach is fundamentally integrated into the organization. Consequently, TBL is woven into the strategic positioning of the organization by being manifested in the strategic priorities designed to ensure the organization's long-term success. The extent of TBL's integration into strategic positioning is influenced by the degree of business alignment between TBL objectives and the organization's products and services. Sequentially, the focus on integrating the TBL approach into strategic positioning is propelled by the business advantages TBL offers. The findings also suggest Thought Leadership (in the sustainability domain) as a new dimension for differentiation in strategic positioning. Regarding the connection between differentiation and image, it was found that differentiation can be achieved through multiple images simultaneously. For instance, the organization's images as a sustainable entity and one that operates with integrity serve as sources of differentiation and are reflected in strategic priorities and external recognitions. This research also uncovered that there is a relationship between image and strategic positioning in the form of Thought Leadership, which is integrated into the strategic priorities. Additionally, portraying the TBL approach in the organization's image, thereby creating the TBL Image, is reflected in various ways (strategic priorities, communication, inclusion in indices, and offerings). Finally, the research suggests that the TBL orientation of the organization, particularly in the social and environmental lines, is a source of differentiation.

TBL and Strategic Positioning

Scholars have explored the relationship between sustainability-related constructs and strategy; my study, however, delves into how TBL influences strategic positioning within an organization, revealing several facets where TBL shapes strategy in a TBL-driven/oriented organization. Specifically, this research found that TBL is woven into the organization's culture and intertwined into its DNA, fabric, and heritage. Therefore, TBL becomes embedded in the strategic priorities that define the organization's strategic position. This research also demonstrates that the degree of business alignment between TBL objectives and the organization's products and services influences TBL's impact on strategic positioning.

TBL Is Embedded in the Organization

Participants' initial thoughts on TBL in Johnson Controls indicated that it is embedded in the organization, being part of its culture, DNA, fabric, and heritage. The connection between TBL and culture suggests that incorporating the TBL approach results from an organizational culture aligned with the TBL construct. For example, Johnson Controls was founded on designing and manufacturing energy-saving products. Additionally, community involvement and charitable contributions are part of the organization's identity. Hence, the elements (environmental and social) of TBL are intertwined with the organization's identity. Respondents echoed this definition, emphasizing that the focus on TBL dimensions is because it is part of the organization's DNA and fabric.

TBL Is Integrated into the Strategic Priorities

The study demonstrates that TBL is embedded in the organization's strategies as part of the 10-year marker, a set of nine strategic priorities developed to ensure the company's long-term success. These priorities include integrity, innovation, sustainability, customer satisfaction, continuous improvement, global growth, employee engagement and leadership, quality, and shareholder value. Analysis of these strategic priorities showed that TBL is embedded in three priorities reflecting the economic, social, and environmental lines of TBL. The economic line of TBL is mirrored in the global growth strategic priority, which states that the organization will thrive in the global economy and seize opportunities to ensure long-term success. The social line of TBL is reflected in the employee engagement and leadership priority, indicating that as the organization grows, its employees will also grow through engagement and involvement in communities to mirror the organization's global markets and population. Lastly, the environmental line of TBL is embodied in the sustainability strategic priority, emphasizing the organization's commitment to environmental sustainability through the design and manufacture of environmentally friendly products and services. Respondents indicated that TBL [and its image] is embedded in Johnson Controls' strategic positioning through strategic priorities.

Integrating TBL into Strategic Positioning Is Influenced by Business Alignment

Another key finding from using TBL in strategic positioning is the influence of the line of business. Data from interviews and document reviews revealed that the extent of TBL's integration into strategic positioning is influenced by the degree of business alignment between TBL objectives and the products/services offered by each of the three groups. Where product and service lines are directly related to TBL elements, the TBL Image is strongly reflected. For example, the review of each business group's site clearly showed a stronger TBL and sustainability image in building efficiency group than in the automotive experience group. This is driven by the direct link between TBL elements and the products and services offered by the building efficiency group. Similarly, respondents indicated that the extent of reflecting the TBL image varied based on the business group.

Strategic Positioning and Differentiation

This research demonstrates that through strategic priorities and thought leadership, the organization differentiates itself to achieve its strategic position. Respondents indicated that among the nine strategic priorities, Global Growth and Integrity are two main differentiators for the organization.

Global Growth

The importance of growth to Johnson Controls is highlighted by using it as the central message to all stakeholders, as shown in the Annual Business and Sustainability Report. To frame global growth as a strategic priority, Johnson Controls aims to be recognized as a global growth company that thrives in the global economy and seizes growth opportunities. Additionally, global growth is reflected in the global footprint, evidenced by Johnson Controls' global operations, which emerged as a differentiation factor enabling the organization to be everywhere customers require. Respondents indicated that global growth and global footprint contribute to Johnson Controls' differentiation.

Integrity

One of the core values for long-term success, integrity, is among the critical constructs in Johnson Controls. Although corporate documents did not explicitly link integrity as a differentiation strategy, integrity plays an integral role in the organization's success, demonstrated by being the first core value on the 10-year marker. One participant indicated that integrity is a differentiator for Johnson Controls.

Thought Leadership

Thought leadership refers to championing new ideas guided by innovation. Participants indicated that thought leadership is a differentiator for the organization. The re-emergence of thought leadership as a category suggests its significance in differentiation and strategic positioning in a TBL-driven/ oriented organization. Document analysis and responses from interviewees revealed that Thought Leadership is linked to innovation, particularly in sustainability. Innovation is one of the five corporate values and one of the nine strategic priorities. As a differentiator, the organization states that "Innovation will set us apart from the competition and will be a significant driver of our global growth and profitability."

Differentiation through Image

This research shows that image is closely related to differentiation and strategic positioning. This connection is expressed in re-emerging categories that linked image to strategic positioning and differentiation, particularly in the thought leadership area. In terms of using image as a tool for differentiation, participants indicated that image is used to differentiate the organization in three areas: strategic priorities. Prior to the interruption, the document discussed how image, particularly in terms of thought leadership, serves as a tool for differentiation in strategic positioning. Let's continue to build on this:

Thought Leadership in Innovation

Thought leadership emerged as a critical differentiator, especially in the context of sustainability and innovation. Johnson Controls demonstrates thought leadership through its innovative approaches to sustainability, aligning with one of its core values. The company's focus on innovation as a strategic priority positions it as a leader in sustainability initiatives, which, in turn, enhances its image and differentiation in the market.

Johnson Controls' innovative projects, such as the energy-efficient retrofitting of the Empire State Building, underscore their commitment to sustainability. These projects not only highlight their expertise but also serve as powerful marketing tools that reinforce their image as a thought leader in sustainability. This emphasis on innovation and sustainability resonates with stakeholders, including customers and investors, who value environmentally conscious and forward-thinking companies.

TBL Orientation as a Source of Differentiation

The study found that Johnson Controls' orientation toward TBL—encompassing economic, social, and environmental lines—acts as a differentiator. This orientation is evident in their strategic priorities and operational practices. By embedding TBL into its business model, Johnson Controls can differentiate itself from competitors who may not prioritize sustainability to the same extent.

Social Line

The social aspect of TBL is manifested in Johnson Controls' commitment to community involvement and employee engagement. This social responsibility is a key differentiator, as it enhances the company's reputation and fosters stronger relationships with local communities. Engaging in community dialogues and promoting employee welfare are strategic moves that not only improve internal morale but also boost external perceptions of the company.

Environmental Line

On the environmental front, Johnson Controls' dedication to sustainability is demonstrated through its innovative products and services. These include energy-efficient building solutions and advanced battery technologies. By focusing on environmentally friendly products, Johnson Controls not only meets regulatory requirements but also appeals to eco-conscious consumers and businesses looking to reduce their environmental footprint.

Integrating TBL into Strategic Priorities

The integration of TBL into strategic priorities is influenced by the degree of alignment between TBL objectives and the company's products and services. For Johnson Controls, the building efficiency group exemplifies this alignment, as their offerings directly relate to energy efficiency and sustainability. This alignment strengthens the group's strategic position and reinforces the company's overall TBL image.

Business Advantages of TBL Image

The TBL Image offers several business advantages, which drive the integration of TBL into strategic positioning:

- Business Growth: The TBL image helps Johnson Controls secure new business opportunities, particularly in markets that prioritize sustainability. The perception of being a green and responsible company attracts customers and partners, fostering business growth.
- Talent Acquisition and Retention: The company's commitment to TBL makes it an attractive employer, especially for younger talent who value sustainability. This commitment aids in recruiting and retaining top talent, which is crucial for maintaining a competitive edge.
- Shareholder Value: Emphasizing TBL can enhance shareholder value by attracting socially responsible investors. These investors prioritize companies with strong sustainability practices, potentially leading to higher stock valuations and better financial performance.

Practical Implications

For practitioners, the findings from this study offer valuable insights into leveraging TBL for strategic differentiation. The influence of TBL on Strategic Positioning Framework provides a practical tool for integrating TBL into business strategies. By understanding the business advantages of TBL and aligning them with strategic priorities, companies can enhance their competitive position and achieve long-term success.

Human resources practitioners can also benefit from these insights by incorporating TBL into talent acquisition and retention strategies. Promoting the company's TBL initiatives can attract top talent and improve employee engagement, contributing to overall organizational performance.

Conclusion

This study highlights the significant impact of TBL on strategic positioning through image differentiation. By adopting a TBL-driven approach, organizations can enhance their competitive advantage, attract top talent, and build strong relationships with customers and local communities. The theoretical contributions and practical implications of this research provide valuable insights for organizations seeking to leverage sustainability as a strategic differentiator in today's competitive business environment.

The study underscores the importance of embedding TBL into the organization's culture and strategic priorities. This integration not only enhances the company's image but also drives business growth, talent acquisition, and shareholder value. By understanding and leveraging the dynamics between TBL, strategic positioning, differentiation, and image, companies can navigate the complexities of the modern business landscape and achieve sustainable success.

Chapter 8

Shakeout: Adapt to Survive

Set-the-Stage Mini Case

Sprint Corporation

Sprint Corporation, once a major player in the U.S. telecommunications market, provides a compelling example of how companies navigate the shakeout phase of their industry. During the early 2000s, the telecommunications industry experienced rapid growth and expansion, with numerous competitors vying for market share. However, as the industry matured, competition intensified, and market consolidation became inevitable. Sprint found itself in a challenging position, facing fierce competition from industry giants such as Verizon, AT&T, and T-Mobile. The shakeout phase in the telecommunications industry was marked by significant mergers and acquisitions, regulatory changes, and a relentless push for technological advancements.

To survive and thrive during this phase, Sprint undertook a series of strategic initiatives aimed at adapting to the changing market dynamics. The company focused on differentiating its services by enhancing its network infrastructure and investing heavily in 4G LTE technology to improve coverage and speed. Additionally, Sprint pursued aggressive pricing strategies and promotional offers to attract and retain customers. One of the most notable moves during this

 DOI: 10.4324/9781003564133-10

period was Sprint's merger with T-Mobile in 2020, a strategic alliance that allowed the combined entity to leverage economies of scale, expand its customer base, and strengthen its competitive position in the market. This merger marked a significant consolidation in the U.S. telecommunications industry, reflecting the shakeout phase's characteristic market stabilization and the emergence of fewer, more formidable competitors.

Sprint's journey through the shakeout phase illustrates the critical importance of strategic adaptation, technological investment, and market consolidation in navigating a mature and highly competitive industry.

Defining the Shakeout Phase

During the shakeout phase of the industry life cycle, the industry experiences increased competition and a more stable market environment compared to the earlier phases.

In the shakeout phase, the industry stabilizes as weaker players are gradually eliminated or acquired, leading to a consolidation of market share among the stronger competitors. This phase is characterized by slower but more sustainable growth, and the industry landscape starts to take shape with a smaller number of dominant players. The regulatory environment during the shakeout phase can vary depending on the industry. In some cases, regulations may become stricter as the industry matures and regulators aim to ensure fair competition and protect consumer interests. Regulatory bodies may impose industry-specific regulations and standards to maintain market stability and prevent anti-competitive practices.

The competitive landscape in the shakeout phase is characterized by intense rivalry among the remaining players. As weaker competitors exit the market, the number of rivals decreases, resulting in a smaller pool of more formidable competitors. This phase often witnesses an increase in competitive intensity as companies vie for market share and strive to differentiate themselves from their rivals. Price competition becomes more significant during the shakeout phase as competitors try to capture a larger market share. The pressure to differentiate intensifies, leading to price wars and promotional activities to attract customers. Companies may focus on refining their value propositions, improving product quality, or introducing innovative features to stand out in the market.

Several industries in different sectors can be observed in the shakeout phase. One example is the ride-sharing industry, which experienced significant growth during the embryonic and growth phases but eventually entered the shakeout phase. Companies like Uber, Lyft, and Didi Chuxing emerged as dominant players, while smaller competitors struggled to compete and eventually exited the market. The industry witnessed increased consolidation through acquisitions and partnerships, signaling the maturing and stabilization of the market.

SHAKEOUT PHASE IN BRIEF: The shakeout phase of the industry life cycle represents a more stable market environment with increased competition and consolidation among the remaining players. Organizations operating within this phase must focus on differentiating themselves from competitors, refining their value propositions, and navigating regulatory challenges. By strategically positioning themselves and adapting to the changing market dynamics, companies can seize opportunities and thrive in this phase of the industry life cycle.

Key Characteristics of This Phase

✓ Increased Competition: During the shakeout phase, competition intensifies as weaker players are gradually eliminated or acquired. The number of competitors decreases, leading to a smaller pool of more formidable players. This heightened competition drives companies to differentiate themselves and strive for sustainable competitive advantage.

✓ Market Consolidation: The shakeout phase often witnesses a consolidation of market share among the remaining players. Stronger companies acquire or merge with weaker competitors, leading to a concentration of power in the industry. This consolidation can create barriers to entry for new entrants and solidify the positions of the dominant players.

✓ Slower but Sustainable Growth: Compared to the earlier phases of the industry life cycle, the shakeout phase experiences slower but more sustainable growth. Market saturation and increased competition contribute to a more stable growth rate. Companies must focus on capturing market share from their competitors rather than relying solely on industry expansion.

✓ Price Competition and Value Differentiation: Price competition becomes more significant during the shakeout phase as companies vie for market share. Price wars and promotional activities may emerge as competitors seek to attract customers. To stand out in the market, companies must differentiate their products or services through value-added features, superior quality, or innovative solutions.

✓ Regulatory Considerations: The regulatory environment in the shakeout phase can become more stringent as the industry matures. Regulatory bodies may impose industry-specific regulations and standards to ensure fair competition, protect consumer interests, and maintain market stability. Companies must navigate these regulations and comply with the evolving legal framework.

✓ Shift toward Efficiency and Cost Optimization: As competition increases, companies focus on enhancing operational efficiency and cost optimization. This entails streamlining processes, improving productivity, and controlling expenses to maintain profitability and competitive pricing. Successful companies in the shakeout phase leverage economies of scale and operational excellence to gain a competitive edge.

✓ Strategic Alliances and Mergers: The shakeout phase often prompts strategic alliances, collaborations, and mergers among industry players. Companies seek synergies and economies of scale through partnerships to strengthen their market position and enhance competitiveness. Strategic alliances can provide access to new markets, technologies, or resources that drive growth and market expansion.

✓ Customer Loyalty and Brand Building: Building strong customer loyalty and brand equity becomes critical in the shakeout phase. With increased competition, companies must differentiate themselves through superior customer experiences, personalized services, and brand reputation. Cultivating customer loyalty and trust becomes a key driver of success and market share growth.

The Recommended Approach to Strategy During This Phase and Why

During the shakeout phase of the industry life cycle, the recommended approach to strategy is centered around adaptation. Organizations are advised to adapt to the changing market dynamics, intensifying competition, and evolving customer needs. Let's examine the rationale behind the adaptation strategy and its significance in this phase:

■ Recognizing Market Shifts: The shakeout phase is characterized by a shifting market landscape, with changes in customer preferences, technology advancements, and competitive dynamics. Organizations need to closely monitor these shifts and be agile in responding to them. By adapting their strategies, products, and services, companies can stay aligned with the evolving market demands and gain a competitive edge.

■ Surviving Intensified Competition: As the industry shakeout occurs, competition becomes more intense, and weaker players exit the market.

To survive and thrive in this phase, organizations must differentiate themselves from competitors and continuously improve their offerings. By adapting their strategies, companies can differentiate their products, enhance customer experiences, and secure a stronger market position.

- Leveraging Organizational Flexibility: Organizations, as CASs, possess inherent flexibility and the ability to respond to changing circumstances. By embracing the adaptation strategy, companies tap into their capabilities as CAS, enabling them to adjust their strategies, structures, and processes in response to market conditions. This flexibility allows organizations to navigate through uncertainties, seize opportunities, and mitigate potential risks.
- Embracing Innovation and Continuous Improvement: Adaptation goes hand in hand with innovation and continuous improvement. Organizations in the shakeout phase should foster a culture of innovation, encouraging employees to generate new ideas, explore emerging technologies, and improve existing processes. By adopting innovative approaches, companies can differentiate themselves from competitors, introduce novel solutions, and meet evolving customer needs.
- Creating Strategic Alliances: The shakeout phase often necessitates strategic alliances and partnerships to leverage complementary resources, capabilities, and market access. By adapting their strategies to include collaborative initiatives, organizations can strengthen their competitive position, enhance market reach, and share risks and costs. Strategic alliances can provide access to new markets, technologies, and resources, enabling organizations to adapt more effectively.
- Customer-Centric Focus: The adaptation strategy in the shakeout phase emphasizes a customer-centric approach. Organizations should closely engage with customers, gather feedback, and understand their evolving preferences and needs. By adapting products, services, and experiences to meet customer expectations, companies can build customer loyalty, enhance brand reputation, and secure market share.

By embracing adaptation as a strategic approach, organizations can navigate the challenges of the shakeout phase. Adapting allows companies to stay relevant, differentiate themselves, leverage their CAS capabilities, and seize opportunities for growth. The ability to adapt positions organizations for long-term success in a dynamic and competitive business environment.

Special Note on Staying Relevant: The shakeout phase is a critical period where market conditions change rapidly, and customer preferences evolve. Organizations that fail to adapt risk becoming obsolete or losing their competitive edge. By embracing adaptation, companies can proactively respond to market shifts, emerging technologies, and changing customer needs. They can stay relevant by continuously improving their offerings, refining their value proposition, and addressing new market demands. Nokia's transformation is an example: Nokia, once a leading mobile phone manufacturer, faced a significant challenge during the shakeout phase of the industry life cycle when smartphones emerged as a disruptive force. Despite its initial resistance to change, Nokia eventually embraced adaptation by shifting its focus to smartphones and forming a strategic alliance with Microsoft. This move allowed Nokia to stay relevant in the evolving mobile industry and regain market share.

RECOMMENDED APPROACH IN BRIEF: Embracing adaptation as a strategic approach allows organizations to navigate the challenges of the shakeout phase effectively. It enables companies to stay relevant, differentiate themselves from competitors, leverage their CAS capabilities, and seize growth opportunities. By continuously adapting their strategies, products, and services, organizations position themselves for long-term success in a dynamic and competitive business environment. The ability to adapt becomes a core competency, empowering organizations to thrive in the face of uncertainties and emerge as industry leaders.

Assess: is your organization competing during this phase

Assessing the phase of the industry life cycle is crucial for business leaders to make informed strategic decisions. Here is a detailed guideline to help business leaders assess if their organization is in the shakeout phase:

- ✓ Evaluate Competitive Intensity: Assess the level of competition in the industry. Look for signs of increasing rivalry, such as price wars, aggressive marketing tactics, or heightened product differentiation. Monitor the entry and exit of competitors. Note the number of players exiting the market due to financial difficulties or inability to sustain operations. Analyze market share dynamics. Identify whether market shares are consolidating among a few dominant players or spreading across multiple competitors.
- ✓ Analyze Market Consolidation: Determine if the industry is undergoing consolidation through mergers, acquisitions, or partnerships. Look for indications of companies strategically aligning themselves to strengthen their market positions. Assess if larger, more established companies are acquiring smaller competitors or absorbing their market share. Evaluate the impact of consolidation on the competitive landscape and the potential barriers it creates for new entrants.
- ✓ Monitor Pricing and Profitability: Assess pricing trends within the industry. Look for signs of price stabilization or declining profit margins due to

heightened competition. Analyze the pricing strategies of competitors. Identify if price competition is intensifying, indicating a shakeout phase where organizations fight for market share. Evaluate the profitability of industry participants. Determine if profitability is declining, suggesting a challenging business environment.

✓ Assess Market Offerings: Analyze the diversity of product or service offerings in the market. Determine if companies are expanding their portfolios to cater to evolving customer demands or to differentiate themselves from competitors. Identify innovative products or services that are disrupting the market. Note if organizations are introducing new technologies or business models to gain a competitive edge. Evaluate the level of customer demand and market saturation. Assess if market saturation is leading to a decline in demand or if there are untapped customer segments to explore.

✓ Consider Regulatory Environment: Evaluate the regulatory landscape within the industry. Determine if regulations are becoming more stringent, impacting market entry or limiting competitive actions. Assess the potential influence of government policies or industry regulations on market dynamics, barriers to entry, or pricing strategies. Analyze how regulatory changes may favor larger, more established players or create challenges for smaller, emerging organizations.

✓ Understand CAS Behavior: Recognize that organizations, as CASs, exhibit certain behaviors during the shakeout phase. CAS tends to adapt their strategies and business models to respond to changing market conditions and competitive pressures. Look for signs of organizations adjusting their value propositions, exploring new markets, or seeking partnerships and collaborations to survive the shakeout phase.

✓ Consider External Influences: Take into account external factors such as technological advancements, changes in customer preferences, or shifts in the macroeconomic environment that may impact the industry's shakeout phase. Assess the influence of disruptive innovations, new business models, or emerging trends that can accelerate industry transformation. Monitor the industry's susceptibility to external shocks, economic downturns, or changes in global trade dynamics that may impact competition and shakeout dynamics.

Kraft Heinz

Kraft Heinz provides a notable example of a company navigating the shakeout phase in the food industry. Following the merger of Kraft Foods Group and H.J. Heinz Company in 2015, the newly formed

Kraft Heinz faced an increasingly competitive and saturated market. The food industry was undergoing significant transformations, driven by changing consumer preferences toward healthier and more sustainable food options, as well as the rise of private label brands and niche competitors. The merger aimed to leverage synergies between the two companies, reduce costs, and enhance market positioning in an environment characterized by slow growth and intense competition.

During the shakeout phase, Kraft Heinz implemented several strategic initiatives to adapt and survive. The company focused on operational efficiency, cost reduction, and innovation to maintain profitability and market share. This included closing underperforming plants, streamlining supply chains, and investing in new product development to meet the evolving demands of health-conscious consumers. Additionally, Kraft Heinz sought to rejuvenate its brand image through marketing campaigns and partnerships, emphasizing its commitment to quality and sustainability. Despite these efforts, the company faced challenges in revitalizing stagnant brands and competing with agile, innovative rivals in the market.

Develop the Strategy for This Phase

1. Assess the Competitive Landscape: Conduct a thorough analysis of the industry's competitive dynamics, including the number of rivals and their market positions. Identify the key players and their strategies to understand the level of competition and market saturation. Evaluate the strengths and weaknesses of competitors to identify gaps and opportunities for differentiation.
2. Focus on Differentiation: Emphasize unique value propositions and differentiate your offerings from competitors. Identify customer needs that are not adequately addressed in the market and develop products or services to fulfill those needs. Invest in research and development to innovate and create distinctive features or capabilities that set your organization apart.
3. Adapt to Changing Consumer Preferences: Stay attuned to evolving consumer trends and preferences. Regularly gather customer feedback and use it to refine your offerings. Leverage market research and consumer insights to anticipate changing demands and tailor your products or services accordingly.

4. Embrace Digital Transformation: Emphasize digital innovation to enhance customer experiences and streamline operations. Invest in technologies that improve efficiency, such as automation, data analytics, and cloud computing. Leverage digital platforms to engage with customers, offer personalized experiences, and gather valuable data for decision-making.

5. Enhance Operational Efficiency: Optimize internal processes to increase efficiency and reduce costs. Streamline supply chain management to ensure timely delivery and cost-effectiveness. Implement lean practices and continuous improvement methodologies to eliminate waste and enhance productivity.

6. Foster Collaboration and Partnerships: Seek opportunities for collaboration with complementary organizations to leverage synergies and expand market reach. Form strategic alliances or partnerships to access new markets, technologies, or distribution channels. Establish relationships with suppliers, distributors, or other stakeholders to enhance competitiveness and adaptability.

7. Monitor and Respond to Regulatory Changes: Stay informed about regulatory developments and anticipate their impact on the industry. Adjust strategies and operations to comply with new regulations or leverage opportunities arising from regulatory changes. Engage in dialogue with regulatory bodies to influence favorable policies that support your organization's goals.

Practical Implications for Strategy Development

Embracing adaptation as a core strategic approach allows organizations to navigate the challenges of the shakeout phase effectively.

A. Continuous monitoring of the competitive landscape and customer preferences is crucial for identifying opportunities and staying ahead of the curve.

B. Agility and flexibility are key attributes for organizations in the shakeout phase, as they need to respond quickly to market changes and seize emerging opportunities.

C. Effective execution of strategies requires cross-functional collaboration, a focus on operational efficiency, and leveraging technology to enhance customer experiences.

D. Developing a strong organizational culture of innovation, agility, and customer-centricity is essential to thrive in the dynamic shakeout phase.

By following this guideline, business leaders can navigate the complexities of the shakeout phase, adapt their strategies to changing market conditions, and position their organizations for long-term success in the industry.

Deploy the Strategy for This Phase

1. Communicate and Align Strategy: Ensure clarity in communicating the strategic direction and goals to all employees. Foster a shared understanding of the competitive challenges and the need for adaptation. Ensure alignment across all departments and functions to drive cohesive execution.

2. Build Organizational Agility: Develop a flexible and agile organizational structure that enables quick decision-making and adaptability. Encourage a culture of experimentation, learning, and continuous improvement. Empower employees to take ownership of their roles and contribute to the organization's adaptive capabilities.

3. Invest in Talent Development: Identify key competencies required for success in the shakeout phase. Provide training and development programs to enhance employees' skills and knowledge. Foster a learning environment that encourages innovation and creativity.

4. Monitor and Anticipate Market Changes: Implement robust market intelligence systems to gather real-time data on industry trends and competitors. Regularly assess the competitive landscape and monitor shifts in customer preferences. Anticipate potential disruptors and proactively respond to emerging threats.

5. Optimize Resource Allocation: Prioritize resource allocation based on strategic objectives and the organization's core competencies. Continuously evaluate the return on investment of various initiatives and make data-driven decisions. Allocate resources to areas that provide the greatest potential for growth and differentiation.

6. Foster Customer Relationships: Strengthen relationships with existing customers and actively seek feedback. Develop customer loyalty programs to retain customers and enhance their experience. Engage in targeted marketing and promotional activities to attract new customers.

7. Collaborate with Partners and Stakeholders: Identify potential collaboration opportunities with industry partners or complementary organizations. Build strategic alliances and partnerships to leverage shared resources and capabilities. Engage with stakeholders, such as suppliers and distributors, to enhance supply chain efficiency and flexibility.

8. Continuously Evaluate and Adjust: Establish performance metrics and regular reporting mechanisms to track progress. Conduct periodic reviews of strategy implementation and assess the effectiveness of initiatives. Stay open to feedback and be willing to make adjustments based on market dynamics and new information.

Practical Implications for Strategy Deployment

Successful strategy deployment in the shakeout phase requires a combination of organizational agility, talent development, and market intelligence.

A. Continuous monitoring of market changes and customer preferences is essential for staying competitive and adapting strategies as needed.
B. Effective resource allocation and prioritization enable organizations to optimize their efforts and focus on areas that drive differentiation and growth.
C. Building strong relationships with customers, partners, and stakeholders enhances market positioning and supports strategic initiatives.
D. By following this guideline, organizations can effectively deploy their strategies in the shakeout phase, adapt to market challenges, and capitalize on emerging opportunities for sustainable success.

Failing to Strategize Effectively during the Shakeout Phase

Failing to strategize effectively during the shakeout phase can have significant implications for organizations, leading to missed opportunities, loss of market share, and even business failure. Let's explore some reasons for failure and their consequences using specific examples from real organizations:

■ Lack of Differentiation:
  – Consequence: Similar to the growth phase, organizations that fail to differentiate their products or services from rivals are likely to struggle with the acquisition and retention of customers. Without a clear direction for differentiation be it broad or focused, these organizations risk becoming irrelevant in an increasingly sophisticated customer market. Sequentially, they lose their unique value proposition, they become susceptible to price wars and eroding profit
    • Example: Borders Group Inc. Borders, a former bookstore chain, failed to differentiate itself in the rapidly changing retail landscape. The company struggled to compete with online retailers like Amazon and failed to adapt to the shift toward digital content. As a result, Borders faced declining sales, filed for bankruptcy, and eventually closed its stores.
■ Inability to Adapt to Technological Advances:
  – Consequence: Blockbuster's failure to recognize and adapt to technological advances resulted in the company's obsolescence,

underscoring the need for organizations to proactively embrace disruptive technologies.

- Example: Blockbuster Inc. Blockbuster, a video rental company, failed to adapt to the emergence of online streaming and digital distribution. Despite having opportunities to acquire Netflix, Blockbuster declined the offer, believing that its brick-and-mortar model would continue to dominate. This decision proved costly as consumers increasingly embraced the convenience of streaming services, ultimately leading to Blockbuster's bankruptcy.

■ Poor Market Analysis and Competitive Intelligence:
  - Consequence: Kodak's failure to conduct adequate market analysis and competitive intelligence resulted in missed opportunities to capitalize on the digital photography revolution, leading to a significant loss of market share and eventual bankruptcy.
    - Example: Kodak—Kodak, once a dominant player in the photography industry, failed to recognize the rapid rise of digital photography. Despite inventing the digital camera, Kodak did not fully leverage the technology and underestimated its potential impact. The company focused heavily on traditional film-based products and failed to adapt to changing consumer preferences, leading to its decline.

■ Ignoring Customer Preferences and Needs:
  - Consequence: Nokia's failure to address evolving customer preferences and meet their needs led to a significant decline in market share and eventually forced the company to sell its mobile phone business.
    - Example: Nokia—Nokia, a leading mobile phone manufacturer, initially dominated the market with its feature phones. However, the company failed to recognize the growing demand for smartphones and the emergence of touchscreen technology. Nokia was slow to innovate and adapt to the changing landscape, resulting in a loss of market share to competitors like Apple and Samsung.

Lesson from a leader

Shantanu Narayen

Adobe Systems, a software company known for its creative and multimedia solutions, experienced a significant shift in its business model under the leadership of CEO Shantanu Narayen. In the early 2000s, Adobe faced challenges as the market for its traditional software products started to change with the rise of cloud-based software and subscription models.

Recognizing the need to adapt to the evolving market dynamics and customer preferences, Narayen led Adobe through a strategic transformation. He initiated the shift from a traditional software licensing model to a subscription-based model called Adobe Creative Cloud. This change allowed customers to access Adobe's software as a service (SaaS) through subscription plans, providing greater flexibility and affordability.

Narayen's vision and strategic decision to embrace the subscription-based model proved successful for Adobe. The company experienced significant growth in recurring revenue, strengthened customer relationships, and increased market share. By adapting its business model, Adobe successfully navigated the shakeout phase and positioned itself as a leader in the digital creative industry.

This example highlights the importance of leadership and strategic adaptation in response to changing market dynamics. By embracing new business models and technologies, organizations can remain competitive, retain customer loyalty, and drive sustainable growth.

CASE STUDY: ELECTRIFICATION STRATEGY AT VOLKSWAGEN GROUP

Introduction

Electrification has become a central goal for many automakers as they strive to meet global environmental regulations and consumer demand for sustainable mobility. Volkswagen Group, one of the world's largest automotive manufacturers, has made significant strides in this area, particularly after the 2015 diesel emissions scandal. The company's ambitious electrification strategy aims to restore its reputation and position itself as a leader in the electric vehicle (EV) market.

Volkswagen's journey toward electrification was catalyzed by both regulatory pressures and strategic realignment. The European Union's stringent emissions targets and the global push for zero-emission vehicles have driven automakers to innovate rapidly. Volkswagen has committed to investing approximately €60 billion by 2024 in the development of electric, hybrid, and digital technologies, showcasing its dedication to transforming its product lineup and infrastructure (Volkswagen Group, 2020).

Evolution of Electric Vehicles

Volkswagen's early forays into electric mobility included the e-Golf and e-Up!, which offered modest ranges and performance compared to today's standards. These models were crucial in laying the groundwork for the company's future EV initiatives. The major breakthrough came with the launch of the ID.3 in 2020, the first model based on the new Modular Electric Drive Matrix (MEB) platform. The ID.3 marked Volkswagen's transition from conventional vehicle adaptations to purpose-built electric cars (Volkswagen Group, 2020). The MEB platform represents a significant technological leap, designed exclusively for electric vehicles. It offers scalable solutions that can be used across various segments, enabling Volkswagen to streamline production and reduce costs. The ID.3, followed by the ID.4 SUV, demonstrated Volkswagen's capability to produce competitive EVs with substantial range, advanced features, and wide market appeal. By 2021, Volkswagen delivered more than 263,000 electric vehicles worldwide, doubling its previous year's sales and underscoring its growing presence in the EV market (Volkswagen Group, 2022). Volkswagen's commitment to electrification extends beyond just new models. The company plans to electrify its entire portfolio, ensuring that each of its brands, including Audi, Porsche, and Skoda, offers electric alternatives. This comprehensive strategy highlights Volkswagen's goal to become a leader in the global transition to electric mobility.

Mass Production and Scaling Challenges

Volkswagen's aggressive electrification plan involves overcoming substantial challenges in production and supply chain management. The company has committed to building six battery cell production facilities in Europe by 2030, with a combined capacity of 240 gigawatt-hours per year. These factories aim to secure the supply of battery cells, which are critical for the scalability of EV production (Volkswagen Group, 2021a). One notable facility is the Salzgitter plant in Germany, which is being transformed into a key hub for battery technology. Volkswagen has partnered with companies like Northvolt to develop sustainable and high-performance battery solutions. By investing in these facilities, Volkswagen aims to control the supply chain, reduce dependency on external suppliers, and lower production costs (Volkswagen Group, 2021a). Volkswagen's investment in battery production also includes innovative research into new battery technologies. The company is focused on developing solid-state batteries, which promise greater energy density and faster charging times compared to current lithium-ion batteries. Volkswagen's collaboration with QuantumScape, a leader in solid-state battery technology, is a testament to its commitment to innovation and sustainability (QuantumScape, 2021).

Infrastructure and Market Expansion

Volkswagen's strategy also involves significant investment in charging infrastructure. Through its subsidiary, Electrify America, Volkswagen is expanding the availability of fast-charging stations across North America. By 2025, the company plans to have more than 3,500 charging points at 800 locations, significantly enhancing the accessibility of charging options for EV owners (Electrify America, 2021). In Europe, Volkswagen is part of the Ionity network, a joint venture with other major automakers, which aims to build a high-power charging network along major highways. These initiatives are critical in addressing range anxiety and supporting the broader adoption of electric vehicles (Ionity, 2021).

To further support the adoption of EVs, Volkswagen is integrating advanced charging solutions into its vehicles. The company's We Charge service provides seamless access to over 150,000 charging points across Europe, allowing customers to easily find and use charging stations. This integration of hardware, software, and services is a key component of Volkswagen's strategy to make electric mobility convenient and accessible for all (Volkswagen Group, 2021b).

Research and Development

Volkswagen continues to prioritize research and development to stay ahead in the competitive EV market. The company is exploring next-generation battery technologies, including solid-state batteries, which promise greater energy density and shorter charging times. Volkswagen has invested in QuantumScape, a company specializing in solid-state battery technology, to accelerate the commercialization of these advanced batteries (QuantumScape, 2021). Additionally, Volkswagen is integrating digital and autonomous driving technologies into its EVs. The ID.4, for instance, features advanced driver-assistance systems and over-the-air software updates, ensuring that the vehicle remains up-to-date with the latest features and improvements (Volkswagen Group, 2021b). Volkswagen's investment in autonomous driving technology is another critical area of focus. The company is working on integrating Level 4 autonomous driving capabilities into its vehicles, which will enable fully autonomous driving in certain conditions. Volkswagen's partnership with Argo AI, a leading autonomous vehicle technology company, is a key component of this strategy. Together, they are developing advanced autonomous driving systems that will be integrated into Volkswagen's commercial and passenger vehicles (Volkswagen Group, 2021b).

Consumer Education and Advocacy

Volkswagen recognizes the importance of consumer education in promoting EV adoption. The company engages in extensive marketing campaigns to highlight the benefits of electric mobility, including lower operating costs, environmental impact, and the driving experience. By positioning itself as a pioneer in the transition to sustainable transportation, Volkswagen aims to build consumer trust and brand loyalty (Volkswagen Group, 2020). Volkswagen's ID. Family marketing campaigns have been particularly effective in educating consumers about the benefits of electric mobility. The campaign emphasizes the environmental benefits, cost savings, and advanced technology of Volkswagen's electric vehicles. By highlighting real-world examples and testimonials, Volkswagen is able to convey the advantages of electric mobility in a relatable and compelling way (Volkswagen Group, 2021c).

Challenges and Opportunities

Despite its progress, Volkswagen faces several challenges. The automotive industry is highly competitive, with new entrants and established players alike vying for a share of the growing EV market. Volkswagen must continue to innovate and differentiate its offerings to maintain its competitive edge (Volkswagen Group, 2020).

Another challenge is achieving cost parity with traditional combustion engine vehicles. Although battery costs have been decreasing, they remain a significant component of the total vehicle cost. Volkswagen is focused on achieving economies of scale and advancing battery technology to make EVs more affordable for a broader range of consumers (Volkswagen Group, 2021b).

Volkswagen also faces regulatory challenges as different regions have varying standards and requirements for electric vehicles. The company must navigate these complexities to ensure compliance and maintain its market position. Additionally, Volkswagen must address the environmental impact of battery production and disposal, as sustainability is a key component of its brand promise (Volkswagen Group, 2021b).

Conclusion

Volkswagen Group's comprehensive electrification strategy reflects its commitment to becoming a leader in the electric vehicle market. By investing heavily in battery technology, charging infrastructure, and R&D, Volkswagen aims to overcome the challenges of scaling production and meeting consumer demand. The company's efforts to educate consumers and promote the benefits of electric mobility are crucial in driving broader adoption. Volkswagen's journey underscores the transformative potential of electrification in the automotive industry and its critical role in achieving a sustainable future (Volkswagen Group, 2022).

Chapter 9

Maturity: Compete Until Blue Oceans Turn Red

Set-the-stage Mini Case

AstraZeneca is a multinational pharmaceutical company headquartered in Cambridge, England. Formed in 1999 through the merger of Swedish Astra AB and British Zeneca Group, the company has established itself as a significant player in the global pharmaceuticals market. Renowned for its innovative drug development, AstraZeneca has a diverse portfolio of products across various therapeutic areas, including oncology, cardiovascular, and respiratory health. The company faced several challenges in the competitive pharmaceutical landscape. Intensifying competition from generic drug manufacturers has led to price pressures, necessitating strategic differentiation. The company had to continuously innovate within its existing portfolio, focusing on incremental improvements and enhancements to retain customer loyalty. Furthermore, despite the regulatory landscape remaining stable, yet it required ongoing compliance to ensure product quality and safety. Despite these challenges, AstraZeneca has numerous opportunities for growth. The company explored partnerships and collaborations to leverage its research and development capabilities. By focusing on personalized medicine and advancing digital health initiatives, AstraZeneca addressed evolving customer demands and capture new market segments. To navigate the competitive environment effectively, the company adopted three key strategic initiatives. 1) Product Differentiation:

The company invests heavily in research and development to introduce new formulations and combination therapies that enhance the efficacy of existing drugs. 2) Cost Optimization: AstraZeneca emphasizes operational efficiency to manage costs while maintaining high standards of quality and compliance. 3) Customer Engagement: The company enhances customer relationships through tailored marketing strategies and patient support programs that foster brand loyalty.

Defining the Maturing Phase

In the maturity phase of the industry life cycle, the market becomes more stable, and the industry experiences a slower rate of growth compared to previous phases. The industry reaches a point where most potential customers have adopted the product or service, resulting in a saturated market. During this phase, organizations focus on sustaining their market position, optimizing operations, and maximizing profitability. In the maturity phase, the industry tends to stabilize as market conditions become more predictable. Companies have a better understanding of customer demands and preferences, and market trends are relatively well-established. This stability allows organizations to focus on refining their strategies and operations rather than aggressively seeking new market opportunities. The regulatory environment in the maturity phase can vary depending on the industry. Some industries may face increased government oversight and regulations aimed at maintaining fair competition and protecting consumer interests. Regulatory frameworks may be put in place to prevent monopolistic behaviors or anticompetitive practices. However, the regulatory environment is generally more stable compared to the earlier phases, with fewer disruptive changes.

The competitive landscape in the maturity phase is characterized by a moderate number of established competitors. Industry consolidation may have occurred, resulting in fewer players due to mergers, acquisitions, or the exit of less successful firms. The focus shifts from aggressive competition for market share to maintaining existing customer relationships and fending off potential new entrants. Differentiation strategies become crucial for organizations to stand out from competitors and retain market share. In the maturity phase, price competition becomes more prominent as companies strive to maintain market share and maximize profitability. Price wars among competitors may arise, leading to margin pressure. Organizations also focus on product/service differentiation, bundling, or offering additional value-added services to attract and retain customers. Market offerings may become more standardized, and innovation shifts toward incremental improvements rather than radical breakthroughs.

THE MATURITY PHASE IN BRIEF: In summary, the maturity phase of the industry life cycle represents a period of stability, moderate competition, and a focus on sustaining market position and optimizing operations. Organizations in this phase emphasize differentiation, pricing strategies, and refining their product offerings to maintain market share and maximize profitability.

Key Characteristics of This Phase

✓ Market Stability: The maturity phase is characterized by a stable market environment. Customer preferences, market trends, and competitive forces are well-established, leading to a more predictable business landscape. Market conditions become relatively stable, allowing organizations to focus on optimizing their operations and sustaining their market position.

✓ Slower Growth Rate: In the maturity phase, industry growth rates tend to slow down compared to the earlier stages of the industry life cycle. Most potential customers have already adopted the product or service, resulting in a saturated market. This slower growth rate necessitates a shift in focus toward maintaining market share and maximizing profitability through operational efficiencies and cost management.

✓ Established Competitors: The competitive landscape in the maturity phase typically consists of a moderate number of established competitors. Industry consolidation may have occurred, resulting in fewer players due to mergers, acquisitions, or the exit of less successful firms. The competition shifts from gaining new customers to retaining existing ones. Differentiation strategies become crucial for organizations to differentiate their offerings from competitors and maintain customer loyalty.

✓ Price Competition: Price competition becomes more prominent in the maturity phase as organizations strive to maintain or increase market share. Price wars may arise as competitors attempt to capture a larger customer base. This increased price competition can put pressure on profit margins, making cost management and operational efficiency critical for success.

✓ Product Standardization: As the market matures, product offerings tend to become more standardized. Organizations focus on incremental improvements and variations of existing products rather than radical innovations. The emphasis shifts toward refining features, quality, and customer experience to differentiate their offerings.

✓ Focus on Customer Retention: With a saturated market and established competitors, customer retention becomes a key priority in the maturity phase. Organizations invest in building and maintaining strong customer relationships through excellent customer service, loyalty programs, and personalized offerings. Retaining existing customers becomes more cost-effective than acquiring new ones.

✓ Marketing and Branding: In the maturity phase, marketing efforts focus on maintaining brand awareness and loyalty. Organizations use marketing strategies to differentiate their offerings, communicate value, and reinforce customer perceptions of their brand. Effective branding and targeted marketing campaigns become essential for sustaining market share.

✓ Operational Efficiency: With market stability and slower growth, organizations in the maturity phase emphasize operational efficiency. Streamlining processes, reducing costs, and optimizing resource allocation are crucial for maintaining profitability. This may involve implementing lean practices, adopting new technologies, and continuously improving operational performance.

It is important to note that the characteristics mentioned above are not fixed or absolute but provide a general framework for understanding the maturity phase of the industry life cycle. Different industries and companies may exhibit variations based on their specific circumstances.

The Recommended Approach to Strategy During This Phase and Why

Competitive Strategy

In the maturity phase, where market conditions become stable and competition intensifies, organizations are advised to adopt competitive strategies to maintain their market share and profitability. Competitive strategy, as described by Michael Porter, involves positioning the organization in a way that it can outperform competitors in the industry. This can be achieved through differentiation or cost leadership.

- Differentiation Strategy: Organizations can differentiate their products or services from competitors by focusing on unique features, superior quality, exceptional customer service, or innovative design. By offering differentiated value, organizations can attract customers and create a perceived competitive advantage. For example, in the smartphone industry, Apple has successfully differentiated itself through its user-friendly interface, ecosystem integration, and emphasis on design aesthetics.

- Cost Leadership Strategy: Alternatively, organizations can pursue a cost leadership strategy by optimizing their operations, achieving economies of scale, and delivering products or services at a lower cost than competitors.

This allows organizations to offer competitive pricing and appeal to cost-conscious customers. Walmart is a notable example of a company that has implemented a successful cost leadership strategy, leveraging its operational efficiencies and large-scale purchasing power to provide affordable products to consumers.

Blue Ocean Strategy

Blue ocean strategy, coined by W. Chan Kim and Renée Mauborgne, suggests that organizations should seek uncontested market spaces or "blue oceans" rather than competing in crowded and highly competitive "red oceans." In the maturity phase, where competition is fierce and market saturation is prevalent, organizations are advised to explore untapped market segments or create new demand through innovation and value creation.

Blue ocean strategy involves identifying new customer needs, developing innovative products or services, and creating a unique market space where competition is limited. By doing so, organizations can unlock new growth opportunities and escape the confines of intense competition in the mature market. One example of a company that successfully implemented a blue ocean strategy is Cirque du Soleil. Instead of competing in the traditional circus industry, Cirque du Soleil created a new market space by combining elements of theater, circus arts, and music, appealing to a broader audience and offering a unique entertainment experience.

The rationale behind both competitive strategy and blue ocean strategy during the maturity phase is to maintain relevance, differentiate from competitors, and sustain growth. Organizations as CAS must adapt and evolve their strategies to navigate the challenges of a mature industry. By strategically positioning themselves through differentiation or cost leadership, they can leverage their CAS capabilities to respond to changing market dynamics and customer preferences.

Moreover, by exploring blue ocean opportunities, organizations can create new demand, unlock untapped markets, and extend their product or service offerings. This approach aligns with the characteristics of the maturity phase, where product standardization and price competition are prevalent. Organizations that proactively pursue competitive and blue ocean strategies are more likely to secure a sustainable competitive advantage and thrive in the mature market.

In the maturity phase of an industry life cycle, organizations face challenges such as product standardization and price competition. The market becomes saturated, and differentiation becomes more difficult to achieve. To thrive in such an environment, organizations need to go beyond incremental improvements and explore new avenues for growth. This is where the concept of blue ocean strategy comes into play.

Blue ocean strategy emphasizes the creation of uncontested market spaces or "blue oceans" where competition is limited or non-existent. By venturing into these blue oceans, organizations can create new demand, unlock untapped markets, and extend their product or service offerings. This approach aligns well with the characteristics of the maturity phase, where differentiation becomes critical for sustained success.

Exploring blue ocean opportunities allows organizations to break away from the crowded "red oceans" characterized by fierce competition and price wars. Instead of battling with competitors over a limited customer base, organizations can seek out new customer segments or create innovative offerings that meet previously unaddressed needs. This strategy enables organizations to escape the constraints of price competition and find new sources of value creation.

By creating new demand, organizations can expand the boundaries of the market and attract customers who were previously not served or underserved. This expansion opens up growth possibilities and reduces the reliance on a shrinking customer base. By unlocking untapped markets, organizations can establish themselves as pioneers and market leaders, capturing significant market share and enjoying higher profitability.

Moreover, by extending their product or service offerings into blue ocean spaces, organizations can diversify their revenue streams and reduce the risk associated with relying on a single product or market. This diversification enables them to adapt to changing market dynamics and customer preferences, ensuring long-term sustainability.

The proactive pursuit of competitive and blue ocean strategies in the maturity phase offers several benefits for organizations. First, it allows them to differentiate themselves from competitors by offering unique value propositions. Instead of competing solely on price, organizations can focus on creating distinctive features, delivering superior customer experiences, or introducing innovative solutions.

Second, by exploring blue ocean opportunities, organizations can reduce the intensity of competition and avoid the downward pressure on prices. Instead of fighting for a share of the existing pie, they can carve out new markets or create entirely new industries, giving them a higher degree of control over pricing and profitability.

Third, pursuing blue ocean strategies encourages organizations to innovate and think outside the box. It pushes them to challenge industry norms and question traditional assumptions. This mindset of continuous innovation and value creation keeps organizations agile, adaptable, and responsive to market changes.

By proactively pursuing competitive and blue ocean strategies, organizations can secure a sustainable competitive advantage and thrive in the mature market. They are more likely to outperform competitors, attract loyal customers, and achieve long-term profitability. Examples of organizations that have successfully embraced blue ocean strategies include Cirque du Soleil, which revolutionized the circus industry, and Yellow Tail, which disrupted the wine market with its approachable and affordable wines.

> **THE RECOMMENDED APPROACH IN BRIEF**: Exploring blue ocean opportunities is a powerful strategy for organizations in the maturity phase of the industry life cycle. By breaking away from the red ocean of intense competition and venturing into uncontested market spaces, organizations can create new demand, unlock untapped markets, and extend their product or service offerings. This proactive and innovative approach aligns with the characteristics of the maturity phase, where product standardization and price competition prevail. By embracing competitive and blue ocean strategies, organizations can secure a sustainable competitive advantage and thrive in the mature market.

Assess: is your organization competing during this phase

✓ Evaluate Market Saturation: Assess the level of market saturation in your industry. Look for signs of intensified competition, price stabilization, and limited opportunities for differentiation. Analyze whether the market has reached a point where growth is slowing down, and competitors are fighting for market share.

✓ Assess Product Standardization: Examine the level of product standardization in your industry. Determine if there is a convergence of offerings among competitors, with little variation in features, functionalities, or quality. Look for indications that customers perceive products as interchangeable.

✓ Analyze Customer Preferences: Study customer preferences and behaviors within your industry. Determine if customers exhibit a higher degree of brand loyalty or if they are more price-sensitive. Assess whether customers are seeking differentiated products or if they are primarily driven by price considerations.

✓ Monitor Technological Advancements: Keep an eye on technological advancements and their impact on the industry. Evaluate the level of innovation and disruptive technologies entering the market. Determine if new technologies are reshaping customer expectations and challenging traditional industry norms.

✓ Study Competitive Landscape: Analyze the competitive landscape within your industry. Identify the number of rivals and their market positions. Assess the intensity of competition, pricing strategies, and the level of rivalry among competitors. Look for signs of consolidation or the emergence of dominant players.

✓ Consider Industry Growth Rates: Evaluate the historical growth rates of your industry. Compare them to current growth rates to determine if the industry is experiencing a slowdown in overall growth. Assess the growth potential of your market segment and whether it aligns with the overall industry trends.

✓ Assess Customer Demographics: Study the demographics and characteristics of your target customer segment. Determine if there are any shifts in customer preferences, demographics, or buying behaviors that could impact the industry. Analyze whether the target market is reaching a saturation point or if there are untapped customer segments to explore.

✓ Monitor Regulatory Environment: Stay updated on regulatory changes and their impact on the industry. Assess the level of government intervention, industry regulations, and compliance requirements. Determine if regulatory changes are creating barriers to entry or affecting the competitive dynamics within the industry.

✓ Consider Organizational Capabilities: Evaluate your organization's capabilities and resources in relation to the demands of the maturity phase. Assess your ability to differentiate your offerings, adapt to changing customer needs, and effectively compete on cost. Determine if your organization has the necessary flexibility, agility, and innovation capacity to succeed in the mature market.

✓ Reflect on CAS Characteristics: Consider the characteristics of organizations as CAS. Recognize that CAS are inherently adaptable and responsive to changes in the environment. Assess whether your organization has the ability to sense and respond to market dynamics, leverage collective intelligence, and continuously learn and evolve.

By following this guideline, business leaders can gain a deeper understanding of their industry life cycle phase and determine if they are in the maturity phase. It allows them to assess market saturation, product standardization, customer preferences, technological advancements, competitive landscape, industry growth rates, customer demographics, regulatory environment, and their organization's capabilities. By considering the behaviors and characteristics of organizations as CAS, leaders can make informed strategic decisions and position their organizations for success in the mature market.

Peleton

Peloton is a fitness technology company that revolutionized the home fitness industry by combining high-quality exercise equipment with immersive live and on-demand workout classes. Their innovative approach disrupted the traditional gym model and created a new market space.

Peloton's blue ocean strategy involved targeting consumers who were seeking convenient and engaging workout experiences at home. They developed a range of connected exercise equipment, such as stationary bikes and treadmills, that integrated with their digital platform. Users could access a vast library of workout classes led by professional instructors, stream them in real-time, or access them on-demand.

By leveraging technology and connectivity, Peloton provided a unique value proposition to consumers who wanted to exercise from the comfort of their homes without sacrificing the quality of instruction or community engagement. Their immersive and interactive workout experience differentiated them from traditional fitness equipment manufacturers and positioned them as a leader in the connected fitness industry.

Peloton's strategy enabled them to tap into a growing market of fitness enthusiasts who valued convenience, personalization, and community engagement. Their subscription-based revenue model, which offers access to the digital content and classes, provides ongoing customer engagement and recurring revenue streams.

This blue ocean strategy propelled Peloton to significant success, particularly during the COVID-19 pandemic when at-home fitness became even more popular. They experienced rapid growth in sales and subscriptions, expanding their customer base and market share. Additionally, their success has prompted traditional fitness equipment manufacturers and gym chains to adapt their strategies and incorporate digital offerings.

Peloton's ability to identify and cater to unmet customer needs, coupled with their seamless integration of hardware, software, and content, has positioned them as a leader in the connected fitness industry. Their blue ocean strategy allowed them to create uncontested market space and build a strong brand that resonates with health-conscious consumers seeking personalized and convenient workout experiences at home.

Develop the Strategy for This Phase

1. Assess Market Dynamics: Understand the current market dynamics, including the level of competition, customer preferences, and technological advancements. Analyze the maturity level of the industry and identify key trends, such as product standardization and price competition.

2. Segment the Market: Identify distinct customer segments within the mature market based on their unique needs, preferences, and behaviors. Tailor your product or service offerings to address the specific demands of each segment.

3. Focus on Differentiation: Emphasize differentiation to stand out in a crowded marketplace. Identify opportunities to offer unique value propositions, such as superior product quality, innovative features, exceptional customer service, or customization options.

4. Enhance Customer Experience: Invest in enhancing the overall customer experience to build loyalty and differentiate from competitors. Leverage technology and data to personalize interactions, provide seamless purchasing experiences, and offer value-added services.

5. Explore Adjacent Markets: Look for opportunities to expand into related or adjacent markets that are not yet fully saturated. Identify complementary products or services that can leverage your existing capabilities and customer base.

6. Foster Strategic Partnerships: Seek strategic partnerships with other organizations to strengthen your market position and access new customer segments. Collaborate with suppliers, distributors, or complementary businesses to create integrated solutions or bundled offerings.

7. Continuously Innovate: Maintain a culture of innovation and agility to respond to changing customer needs and market trends. Encourage employees to generate and implement ideas for product enhancements, process improvements, and new business models.

8. Optimize Operations: Streamline internal processes, optimize supply chain management, and reduce costs to improve operational efficiency. Explore opportunities for automation, digitalization, and process reengineering to maximize productivity and profitability.

Practical Implications for Strategy Development

It is crucial to balance differentiation with cost-effectiveness. Innovate to create unique value propositions while keeping operational costs in check.

A. Customer retention becomes increasingly important during the maturity phase. Focus on building strong customer relationships and loyalty programs to maintain market share.

B. Regularly monitor market trends and competitive dynamics to identify potential disruptions or emerging opportunities.

C. Embrace digital technologies to enhance customer experience, streamline operations, and enable data-driven decision-making.

D. Foster a culture of continuous learning and adaptation to stay ahead of the competition and identify new growth avenues.

Deploy the Strategy for This Phase

1. Communicate the Strategy: Clearly articulate the strategic direction and objectives to all stakeholders within the organization. Ensure that employees understand their roles and responsibilities in executing the strategy.
2. Align Resources: Allocate resources effectively to support the strategic initiatives. Optimize resource allocation to areas that have the greatest potential for growth and profitability.
3. Monitor Market Trends: Continuously monitor market trends, customer preferences, and competitor activities. Stay informed about emerging technologies, shifts in consumer behavior, and industry regulations.
4. Optimize Product Portfolio: Assess the performance of existing products or services and determine which offerings have the highest potential for growth. Streamline the product portfolio by discontinuing underperforming or obsolete offerings.
5. Pricing Strategies: Evaluate pricing strategies to ensure competitiveness while maintaining profitability. Consider value-based pricing, promotional pricing, or bundle pricing to entice customers and maintain market share.
6. Market Expansion: Explore opportunities to expand into new geographic regions or untapped customer segments. Conduct market research to identify potential growth areas and develop targeted marketing campaigns.
7. Enhance Customer Relationships: Focus on building strong customer relationships and loyalty programs. Leverage customer data to personalize marketing efforts and provide exceptional customer experiences.
8. Strategic Partnerships: Seek strategic partnerships or alliances to access new markets, capabilities, or distribution channels. Collaborate with complementary businesses to offer bundled solutions or cross-promote products.
9. Continuous Improvement: Foster a culture of continuous improvement and innovation. Encourage employees to contribute ideas for process enhancements, cost optimization, and customer value creation.
10. Performance Measurement: Establish key performance indicators (KPIs) aligned with the strategic objectives. Regularly track and evaluate performance against the set targets to ensure progress and make necessary adjustments.

Practical Implications for Strategy Deployment

Balance short-term profitability with long-term growth. Maintain profitability while investing in innovation and market expansion.

A. Stay agile and responsive to changes in the competitive landscape and customer demands.

B. Leverage data analytics to gain insights into customer behavior, market trends, and operational performance.

C. Foster collaboration and cross-functional communication to ensure effective strategy execution.

D. Monitor customer feedback and adjust strategies accordingly to meet evolving customer needs.

By following this guideline, organizations can effectively deploy their strategies during the maturity phase, leveraging their existing market position and maximizing growth opportunities.

Failing to Strategize Effectively During the Maturity Phase

Failing to strategize effectively during the maturity phase of the industry life cycle can have significant implications and consequences for organizations. Let's explore some specific examples of failures and their consequences:

■ Reason for failure: Lack of Differentiation
- Consequence: Failure to differentiate products or services from competitors leads to a commoditized market, resulting in declining market share, price erosion, and reduced profitability.
  • Example: BlackBerry—BlackBerry, a once-prominent smartphone manufacturer, failed to differentiate its smartphones from competitors like Apple's iPhone and Android devices. While BlackBerry was known for its secure messaging features, it struggled to keep up with the app ecosystem and user-friendly interfaces offered by its competitors. As a result, the market perceived smartphones as interchangeable commodities, leading to a significant decline in BlackBerry's market share and financial performance.

■ Reason for failure: Inadequate Innovation
- Consequence: Insufficient investment in research and development (R&D) leads to stagnation and loss of competitive edge.
  • Example: Xerox—Xerox, a pioneer in photocopiers, failed to adequately invest in innovation and research. The company missed the opportunity to transition into digital technology, which allowed competitors to introduce advanced solutions. As a result, Xerox lost its competitive edge and market leadership in the photocopying industry.

- Reason for failure: Failure to Adapt to Changing Customer Needs
  - Consequence: Ignoring evolving customer preferences and failing to respond with appropriate product or service offerings leads to decreased customer satisfaction, loyalty, and market share loss.
    - Example: Kodak—Kodak, a renowned photography company, failed to adapt to the digital camera revolution. While Kodak had invented digital cameras, it did not fully embrace the technology and underestimated its potential impact. The company remained heavily focused on film-based products, leading to a decline in market position as customers shifted to digital photography.
- Reason for failure: Inefficient Cost Management
  - Consequence: Inability to effectively manage costs and maintain competitive pricing in the face of price pressure from rivals results in decreased profitability and potential loss of market share.
    - Example: Circuit City—Circuit City, a consumer electronics retailer, struggled to manage costs and maintain competitive prices in a highly competitive market. The company faced significant price pressure from rivals and failed to adapt its cost structure. As a result, Circuit City experienced decreased profitability and eventually filed for bankruptcy.
- Reason for failure: Resistance to Change
  - Consequence: Resistance to change and reluctance to embrace new business models or technologies lead to missed opportunities and an inability to stay ahead of competitors.
    - Example: Blockbuster—Blockbuster, a video rental company, resisted the shift to online streaming and failed to embrace new technologies in the entertainment industry. The company clung to its traditional brick-and-mortar rental model, despite the growing popularity of digital platforms like Netflix. This resistance to change eventually led to Blockbuster's bankruptcy as it lost relevance in the evolving market.
- Reason for failure: Lack of Strategic Partnership
  - Consequence: Failure to establish strategic partnerships or alliances to expand market reach or access new capabilities results in limited growth opportunities and an inability to leverage synergies.
    - Example: Yahoo—Yahoo, once a dominant player in internet search and services, missed opportunities to form strategic partnerships with other companies. The lack of collaborations limited Yahoo's ability to expand its market reach and access new capabilities, leading to a loss of market share to competitors like Google.

Lesson from a leader

Michael Dubin

Another example of a business leader who successfully implemented a blue ocean strategy is Dollar Shave Club. Founded in 2011 by Michael Dubin and Mark Levine, Dollar Shave Club disrupted the razor industry with its subscription-based model and direct-to-consumer approach.

Dollar Shave Club recognized the high cost and inconvenience associated with purchasing razors from traditional brands, such as Gillette, which dominated the market. By identifying the pain points of consumers and the existing market landscape, Dollar Shave Club pursued a blue ocean strategy to offer a more affordable and convenient solution. Key elements of Dollar Shave Club's successful blue ocean strategy included: Subscription Model: The company introduced a subscription-based business model, allowing customers to receive razor blades and grooming products delivered to their doorstep on a regular basis. This eliminated the need for consumers to make repeated trips to the store and simplified the purchasing process. Price Disruption: Dollar Shave Club positioned itself as a cost-effective alternative to expensive razor brands. By leveraging their direct-to-consumer model, the company was able to offer high-quality razors at significantly lower prices, appealing to price-conscious consumers. Humorous Marketing and Branding: Dollar Shave Club differentiated itself through its unique marketing campaigns, utilizing humor and relatability to stand out from traditional razor brands. The company's viral video, "Our Blades Are F***ing Great," garnered widespread attention, effectively generating brand awareness and attracting a loyal customer base. Product Expansion: While initially focusing on razors, Dollar Shave Club expanded its product offerings to include a range of grooming and personal care products. By diversifying its product portfolio, the company further solidified its position as a comprehensive grooming solution for its customers. The success of Dollar Shave Club's blue ocean strategy is evident in its rapid growth and disruption of the razor industry. Within a few years of its launch, the company gained millions of subscribers and captured a significant market share, challenging established razor brands.

CASE STUDY: GROWTH STRATEGY AT ZAIN

Zain Group is a leading telecommunications provider in the Middle East and North Africa (MENA) region. Founded in 1983, the multinational is the second-oldest of the five leading players in the region yet ranks fifth in revenue. The company had 47.8M active customers in 2020. While high economic risk and developing technological infrastructure characterize the

MENA region, all regional rivals play by the same rules. In a market valued at $65B, Zain Group's market share is only 8.8% despite nearly four decades in operation.

Bader Al-Kharafi, Zain Group's vice chairman and CEO, has been spearheading 4Sight, the company's strategy focusing on eight areas in IT and technology. Informed by 4Sight, the company has launched a venture fund and invested $100M in fintech-based companies. Is this the right move for Zain Group, given its competitive position within the MENA region? Is 4Sight informing an effective strategy for growth?

A $2.56T 1 global industry, telecommunications is a highly contested space with a low market concentration in which five major players2 collectively hold 42.2% of the market share.3 The remaining players are more than 100 regional carriers spread across the globe. The MENA region is home to some of those carriers,4 of which collectively hold 2.34% of the global market share.

Industry experts expected telecommunications revenue in the MENA region to grow at a compound annual growth rate (CAGR) of 0.4% between 2020 and 2025, despite the slight negative impact of the COVID-19 pandemic. Total revenue in the region was expected to increase to $65.4B by 2024 (from $62B in 2018).5 Founded in 1983, Zain is the second-oldest company among the top five players in the region yet ranked fifth in revenue based on 2020 financials.

Zain Group introduced an operational strategy in 2012 aimed at realizing full synergy from a series of developmental projects in its commercial and operational entities to stimulate growth. In 2019, the company rolled out its overarching strategy, 4Sight. The strategy was developed to enable the creation of the company's "sustainable and digital future" by advancing "the company's core telecom business. This enablement intended to maximize value and build on its many strengths through digitization, optimization, and modernization to free up resources and invest selectively in growth verticals beyond standard mobile services."6 Bader Al-Kharafi7 was appointed CEO and vice chairman in 2017 and has been spearheading 4Sight.

As of 2020, Zain's customer base was 47.8M, with revenue of $5.3B, representing 8.8% of the market share in the MENA region. In 2021, Zain launched a venture capital fund with investments worth $100M in fintech and mobility-based startups. Given the company's current growth rate, the potential for business development and expansion is still significant. So, what is the right move for Zain Group to improve its competitive position in the MENA region? Is 4Sight informing an effective strategy for growth? What does CEO Bader Al-Kharafi need to do to accelerate the growth of Zain Group after 40 years of regional operation?

ABOUT ZAIN GROUP

Zain Group provides mobile telecommunications and data services, including voice and roaming, wholesale, cloud, enterprise WAN, and internet services. Zain's customer base of 47.8M includes retail and commercial customers in both the public and private sectors. The company provides services to residents and educational, governmental, and financial institutions. Zain operates in Saudi Arabia, Bahrain, Iraq, Jordan, Sudan (except where noted, "Sudan" includes "South Sudan"), and Kuwait (home to the company's headquarters and most profitable segment). In the 2021 annual letter to the Zain family, and consistent with the 4Sight strategy, Al-Kharafi indicated that Zain does not want to limit itself to being solely a telecom company but instead sees itself as a provider of all digital services (see Exhibit 1).

Zain Group competes in multiple markets with a network of subsidiaries, associates, and joint ventures across the region, Europe, and the US. These markets include mobile and fixed (for voice and data), Internet of Things (IoT), hosted managed services (geared toward commercial customers to ensure business continuity and managed data centers), cloud connectivity, managed security services for businesses, and drones (see Exhibit 2). In 2020, the company reported $5.3B in revenue (38% of which was data revenue), $2.2B in EBITDA8, and $605M in net income while serving 47.8M customers in six countries (Zain Group is a market leader in Kuwait, Iraq, Sudan, and Jordan). From 2019 to 2020, revenue and profit for the year dropped by 2% and 16%, respectively (primarily due to the effects of the COVID-19 pandemic). Like other telecommunications companies, Zain saw its revenue drop (by $112M) mainly because of a decrease in airtime and roaming revenue (due to imposed travel restrictions). Zain Group concentrated on cost optimization to offset the impact of the pandemic while receiving $8M in government support in 2020 to aid local employees.

Saudi Arabia accounted for the largest segment of the company's total revenue (39.6%), followed by Kuwait (18.9%), Iraq (17.8%), Sudan (9.4%), Jordan (9.2%), and Bahrain (3.1%). As of 2020, Zain was the number one provider in Iraq (52% of the market share), Sudan (48%, excluding South Sudan), and Jordan (42%). Its market share in Kuwait was similarly substantial (37%). The company's share of the Saudi market was 16.4%, as reported in its 2021 H1 financials. Based on the same set of reported financials, Zain's calculated revenue per customer9 was $385.0 in Kuwait, followed by $300.0 in Saudi Arabia, $245.0 in Bahrain, $135 in Jordan, $28.0 in Sudan, and $5.8 in Iraq.

INDUSTRY LANDSCAPE

Industry experts have projected that both global and regional markets in the telecommunications industry will see growth, primarily due to technological advancements in networking and increased demand for connectivity services.

- Global Telecommunications Market
  The telecommunications market consists of sales of telecom goods and services to retail and commercial customers by entities (partnerships, sole traders, and organizations) that provide communication hardware for transmitting voice, data, text, and video. The market also includes manufacturers' sales of goods such as GPS, cellular, and switching equipment. The telecom market is segmented into wireless telecommunications carriers, wired telecommunications carriers, communications hardware, and satellite and telecommunications resellers. Operators in this industry maintain transmission and switching facilities to provide direct communications via wireless radio transmission. Services in the wireless sector include traditional cellular voice telephony, messaging, and broadband data. Wireless services include mobile backhaul services (transferring data from small subnetworks to a network core). It is common for carriers to sell mobile handsets and other equipment to retail and commercial consumers. The industry does not include mobile virtual network operators. Globally, the industry primarily generates revenue from mobile telephone subscriptions. Therefore, performance relies mainly on the number of mobile telephone subscriptions worldwide. Experts estimated a 6% CAGR growth for the industry by 2025, reaching $3.46T.
- Regional Telecommunications Market
  The MENA region telecommunications industry grew in 2019 following three consecutive years of decline (with a steep drop of 11.5% in 2017 deriving from the trickle-down effect of the Arab Spring). In 2019, the overall market estimate for revenue was $65B, which can be attributed to a rise in tariff prices following years of low prices.

Similar to the global telecommunications market structure, the regional market consists primarily of providers of cellular and mobile services (voice and data). The number of subscribers determines market volume for the industry, whereas the revenue generated from subscriptions and usage determines market value. Zain Group's competitive landscape in the MENA region includes players whose annual revenue and customer base range from $3.4B to $15.7B and from 3.3M to 160M, respectively. These players include Saudi Telcom Company (STC), Etisalat, Ooredoo, and Omantel (see Exhibit 3).

4SIGHT STRATEGY

With existing competition in the regional market, Zain's strategy, 4Sight, was developed to transform the company by pivoting on evolving telecommunications and accelerating growth. 4Sight was organized into two spheres: Evolution of Telco (short for telecommunication) and Growth Verticals (see Exhibit 4). Each sphere consisted of four strategic pillars intended to diversify revenue streams, generate sustainable growth, and increase shareholder value. From a technological perspective, the strategy aimed to optimize the company's high-speed broadband networks, network intelligence, and billing and assets infrastructure. 4Sight was developed as an operational strategy to realize the full synergies of Zain's projects. It evolved into a transformational strategy to accelerate the growth of the company.

Evolution of Telco. This sphere focused on technological evolution in digital transformation, enterprise and government, fixed and convergence (airtime and data), and portfolio optimization. Below is a brief description of each:

1. Digital transformation: Transforming the telecom core to provide customers with the best experience while streamlining the backend and reaping the best analytics for Zain to thrive and lead in the digital era.
2. Enterprise and government: Working closely with organizations of all sizes to provide them with the necessary connectivity and the latest solutions required to achieve their business and operational objectives.
3. Fixed and convergence (airtime and data): The long-term ambition for Zain is to transform into a fixed-mobile convergent player serving consumers and businesses. In other words, the company would change from a mobile-centric telecom into an integrated player that

offers fixed-mobile domestic and international convergence by serving consumers' and businesses' airtime (voice) and data needs. Note: in the telecommunications industry, the term "convergence," or "network convergence," refers to integrating network architectures and telecommunications technologies to migrate multiple communications services into a single network.

4. Portfolio optimization: Continuously seeking opportunities to realize synergies and unlock potential value through M&A activities.

Growth Verticals. This sphere focused on pursuing growth in information and communications technology (ICT), digital transformation, fintech, and digital health. Below is a brief description of each:

1. ICT: Establishing a regional center of excellence developing and providing the latest infrastructure, managed services, and digital solutions. The intent is to enable digital solutions across a technology stack that includes cloud, cybersecurity, IoT, big data, drones, and other emerging technologies.

2. Digital transformation: Leading digital infrastructure in the region by focusing on API, Livestreaming by Zain©, and Zain eSports ©. Zain Group's API connects multiple servers (for example, docomo digital, DIGITAL VIRGO, OSN, Google, PLAY VOD, to name a few) to Zain's infrastructure in the countries where it operates. As of 2020, 26 API-enabled services had generated $28M in revenue to 1.1M active customers.

3. Fintech: Introducing a suite of digital financial and insurance services contributing to the evolution of the region's digital ecosystem. Licensed by the Saudi Central Bank (SAMA), Tamam was the first microfinancing license in the region. The platform is Shari'a10 compliant and offers consumer microfinance in less than five minutes via a seamless digital customer experience through a mobile app. Zain introduced Zain Cash (in Iraq and Jordan), a mobile wallet licensed by the Central Bank of Iraq to offer innovative financial services such as money transfer, electronic bill payment, funds disbursement service, mobile recharge, and e-commerce. Zain Cash and government funding support grew Iraq's customer base and volume. In addition to maintaining its market position as the largest mobile financial services provider in Jordan, Zain Cash Jordan has rapidly expanded its portfolio to cover more services. The company led the processing of disbursements for the government's financial aid programs with a

value exceeding 100M JOD ($140M). In South Sudan, M-Gurush is a digital financial service based on a partnership model with Trinity Technologies. It is licensed by the Central Bank of South Sudan to run mobile money and electronic payment services.

4. Digital health: Introducing a suite of digital financial and insurance services, contributing to the evolution of the region's digital ecosystem. In response to the COVID-19 pandemic, Zain developed a state-of-the-art digital platform application, Shlonik. In collaboration with Kuwait's Ministry of Health and Central Agency for Information Technology, Shlonik managed the quarantine process for those arriving from overseas. Zain also developed Wasfa as an end-to-end e-prescription digital platform. The platform enables the Ministry of Health to control prescription and drug dispensing in Kuwait by connecting pharmacies and prescribing doctors. Wasfa also provided insights and analytics on patients', doctors', and pharmacists' purchasing habits. These insights inform ways to minimize waste, mitigate the risk of fraud, and contribute to generating savings for the Ministry of Health. The platform also introduces the concept of preventive care. Since August 2019, Wasfa has been operational in two sites, generating over 350,000 e-prescriptions.

ZAIN GROUP'S FINANCIAL PERFORMANCE (REGIONAL)

Revenue from operations consisted of recurring revenues—from monthly subscription fees and roaming leased line, and airtime usage fees, for example—and non-recurring revenue, such as one-time connection fees, telephone equipment, and accessory sales. In 2020, the company generated revenue of $5.3B, of which $4.75B (roughly 90%) was allocated to airtime and data.

Zain's largest customer base is in Sudan (17.7M), followed by Iraq (16.2M), Saudi Arabia (7.0M), Jordan (3.6M), Kuwait (2.6M), and Bahrain (0.7M). See Exhibit 5. The variation in customer base resulted in revenue per customer ranging from Zain's largest customer base in Sudan (17.7M), followed by Iraq (16.2M), Saudi Arabia (7.0M), Jordan (3.6M), Kuwait (2.6M), and Bahrain (0.7M). See Exhibit 6.

◼ Operating performance: In a pattern consistent with the rest of the telecommunications industry, the company experienced an overall decline in performance due to the COVID-19 pandemic, which began in 2020. For example, in 2020, the company reported an operating margin of 20.3% compared to 21.2% in 2019. Similarly, operating costs increased to 79.9% in 2020 from 78.8% in the year prior. The net profit margin also decreased from 13.1% in 2019 to 11.4% in 2020. The company's return on equity declined to 14.1% in 2020 from 16.7% in 2019. In revenue allocation, roughly 90% of revenue generated in 2020 was from "airtime, data, and subscription"; the remainder came from "trading income."11 See Exhibit 7.

■ Liquidity: The company reported total liabilities of $4.4M in 2020, compared to $4.1M in 2019, a 7.3% increase. Equity increased in 2020 to $6.4M from $5.6M in 2019, resulting in a total increase in liability and equity to $16.3M from $15.7M in 2019.

■ Currency rates: Because Zain operates in six countries in the MENA region, it was exposed to fluctuations in foreign exchange rates against its reporting currency. As Zain puts it, "Hedges of net investments in foreign operations are accounted for similarly to cash flow hedges. Any gain or loss on the foreign currency forward contracts relating to the effective portion of the hedge was recognized in other comprehensive income and accumulated in the foreign currency translation reserve. The gain or loss relating to the ineffective portion was recognized immediately in profit or loss and was included in the 'other gains and losses' line item. Gains and losses on the hedging instrument accumulated in the foreign currency translation reserve were reclassified to profit or loss on the disposal or partial disposal of the foreign operation."12

■ Strategic partnerships: Zain Group developed several strategic partnerships to deliver value-added products and services to its customers and realize its 4Sight strategy. Zain partnered with various suppliers and vendors to enable its services via Microsoft Azure, Amazon Web Services, Oracle Cloud, Equinix Cloud Exchange, and Pipe.

ADDITIONAL CHALLENGES AFFECTING ZAIN'S STRATEGY IMPLEMENTATION: THE COVID-19 PANDEMIC AND THE TELECOMMUNICATIONS INDUSTRY

■ Global impact: Overall, many telecom players have benefited to some extent from an increase in data and voice traffic. As a result, telecom has been performing slightly better than other infrastructure subsectors. Unlike many other industries, telecom was generally exempted from significant COVID-19-related restrictions, such as stay-at-home orders and quarantine requirements, as it is recognized as an essential service.13 The short-term spike strengthened some telecom companies in data traffic and increased the use of broadband services (as more people work from home and rely on video conferencing to hold meetings). However, the performance of the telecom sector remained cyclical throughout the crisis14 despite the short-term gains from a surge in data and network demand due to the decline in telephony demand. In other words, the rise in connectivity demand was not significant enough to offset other revenue segments.

■ Impact on Zain Group: Zain Group experienced a drop in net income and revenue in Q4 2020 due to disrupted economic activities resulting from the COVID-19 pandemic; the impact varied by country. In the Q4 2020 financial results, Zain sustained a $62M, $176M, $131M, $22M, $11M, and $15M decline in 2020 revenue compared to Q4 2019 in Kuwait, Saudi Arabia, Iraq, Jordan, Sudan, and Bahrain, respectively. Foreign currency devaluation resulted in declines of $33M and $7M in the group's revenue and net income, respectively. Due to COVID-19, Zain's operations were affected by government lockdown measures that resulted in the activation of remote work procedures. Zain instituted a Crisis Management Committee at the enterprise level to establish COVID-19 response plans. Execution of the plans was monitored weekly starting in March 2020. The committee focused on business scenario planning, employee safety, supply chain management, network performance, and work-from-home policies.15 To address disruptions in operations, the company developed business continuity plans, expanded network capacities, and redeveloped payment and distribution of online payment channels (Zain Cash). Al-Kharafi stated that the group's performance reflected the reality of COVID-19 disruption and its "unavoidable impact." He added, "…the board and management are working closely together in minimizing the impact across our footprint with a particular focus on driving efficiencies, cost optimization and monetizing our 4G and 5G networks."16

WHAT'S NEXT FOR ZAIN GROUP?

In 2021, Zain launched a venture capital fund with a total of $100M in investments in Pipe (a fintech startup developing a trading platform founded in 2020) and Swvl (a mobility-based startup founded in 2017). Zain Ventures was established as complementary to the existing investment portfolio of the group to open doors to future investment opportunities in fintech and technology, with a focus on digital innovations in the electronic services and startup ecosystem. After the investment, Bader AlKharafi said,

> [...] the establishment of Zain Ventures is another step in Zain Group's '4Sight' strategy and progression to become a full-fledged digital services company. We have already enjoyed tremendous success in the investments we have made in venture capital entities and startups that show promising potential for boosting our revenues in new and developing verticals and formalizing these investments under a single entity at this time will create shareholder value. We are extremely excited and confident that Zain Ventures' first investments in fast-growing and world-leading entities in their respective industries, Pipe and Swvl will be value accretive to all parties as we accelerate their growth across the region and beyond. We are keen on participating in and encouraging the global entrepreneurial startup ecosystem, said Al-Kharafi."

Regarding Swvl, he stated, "Zain grasped the opportunity to invest in Swvl for reasons that are also core to our Sustainability, Diversity and Inclusion corporate strategy: 1. Supporting national transport infrastructure and optimizing mobility; 2. Serving the underprivileged; 3. Sustainability and environmentally friendly; 4. Women empowerment and safety; 5. Unlimited synergies with Zain's footprint across the region. The Zain team looks forward to playing its strategic role and being part of Swvl's trajectory growth and global success story." 17

Informed by the 4Sight strategy, is this a good move given the company's current competitive position in the market?

To conclude, the $2.56T telecommunications industry is blooming. The MENA region has fierce rivals, so the growth challenge for Zain Group is significant. The 40-year-old company ranked fifth in the region based on revenue against competitors formed years after Zain's establishment. Is it possible that the 4Sight strategy may be sending Zain Group in multiple directions amid significant variations by country in revenue and profit? Is it putting the company on the right growth path? What should Bader Al-Kharafi do to accelerate the growth of a $5.3B company in this $2.56T industry?

Chapter 10

Decline: End Your Game or Play Another One

Set-the-Stage Mini Case

Goldman Sachs

As the financial industry enters the maturity phase, characterized by market saturation and stable growth, Goldman Sachs has effectively navigated these challenges through strategic diversification and digital transformation. This phase is marked by intense competition among established players, necessitating a focus on sustaining market share and maximizing operational efficiencies. Goldman Sachs has embraced these strategies, leveraging its historical strengths while expanding into new avenues such as consumer banking and sustainable finance.

To differentiate itself in a highly competitive market, Goldman Sachs has heavily invested in technology and innovation. The launch of Marcus by Goldman Sachs, a digital consumer bank, has allowed the company to tap into the retail banking sector, traditionally dominated by other financial giants. Marcus provides personal loans, high-yield savings accounts, and other financial products, all through a user-friendly online platform. Additionally, Goldman Sachs' commitment to sustainable finance is evident in its pledge to facilitate $750 billion in sustainable finance initiatives by 2030, supporting

DOI: 10.4324/9781003564133-12

projects that drive environmental progress and inclusive growth. These strategic moves highlight Goldman Sachs' ability to adapt and thrive in the mature phase of the financial industry by exploring new growth opportunities and reinforcing its market position through innovation and sustainability.

Defining the Decline Phase

In the decline phase of the industry life cycle, the stability of the industry diminishes, and signs of decline become more apparent. This phase is characterized by a decreasing demand for products or services, a shrinking customer base, and intense competition. Industry Stability: During the decline phase, the industry experiences a decline in overall growth and market demand. The market becomes saturated, and competition intensifies as companies struggle to maintain their market share. Companies operating in the industry face challenges in generating revenue and growth. In terms of Regulatory Environment, it can vary depending on the industry. In some cases, regulators may introduce stricter regulations to manage declining industries, while in others, the regulatory framework may remain relatively stable. The role of regulations becomes crucial as they can impact the survival and operations of companies in declining industries.

The competitive landscape in the decline phase is characterized by a higher number of rivals competing for a shrinking market. Companies may resort to aggressive pricing strategies and promotions to maintain their market share. Mergers, acquisitions, and consolidations become common as companies aim to gain economies of scale or eliminate competition. Then as the industry declines, price competition intensifies. Companies may engage in price-cutting strategies to attract customers and maintain sales volume. This can lead to decreased profit margins and further industry decline. Product offerings may also become limited as companies focus on core products or services to streamline operations and reduce costs. It is important to note that examples of industries in the decline phase can vary over time, and the pace of decline may differ across industries.

Additional examples across different industries include digital media, landline telecommunication, and traditional retail. The rise of digital media and streaming services has led to a decline in industries such as physical music CDs, DVDs, and print newspapers. With the shift toward digital formats, these industries have faced decreasing demand and revenue. The advent of mobile phones and the widespread adoption of wireless communication technologies have resulted in a decline in landline telecommunication services. As more consumers rely on mobile devices, the demand for landline services has diminished. Finally, the growth of e-commerce and online shopping has impacted traditional brick-and-mortar retail stores. Many retail giants have struggled to adapt to changing consumer preferences and the convenience of online shopping, leading to a decline in sales and store closures.

In the decline phase, organizations must carefully navigate the challenges and make strategic decisions to minimize the impact of the industry decline. While it may be difficult to reverse the decline, companies can explore various strategies to manage the decline effectively. This can include diversification into new markets or industries, innovation to reposition existing products or services, or restructuring to optimize operations and reduce costs. In the decline phase of the industry life cycle, organizations face numerous challenges as they navigate the shrinking market and intense competition. While it may be difficult to reverse the decline, companies can employ strategic decisions to minimize the impact and manage the decline effectively. This section will elaborate on key strategies that organizations can consider during the decline phase.

One strategy for organizations in the decline phase is to explore opportunities for diversification into new markets or industries. By identifying emerging or growing markets, companies can leverage their existing capabilities and resources to enter new sectors. This strategy allows organizations to reduce their dependence on the declining industry and tap into new sources of revenue and growth. An example of successful diversification is the transformation of Nokia, a once-leading mobile phone manufacturer, into a telecommunications infrastructure provider. Another approach for organizations in the decline phase is to focus on innovation to reposition their existing products or services. By understanding evolving customer needs and market trends, companies can introduce product or service enhancements, rebranding, or repackaging efforts to regain customer interest and differentiate themselves from competitors. IBM's successful transition from a hardware-focused company to a leader in IT services and consulting is a prime example of strategic innovation to adapt to changing market dynamics.

Organizations in the decline phase may need to undergo restructuring to optimize their operations and reduce costs. This can involve streamlining processes, consolidating operations, and improving efficiency. By eliminating inefficiencies and reallocating resources, companies can enhance their competitiveness and increase their chances of survival in a declining industry. One example of successful restructuring is the turnaround of Harley-Davidson in the early 1980s, where the company implemented aggressive cost-cutting measures to address financial challenges. Collaborations, strategic alliances, and partnerships can offer opportunities for organizations in the decline phase to access new markets, technologies, or distribution channels. By forming alliances with complementary organizations, companies can leverage each other's strengths and resources to create synergies and explore new growth avenues. A notable example is the partnership between Microsoft and Nokia in the mobile phone industry, which aimed to combine their respective expertise and market reach to compete against industry giants.

In some cases, organizations in the decline phase may opt for exit or harvesting strategies. This involves winding down operations, divesting non-core assets, or focusing on maximizing short-term profitability. Companies may choose to sell their assets, licenses, or intellectual property rights to extract value from their existing business. An example is the exit strategy pursued by Eastman Kodak, once a leader in the photography industry, which involved focusing on its profitable business segments and divesting non-core assets.

It is crucial for organizations in the decline phase to carefully assess their resources, capabilities, and market dynamics before determining the most appropriate strategy. They should conduct a thorough analysis of their competitive position, market trends, and customer preferences to inform their strategic decisions. Moreover, effective communication with stakeholders, including employees, customers, and investors, is vital during this phase to manage expectations and maintain trust.

THE DECLINE PHASE IN BRIEF: While the decline phase presents numerous challenges, it also offers opportunities for organizations to adapt, innovate, and redefine their strategies. By embracing strategic decision-making and exploring new avenues, companies can navigate the decline and position themselves for potential revival or transition into new ventures.

Key Characteristics of This Phase

✓ Market Saturation: In the decline phase, the market becomes saturated as most potential customers have already been reached. Market demand reaches a plateau or begins to decline, resulting in limited growth opportunities. This saturation creates intense competition among existing players as they fight for a shrinking customer base.

✓ Shrinking Profit Margins: As the market becomes saturated, competition increases, leading to price wars and eroding profit margins. Organizations face pressure to reduce prices to attract customers, resulting in reduced profitability. This puts further strain on companies' financial resources and ability to invest in new initiatives.

✓ Technological Obsolescence: In the decline phase, technology advancements and disruptive innovations can render existing products or services obsolete. Organizations must contend with the challenges of keeping up with emerging technologies, staying relevant, and adapting to changing customer preferences.

✓ Industry Consolidation: The decline phase often triggers industry consolidation, as weaker players struggle to survive and stronger competitors seek opportunities to acquire or merge with other organizations. This consolidation leads to a smaller number of larger and more dominant companies in the market.

✓ Declining Customer Base: During the decline phase, organizations face the challenge of a declining customer base. Customers may shift to alternative products, switch to substitute industries, or reduce their overall consumption. Retaining existing customers becomes crucial, and organizations must find ways to attract new customers or target niche markets to compensate for the shrinking customer base.

✓ Regulatory Pressures: In some industries, regulatory pressures may increase during the decline phase. Governments and regulatory bodies may introduce stricter regulations or impose barriers to entry, making it more challenging for organizations to operate or expand. Compliance costs may rise, adding additional strain to already struggling companies.

✓ Limited Innovation and Product Development: The decline phase is typically characterized by limited innovation and reduced investment in new product development. Organizations may shift their focus from R&D to cost-cutting measures, limiting their ability to introduce new products or significantly differentiate themselves from competitors.

✓ Decreased Industry Employment: As the industry declines, job opportunities diminish, leading to reduced employment levels. Organizations may downsize or streamline their operations to cut costs, resulting in job losses and a challenging labor market for industry professionals.

It is essential for organizations to recognize these characteristics and adapt their strategies accordingly during the decline phase. By understanding the dynamics of the market, companies can make informed decisions to manage the decline effectively and mitigate the challenges they face.

The Recommended Approach to Strategy During This Phase and Why

Exit Strategies

When facing a declining industry, organizations should carefully evaluate the viability of their current operations and explore exit strategies. This may involve divesting from declining product lines, markets, or business units that no longer align with the organization's long-term objectives. Exiting unprofitable segments allows companies to reallocate resources to more promising areas and protect their overall profitability.

Diversification

Organizations can pursue diversification as a strategy to counter the decline in their current industry. This involves expanding into new markets or industries that offer growth opportunities. By leveraging their existing capabilities and resources, organizations can enter new markets where they can apply their expertise and generate revenue. Diversification helps mitigate the risks associated with being solely dependent on a declining industry.

Innovation and Repositioning

In the face of industry decline, organizations can seek innovative ways to reposition their existing products or services. By identifying new customer segments or adapting their offerings to meet evolving needs, organizations can extend the product lifecycle and create new demand. This requires a keen understanding of customer preferences, emerging trends, and the ability to leverage technology to revitalize products or services.

Strategic Alliances and Partnerships

Collaboration with other organizations can provide opportunities for shared resources, capabilities, and expertise to navigate the decline. Strategic alliances or partnerships can help organizations access new markets, leverage complementary strengths, and achieve economies of scale. By joining forces with other industry players or even cross-industry collaborations, organizations can maximize their competitive advantage and explore new growth avenues.

Blue Ocean

Despite the declining industry, organizations can still uncover blue ocean spaces – untapped market opportunities with little or no competition. This involves identifying new customer needs, developing innovative products or services, and creating uncontested market spaces. By focusing on customer value and differentiation, organizations can reshape the competitive landscape and rejuvenate their growth trajectory.

By adopting a proactive and strategic approach, organizations can position themselves for renewed growth and profitability even in declining industries. This involves understanding the characteristics of the decline phase, conducting a thorough assessment of their current operations, and embracing strategies that align with their capabilities and growth potential. It requires a commitment to continuous innovation, agility, and a willingness to explore new opportunities beyond traditional industry boundaries.

Nintendo is one organization that successfully pursued a blue ocean strategy during an industry decline phase. In the early 2000s, the gaming industry was dominated by Microsoft's Xbox and Sony's PlayStation, creating a highly competitive and red ocean market. Nintendo recognized the limitations of directly competing in the same space and instead focused on creating a new blue ocean. They introduced the Nintendo Wii, a console with innovative motion-sensing controllers that targeted casual gamers and non-gamers, expanding the market beyond traditional gamers. This strategy proved highly successful, with Nintendo capturing a new segment of customers and outselling its competitors.

Embracing these strategies is crucial for organizations to adapt to the characteristics of the decline phase and leverage their CAS capabilities. CAS refers to the organization's ability to respond and adapt to changing environments, similar to how a living organism adapts to its surroundings. Recognizing the decline phase as a dynamic and evolving situation, organizations can harness their CAS capabilities to proactively shape their future.

Another example of an organization that successfully embraced these strategies during a decline is LEGO. In the early 2000s, LEGO faced a decline in sales and struggled to adapt to changing consumer preferences. To revitalize their business, LEGO adopted a multifaceted strategy that included exit strategies by divesting non-core businesses, diversification into new markets and media platforms, innovation through the introduction of new product lines, strategic alliances with partners like Disney, and seeking blue ocean spaces by focusing on creative play experiences. This strategic approach enabled LEGO to turn the decline around and regain its position as a leading toy brand.

THE RECOMMENDED APPROACH IN BRIEF: In conclusion, by embracing exit strategies, diversification, innovation, strategic alliances, and seeking blue ocean spaces, organizations can effectively navigate the challenges of the decline phase. The key lies in recognizing the characteristics of the decline phase, leveraging CAS capabilities, and adopting a proactive and strategic approach to shape their future. These strategies enable organizations to transform adversity into opportunity, driving renewed growth, and positioning themselves for long-term success.

Assess: is your organization competing during this phase

✓ Monitor Industry Performance: Keep a close eye on key industry performance indicators such as revenue growth rates, market share trends, and profitability. Look for signs of stagnation or decline in these metrics, indicating a potential entry into the decline phase.

✓ Analyze Customer Behavior: Understand your customers' changing preferences, needs, and purchasing patterns. Look for any signs of declining demand, increased customer attrition, or shifting market dynamics. Conduct market research, customer surveys, and competitor analysis to gain insights into customer behavior.

✓ Assess Competitive Landscape: Evaluate the competitive landscape within your industry. Look for indications of intensified competition, market consolidation, or declining profitability among competitors. Assess the number of rivals, their strategies, and their ability to sustain growth.

✓ Review Regulatory Environment: Understand the regulatory landscape and any potential changes or challenges that may impact the industry. Regulatory barriers, increased compliance costs, or changing government policies can influence the industry's stability and growth potential.

✓ Evaluate Technology Disruptions: Examine the impact of emerging technologies on your industry. Rapid advancements or disruptive innovations in technology can either accelerate the decline or present opportunities for reinvention. Assess the adoption of new technologies by competitors and their impact on customer preferences and market dynamics.

✓ Assess Product Life Cycle: Evaluate the life cycle stage of your organization's key products or services. If your offerings are reaching maturity or decline stages, it may be an indication that the industry is entering the decline phase. Look for signs of declining sales, diminishing product differentiation, or increased price competition.

✓ Review Financial Performance: Analyze your organization's financial performance and trends over the past few years. Look for signs of declining revenue, shrinking profit margins, or diminishing market share. Assess the sustainability of your current business model and identify potential challenges.

✓ Consider Industry Expertise: Engage with industry experts, consultants, or advisors who can provide insights into the industry's trajectory. Their knowledge and experience can help assess the overall health of the industry and its potential for decline.

✓ Leverage CAS Capabilities: Consider how your organization's CAS capabilities can influence its behavior and adaptability during the decline phase. Assess your organization's ability to respond to changing market dynamics, explore new opportunities, and adapt its strategies and operations.

✓ Seek External Validation: Validate your assessment by seeking external perspectives and benchmarking against industry reports, market analysis, or expert opinions. This can provide an unbiased evaluation of the industry's life cycle phase and help confirm your findings.

✓ Reflect on CAS characteristics: Recognize the need for strategic agility and adaptability in response to declining industry conditions. Leverage CAS capabilities such as resilience, learning, and flexibility to explore new avenues for growth or transformation. Foster a culture of innovation and openness to change to drive organizational renewal. Encourage cross-functional collaboration and knowledge-sharing to identify and pursue new opportunities. Evaluate the potential for diversification, strategic partnerships, or acquisitions to mitigate the impact of decline and explore new markets or industries.

By following this guideline, business leaders can gain a clearer understanding of their industry life cycle phase and assess if they are in the decline phase. This knowledge can inform strategic decision-making, help identify potential risks and opportunities, and guide organizations toward appropriate actions to manage the decline effectively.

Xerox

Xerox, a well-known company in the printing and copying industry, provides an example of a successful exit strategy. In the early 2000s, the company faced significant challenges as digitalization reduced the demand for traditional printing and copying services. To navigate this changing landscape, Xerox strategically decided to shift its focus and exit certain business segments. The company recognized that the decline in demand for printing and copying presented an opportunity to redirect its resources and expertise toward other emerging markets. Xerox's exit strategy involved the following key elements:

■ Portfolio Analysis: Xerox conducted a thorough analysis of its business portfolio, identifying business segments that were no longer aligned with its long-term strategic goals. The company recognized that investing in declining markets would not yield sustainable growth and profitability.

■ Resource Reallocation: Xerox redirected its resources, including capital, talent, and R&D investments, toward high-growth areas and emerging technologies. The company focused on expanding its presence in digital document management, managed print services, and IT consulting, leveraging its expertise and capabilities in these domains.

- Strategic Partnerships and Acquisitions: Xerox pursued strategic partnerships and acquisitions to complement its existing offerings and enter new markets. For example, the company acquired ACS (Affiliated Computer Services), a provider of business process outsourcing services, to strengthen its position in the services sector and diversify its revenue streams.
- Innovation and Technology Focus: Xerox embraced innovation and invested in research and development to develop new products and solutions that aligned with the evolving needs of customers. The company explored technologies such as 3D printing, document workflow automation, and digital imaging to stay ahead of market trends.

As a result of its strategic exit and redirection efforts, Xerox successfully transformed itself from a traditional printing and copying company into a diversified technology and services provider. The company's exit strategy allowed it to adapt to market changes, seize new opportunities, and position itself for long-term growth and profitability. By recognizing the declining market for its core products, Xerox demonstrated the importance of proactively assessing industry trends, making strategic decisions to exit declining businesses, and realigning resources toward emerging opportunities. The successful implementation of its exit strategy enabled Xerox to navigate industry challenges and reinvent itself as a leader in the digital era.

Develop the Strategy for This Phase

1. Assess Industry Dynamics: Conduct a thorough analysis of the industry's current state, including market trends, customer demands, technological advancements, and competitive landscape. Understand the key factors contributing to the decline phase, such as changing customer preferences, disruptive technologies, or regulatory changes.
2. Portfolio Evaluation: Evaluate your organization's product/service portfolio to identify declining or unprofitable offerings. Determine which products/services are no longer viable in the declining market and assess their potential for divestment or restructuring.
3. Exit Strategy Development: Develop a clear exit strategy for the declining products/services, considering options such as divestment, partnerships, or mergers. Evaluate the financial and operational implications of each option and choose the most suitable approach that aligns with your long-term strategic goals.
4. Resource Optimization: Reallocate resources, including financial, human, and technological assets, from declining areas to more promising growth

opportunities. This may involve restructuring operations, downsizing or redeploying workforce, and repurposing assets to maximize their value in the new strategic direction.

5. Diversification and Innovation: Explore new markets, products, or services that align with emerging trends and customer demands. Identify opportunities for diversification by leveraging existing capabilities, technologies, or customer relationships. Foster innovation by encouraging creativity and experimentation to develop new offerings that cater to evolving market needs.

6. Strategic Alliances and Partnerships: Form strategic alliances or partnerships with complementary organizations to access new markets, distribution channels, or technologies. Collaborate with industry players or technology providers to leverage their expertise, resources, or customer base in a mutually beneficial manner.

7. Customer Focus and Value Proposition: Refine your value proposition to address the evolving needs of customers in the declining market. Understand the changing customer preferences, pain points, and price sensitivity. Tailor your offerings, pricing, or service delivery to provide differentiated value and maintain customer loyalty.

8. Continuous Improvement and Efficiency: Streamline operations, reduce costs, and enhance operational efficiency to improve profitability in the declining market. Embrace lean principles, process optimization, and automation to maximize productivity and minimize waste.

9. Talent Management and Organizational Agility: Foster a culture of adaptability and resilience within the organization. Encourage employee engagement, innovation, and continuous learning to enable agility in responding to market changes. Identify and develop talent with skills and competencies relevant to the new strategic direction.

10. Monitoring and Adaptation: Regularly monitor industry dynamics, market trends, and competitive landscape to assess the effectiveness of the strategy and make necessary adjustments. Stay agile and responsive to changes, leveraging feedback from customers, employees, and industry experts to refine the strategy as needed.

Practical Implications for Strategy Development

A. Successful strategy development during the decline phase requires a proactive and forward-thinking approach, embracing change and seeking new opportunities.

B. Organizations must be willing to let go of declining products/services and reallocate resources strategically to capture emerging growth areas.

C. Flexibility and adaptability are crucial to navigate the challenges of the decline phase and explore new avenues for sustainable growth.

D. Collaboration, both within the organization and through strategic partnerships, can provide access to resources and expertise needed to execute the strategy effectively.

E. Continuous monitoring, evaluation, and adaptation are essential to ensure the strategy remains aligned with market dynamics and organizational goals.

Deploy the Strategy for This Phase

1. Communicate the Strategy: Clearly communicate the strategic direction and rationale for the decline phase to all stakeholders, including employees, customers, suppliers, and investors. Ensure everyone understands the challenges, objectives, and expected outcomes of the strategy.

2. Focus on Core Competencies: Identify and leverage your organization's core competencies and unique strengths that can be applied to mitigate the effects of the decline. Concentrate resources and efforts on areas where you have a competitive advantage or expertise.

3. Phased Approach: Implement the strategy in a phased manner, allowing for flexibility and adjustments as the market landscape evolves. Break down the implementation process into manageable stages, ensuring each phase builds upon the previous one and aligns with the overall strategic goals.

4. Resource Allocation: Allocate resources strategically to support the implementation of the decline phase strategy. Prioritize investments, budgets, and manpower to areas that have the greatest potential for success and align with the identified growth opportunities or diversification efforts.

5. Innovation and Adaptation: Foster a culture of innovation and adaptability within the organization. Encourage employees to generate ideas, experiment with new approaches, and adapt to changing market conditions. Embrace emerging technologies and business models that can create new value and differentiation.

6. Customer-Centric Approach: Maintain a strong focus on customer needs and preferences. Continuously gather feedback and insights from customers to understand their evolving demands and adjust your offerings accordingly. Seek ways to enhance the customer experience and maintain customer loyalty during the decline phase.

7. Strategic Partnerships: Collaborate with strategic partners, suppliers, or customers to leverage their capabilities, market reach, or resources. Seek opportunities for joint ventures, alliances, or co-development to access new markets, technologies, or distribution channels. Shared expertise and resources can enhance the implementation of the decline phase strategy.

8. Operational Efficiency: Streamline operations, improve efficiency, and optimize costs to maintain profitability during the decline phase. Implement lean principles, process automation, and performance metrics to identify areas for improvement and eliminate waste. Continuously monitor and adjust operations to maximize productivity.

9. Employee Engagement and Development: Engage and empower employees throughout the implementation process. Provide clear roles, responsibilities, and expectations to ensure alignment with the strategy. Invest in employee training and development to enhance their skills and competencies required for the decline phase strategy.

10. Performance Measurement and Evaluation: Establish key performance indicators (KPIs) and measurement systems to track the progress and effectiveness of the decline phase strategy. Regularly evaluate the outcomes, make necessary adjustments, and communicate the results to stakeholders. Stay agile and responsive to market changes.

Practical Implications for Strategy Deployment

Successful strategy deployment during the decline phase requires strong leadership, effective communication, and engagement at all levels of the organization.

A. Flexibility and adaptability are key to navigate the changing market conditions and seize opportunities.

B. Collaboration and partnerships can provide access to resources and expertise that enhance the implementation of the decline phase strategy.

C. Continuous monitoring and evaluation of performance metrics are essential to ensure the strategy remains on track and delivers the desired outcomes.

D. Employee empowerment and development foster a culture of resilience, innovation, and commitment to the decline phase strategy.

E. Note: It is important to customize this guideline based on the specific characteristics and dynamics of the industry in which your organization operates.

Failing to Strategize Effectively During the Phase

Failing to strategize effectively during the decline phase can have significant implications and consequences for organizations. Here are some examples of specific reasons for failure and their corresponding consequences:

■ Reason for failure: Lack of Adaptation
  – Consequence: Loss of market share, declining revenues, and eventual bankruptcy or business closure.
    • Example: Blockbuster. A once-dominant video rental company that failed to respond effectively to the rise of online streaming services like Netflix. Blockbuster's failure to adapt its business model and embrace digital technology ultimately led to its downfall, as customers shifted to more convenient and cost-effective alternatives.
■ Reason for failure: Ineffective Cost Management
  – Consequence: Erosion of profitability, financial distress, and potential business insolvency.
    • Example: Kodak. A renowned photography company that struggled to adapt to the digital era. Kodak's inability to manage costs and transition its business from film to digital photography resulted in significant financial losses and a decline in its market position.
■ Reason for failure: Lack of diversification
  – Consequence: Loss of competitive advantage, decline in market share, and reduced revenue streams.
    • Example: Nokia. A once-leading mobile phone manufacturer failed to diversify its product offerings and adapt to the emergence of smartphones. As a result, Nokia lost significant market share to competitors like Apple and Samsung.
■ Reason for failure: Ignoring Innovation
  – Consequence: Decline in sales, erosion of brand equity, and reduced customer loyalty.
    • Example: Polaroid. A renowned instant camera manufacturer. Polaroid failed to embrace digital photography and neglected to innovate its product line, which resulted in declining sales and a loss of market relevance.
■ Reason for failure: Inadequate Strategic Leadership
  – Consequence: Loss of market share, financial instability, and potential organizational collapse.

- Example: Sears. A once-prominent department store chain. Sears faced challenges in keeping up with evolving consumer preferences and failed to respond effectively to the rise of e-commerce. The lack of strategic leadership and timely decision-making contributed to its decline.

Lesson from a leader

Lou Gerstner

During his CEO tenure from 1993 to 2002, Gerstner led IBM through a transformative phase, implementing strategic changes that ultimately allowed the company to survive and thrive.

When Gerstner took over as CEO, IBM was facing significant challenges, including declining revenues and losses in key business units. Rather than sticking to a traditional exit strategy of divesting or shutting down underperforming divisions, Gerstner recognized the inherent value in IBM's existing capabilities and assets. He strategically repositioned the company and focused on its core competencies to revitalize its performance. One of Gerstner's key moves was to shift IBM's focus from hardware to services and software. He understood that the technology landscape was changing rapidly, and IBM needed to adapt to remain relevant. By leveraging its expertise in enterprise-level services and software development, IBM was able to tap into emerging markets and capitalize on the growing demand for IT solutions.

Gerstner also implemented a culture of customer-centricity and innovation within IBM. He encouraged collaboration and broke down internal silos, allowing the company to respond more effectively to customer needs and market trends. This customer-driven approach helped IBM regain customer trust and loyalty, boosting its reputation and revenue.

Furthermore, Gerstner strategically formed partnerships and alliances with other companies, expanding IBM's reach and diversifying its offerings. For example, he orchestrated a landmark partnership with Apple in 1991, which allowed IBM to gain access to the growing personal computer market and enhance its software portfolio.

By executing this comprehensive exit strategy, Gerstner successfully guided IBM through a period of transformation and reestablished its position as a leading technology company. Under his leadership, IBM experienced significant growth and regained its financial stability. The example of Lou Gerstner and IBM highlights the importance of a strategic and adaptive approach to executing an exit strategy. Instead of simply divesting or shutting down underperforming divisions, Gerstner recognized the untapped potential within the organization and strategically realigned its focus and resources to capitalize on emerging opportunities.

LEADERSHIP AND PRACTICE

Chapter 11

Strategy Tiers: The Magnifying Lenses

Prelude

We will begin this section by presenting a mini case study that sets the stage for understanding the importance of strategy tiers and the concept of magnifying lenses. The case study will highlight a real-world scenario where an organization's strategy was impacted by misalignment or missing strategy tiers.

Next, we will define and explain the three tiers of strategy. These tiers represent different levels of strategic focus within an organization: corporate, business, and functional. Each tier corresponds to a specific scope and responsibility in strategy development. Then, we will provide clear definitions of each tier and highlight their interdependence. We will introduce the concept of magnifying lenses as a new perspective in understanding strategy. Just as magnifying lenses amplify and bring clarity to smaller objects, the magnifying lens concept highlights the importance of viewing strategy through tiered lenses that drill-down to a smaller scope but greater detail on strategy at each tier. We will discuss how these lenses provide a deeper understanding of strategic decisions and their impact on the overall organization. After that, we will explore the consequences of missing or misaligning the magnifying lenses in an organization's strategy. We will discuss the potential pitfalls and challenges that arise when strategy tiers are not properly integrated or when one tier dominates the others. This misalignment can lead to inefficiencies, lack of strategic coherence, and missed opportunities.

DOI: 10.4324/9781003564133-14

Set-the-Stage Mini Case

Nike

Nike is a global leader in athletic footwear, apparel, equipment, and accessories. The company has effectively aligned its strategies across all three levels to establish a strong competitive position and drive growth.

1. ***Corporate-Level Strategy***: Nike's corporate-level strategy focuses on brand management, innovation, and global expansion. The company's vision is to "bring inspiration and innovation to every athlete in the world." Nike achieves this through strategic initiatives such as:

   a. Brand Building: Nike has invested heavily in building a strong brand image and reputation worldwide. The "Just Do It" slogan and iconic swoosh logo are recognized globally, creating a strong brand identity.

   b. Product Innovation: Nike emphasizes continuous innovation to stay ahead of competitors. The company invests in research and development, collaborates with athletes and sports teams, and leverages advanced technologies to develop cutting-edge products.

   c. Global Expansion: Nike has a strong global presence, with operations in various countries. The company strategically expands into new markets, targeting emerging economies and capitalizing on growing consumer demand for athletic apparel and footwear.

2. ***Business-Level Strategy***: Nike's business-level strategy revolves around differentiation and a focus on key market segments. The company understands the importance of catering to diverse customer needs and preferences. Key elements of Nike's business-level strategy include:

   a. Product Differentiation: Nike offers a wide range of products tailored to different sports, activities, and consumer preferences. They provide performance-driven footwear, apparel, and equipment designed for specific sports, such as basketball, running, and soccer.

   b. Brand Positioning: Nike targets various customer segments, including athletes, sports enthusiasts, and fashion-conscious consumers. The company positions itself as a premium brand, offering high-quality, innovative, and stylish products that embody performance and athleticism.

   c. Marketing and Sponsorship: Nike's marketing campaigns and partnerships with athletes and sports teams contribute to its business-level strategy. The company leverages endorsements and sponsorships to enhance brand visibility, connect with target audiences, and strengthen brand loyalty.

3. ***Functional-Level Strategy***: Nike's functional-level strategies focus on attaining competitive advantage through key functional areas such as

operations, marketing, and supply chain management. These strategies support the overall corporate and business objectives. Examples of functional-level strategies employed by Nike include:

a. Efficient Supply Chain: Nike has implemented a robust supply chain management system to ensure timely delivery, manage inventory effectively, and optimize operational efficiency. This enables the company to respond to changing customer demands quickly.

b. Marketing and Advertising Excellence: Nike excels in marketing and advertising campaigns that resonate with its target market. The company leverages various channels, including digital marketing, social media, and athlete endorsements, to create engaging and impactful marketing initiatives.

c. Product Development and Design: Nike's functional-level strategy emphasizes continuous product development and design to meet customer preferences and stay ahead of trends. The company invests in research and development, collaborates with athletes and designers, and utilizes customer feedback to enhance product offerings.

Nike's successful strategy integration across the corporate, business, and functional-levels has contributed to its strong market position and sustained growth. The alignment of its corporate mission, differentiation-focused business strategies, and effective functional strategies has enabled Nike to consistently meet customer needs, maintain a competitive edge, and capture market share.

Strategy Tiers: A Perspective from Photography

In photography, aperture and depth of field are crucial concepts that determine how much light enters the camera and what is in focus. Aperture refers to the opening in the lens through which light passes, and it is measured in f-stops. A lower f-stop (e.g., f/2.8) means a larger aperture, allowing more light and creating a shallower depth of field. Conversely, a higher f-stop (e.g., f/16) means a smaller aperture, letting in less light and creating a deeper depth of field.

Now, let's draw an analogy between aperture and depth of field in photography and the levels of strategy in organizations:

Corporate-Level: At the corporate-level, think of a wide aperture setting with a shallow depth of field in photography. This setting captures a broad view, akin to a wide-angle lens that encompasses the entire landscape. The focus is on the big picture, with less detail on specific elements.

Business-Level: Moving to the business-level is like adjusting the aperture to a medium setting, which increases the depth of field. This setting narrows the focus slightly, allowing for more detail to be captured in the middle ground while still maintaining some awareness of the broader context.

Functional-Level: Finally, at the functional-level, imagine using a narrow aperture setting with a deep depth of field. This setting focuses sharply on specific elements in the foreground, capturing intricate details and nuances while minimizing the visibility of the background.

Just as a photographer adjusts the aperture to control the amount of light and the depth of field in a photo, organizations adjust their strategic focus to different levels to manage complexity and detail according to their objectives.

Defining the three tiers of strategy

Corporate-level strategy: At the highest tier, the corporate-level strategy focuses on the strategic direction for the organization manifested in its growth and the enabling business model. The scope at this level encompasses the entire organization and its various business units or divisions. Despite the common belief that corporate strategy is near abstract, it is (or should be) an actual process that involves assessing the organization's current position, defining its mission and vision, setting long-term objectives, and making decisions regarding resource allocation, diversification, mergers and acquisitions, and other strategic initiatives.

To be at a "corporate-level" should not mean to be in isolation of the business units. In other words, corporate-level strategy is not necessarily superior to the other tiers but rather the umbrella under which the remaining tiers fall under, cohesively. The intent of strategy at this level—when it comes to business units—is to envision the growth of the organization, in a way that realizes synergies among the business units. This of course may mean different things to different organizations based on the type (i.e., conglomerates) and the scope of diversification (related vs. unrelated). The deliverables of corporate-level strategy include strategic plans, portfolio management decisions, and governance structures.

> **What does it mean to strategically align the tiers at this level?:** Strategic alignment between the corporate-level strategy and the other two tiers is critical to the effectiveness of the overall strategy. The corporate-level strategy provides the overarching strategic direction that sets the context for the business-level and functional-level strategies. It provides the strategic boundaries and priorities within which the lower tiers operate. Just like a magnifying lens brings focus and clarity, the corporate-level strategy ensures that the business-level and functional-level strategies align with the organization's mission, vision, and long-term objectives.

Business-level strategy: The business-level strategy focuses on how a specific business unit or division of the organization competes in its chosen market.

Common bases of competition at this level are differentiation or cost leadership (i.e., low cost). It involves making strategic decisions to achieve a competitive advantage within a particular industry or market segment. The scope of business-level strategy is narrower than the corporate-level and is specific to a particular business unit or product/service line. Again, the thought process here is that the growth (and the enabling business model) has been envisioned at the corporate-level. Now, the focus is on how to realize that growth: by differentiation from competition or cost leadership (in the simplest terms: at this level, the organization decides on whether it wasn't to grow as Rolex or Walmart). Note: every time I taught a strategy class, I follow this example by emphasizing that the difference between differentiation and cost leadership does not necessarily reside in premium-priced offerings. It is all about how the organization wants to make its money….is it by selling high quantities and collecting small profits or by selling small quantities and collecting higher profits (irrespective of price point). The process of developing business-level strategy includes analyzing the competitive landscape, understanding customer needs and preferences, identifying target markets, and formulating strategies to differentiate from competitors or achieve cost leadership. Worthy of mention that deciding between differentiation and cost leadership is not binary, it can be along a spectrum as long as the company is aware of its position on the Efficiency Frontier. And so, business-level strategies may include product differentiation, cost leadership, focused/niche strategies, or a combination thereof.

Efficiency Frontier Description:

The efficiency frontier, also known as the production possibility frontier (PPF) or the efficiency curve, is a graphical representation of the maximum output that can be produced with a given set of inputs. It illustrates the trade-offs between producing different goods or services efficiently. Points along the frontier represent the most efficient allocation of resources, where any increase in the production of one good can only be achieved by decreasing the production of another.

Efficiency Frontier Relative to Differentiation or Cost Leadership:

Cost Leadership: A firm following a cost leadership strategy seeks to produce goods or services at the lowest possible cost. The efficiency frontier is crucial for cost leadership as it represents the boundary of what is achievable in terms of cost efficiency. A firm pursuing cost leadership aims to operate on or near the efficiency frontier to minimize costs and maximize profits.
Differentiation: On the other hand, a differentiation strategy focuses on creating unique products or services that are perceived as distinct by customers. The efficiency frontier is relevant to differentiation as well, but in a different way. A firm pursuing differentiation must balance the costs of creating unique features

or attributes with the value that customers are willing to pay. This means oper-
ating efficiently on the efficiency frontier while also investing in differentiation
factors that set the product or service apart from competitors.

The intent of business-level strategy is to position the business unit for success, achieve sustainable competitive advantage, and deliver value to customers. But at this lower level (from corporate-level), the focus is on how the growth will be realized: through differentiation or cost leadership. The deliverables of business-level strategy include strategic plans for the business unit, marketing and sales strategies, and operational plans. These plans should be developed with a clear lens: differentiation or cost leadership. Now, it is possible that some organizations select a position in between but let's remember where the importance of this tiered approach lies....it is to ensure strategic alignment as visions for growth and abstract conceptualizing of business models at the corporate-level get translated into actionable items that skill teams can deliver.

What does it mean to strategically align the tiers at this level? The business-level strategy must be aligned with the corporate-level strategy to ensure coherence and consistency. The business-level strategy should support the overall strategic direction set by the corporate-level. It should leverage the organization's core competencies and resources in line with the corporate-level goals and priorities. The magnifying lens analogy illustrates how the business-level strategy zooms in on the specific market and competitive dynamics, while staying aligned with the broader corporate strategy.

Functional-level strategy: The functional-level strategy focuses on the activities and operations within a specific functional area, such as marketing, operations, finance, or human resources with the aim of attaining sustainable competitive advantages based on 4 commonly known building blocks (quality, operational efficiency, innovation, and customer responsiveness). The scope of functional-level strategy is even narrower than the business level and is specific to a particular function. Why? Because at this level, the organization is laser-focused on utilizing its functional departments (or teams) to excel in the selected building blocks (here we say selection because it is not realistic that a company aims to excel in all four simultaneously, this will deplete its resources). Essentially, at the functional-level, the intent is to develop strategies to enhance functional capabilities, improve efficiency, innovate processes, and align functional activities with the overall business goals. The process of developing functional-level strategy involves analyzing internal and external factors impacting the function, setting functional objectives, and formulating action plans to achieve those objectives.

Functional-level strategies may include quality improvement initiatives, talent development programs, cost reduction efforts, or technology adoption plans.

The intent of functional-level strategy is to support the business-level strategy by ensuring that functional activities are aligned and contribute to the achievement of business goals, through the attainment of sustainable competitive advantages that will enable the company to achieve its desired position of differentiation or cost leadership in the market. The deliverables of functional-level strategy include functional plans, performance metrics, and initiatives specific to each functional area.

What does it mean to strategically align the tiers at this level? The functional-level strategy should be closely aligned with both the business-level and corporate-level strategies to ensure coordination and integration. It should support the business-level strategy by providing the necessary capabilities and resources within each functional area. The magnifying lens analogy emphasizes how the functional-level strategy zooms in further, focusing on optimizing specific functions while maintaining alignment with the broader business and corporate strategies.

Overall, the strategic alignment among the corporate-level, business-level, and functional-level strategies is critical to the effectiveness of the strategy. Rather than being different strategies, these tiers represent different levels of focus and scope within the same strategic direction. Just like magnifying lenses bring different perspectives to the same object, the three tiers provide different lenses to view and execute the strategy at various levels of the organization. This alignment ensures that the organization moves forward cohesively, capitalizing on its strengths and opportunities while addressing challenges and minimizing conflicts. By adhering to this integrated approach and recognizing the interconnectedness of the three tiers, organizations can optimize their strategic decision-making, resource allocation, and performance across the entire organization. The magnifying lens concept serves as a powerful metaphor for understanding the importance of strategic alignment and the unified nature of strategy development at different levels within a CAS like an organization.

THE MAGNIFYING LENS IDEA IN BRIEF: the corporate-level, business-level, and functional-level strategies are not separate entities but interconnected layers of the same strategy. Like magnifying lenses, each tier brings a unique perspective to the strategic decision-making process, enabling organizations to focus, align, and drive their efforts toward achieving their overarching goals. The strategic alignment among these tiers is crucial to ensuring a harmonized and effective approach to strategy development and execution.

Through the integration of the magnifying lenses, organizations can effectively navigate the complexities of the business environment, make informed strategic choices, and enhance their competitive advantage. This alignment fosters strategic coherence, agility, and adaptability, allowing organizations to respond to changing market conditions, seize opportunities, and achieve long-term success.

Illustrating the magnifying lens concept as NEW PERSPECTIVE

Apple Inc.

Apple provides a compelling illustration of how the three tiers of strategy work in harmony. At the corporate-level, Apple sets strategic direction and overarching goals for the entire organization. Their corporate-level strategy focuses on innovation, design, and delivering seamless user experiences across a range of products and services. This strategic direction influences the business-level strategies of their various product divisions, such as the iPhone, iPad, Mac, and services like Apple Music and Apple TV+.

At the business-level, Apple designs specific strategies tailored to each product line. For instance, their iPhone business-level strategy involves continuous product innovation, differentiation through cutting-edge technology and design, and establishing a strong ecosystem of complementary services. The business-level strategies align with the corporate-level strategy of delivering innovative and user-centric products and services.

On the functional-level, Apple's functional strategies in areas such as marketing, operations, and R&D support the business-level strategies. For example, their marketing strategy emphasizes creating emotional connections with customers through compelling advertising and brand positioning. Their operational strategy includes supply chain management to ensure timely and efficient delivery of products worldwide. The functional strategies are aligned with the business-level strategies, reinforcing the overarching corporate strategy.

The strategic alignment among these tiers is evident in Apple's success. Their corporate-level focus on innovation and design translates into differentiated products (business-level) that resonate with customers. The functional strategies in marketing and operations further support the execution of the business-level strategies, enhancing Apple's competitive advantage. This interconnectedness allows Apple to consistently deliver on their strategic goals and maintain their position as a leader in the technology industry.

The Coca-Cola Company

The Coca-Cola Company provides another example of the interplay between the three tiers of strategy. At the corporate-level, Coca-Cola's strategy revolves around building a strong portfolio of beverage brands, expanding their global presence, and diversifying into new product categories. This corporate-level strategy sets the direction for the company's overall growth and profitability.

On the business-level, Coca-Cola develops specific strategies for each of its product lines, such as Coca-Cola, Sprite, Fanta, and Dasani. These business-level strategies focus on market segmentation, branding, and product innovation. For instance, Coca-Cola's business-level strategy includes tailoring its marketing campaigns to target different consumer segments and adapting product offerings to local preferences in various markets.

At the functional-level, Coca-Cola's functional strategies in areas like marketing, supply chain, and research and development support the business-level strategies. Their marketing strategy includes brand building, sponsorships, and partnerships to drive customer engagement. Their supply chain strategy ensures efficient distribution and availability of products worldwide. The functional strategies are aligned with the business-level strategies to enable effective execution and implementation.

The strategic alignment among these tiers has been instrumental in Coca-Cola's success. Their corporate-level strategy of portfolio diversification and global expansion aligns with their business-level strategies for each product line. The functional strategies in marketing and supply chain support the execution of the business-level strategies, contributing to Coca-Cola's brand strength, market share, and financial performance.

These examples highlight how the corporate-level, business-level, and functional-level strategies are interconnected and mutually reinforcing. The strategic alignment among the tiers ensures that organizations like Apple and Coca-Cola can effectively navigate the complexities of their respective industries, capitalize on opportunities, and deliver value to their customers.

By recognizing the interdependence of these strategy tiers and actively aligning them, organizations can optimize their resources, capabilities, and efforts to achieve their overarching goals. The magnifying lens analogy captures the essence of this alignment, as each tier brings a distinct perspective that, when combined, provides a comprehensive and focused view of the strategic landscape. This alignment enhances decision-making, resource allocation, and performance across all levels of the organization, ultimately leading to sustainable success.

Bringing the strategic alignment among the tiers together:
Strategic alignment among different tiers of an organization is essential for cohesive and effective strategy execution. At the corporate-level, the overarching strategy envisions the growth and sets the direction for the entire organization. This includes defining the enabling business model, which outlines how the organization will create value and generate revenue.

For example, if a company aims to achieve growth similar to Rolex, known for its luxury watches, pursuing a cost leadership strategy at the business-level would be counterproductive. Rolex's success lies in its differentiation strategy, focusing on craftsmanship, brand prestige, and exclusivity. Therefore, the business-level strategy must align with the corporate vision of differentiation.

At the business-level, the company selects how to realize this growth by choosing between pursuing a differentiation strategy or cost leadership. A differentiation strategy aims to create unique products or services that are valued by customers, while a cost leadership strategy focuses on minimizing costs to offer products or services at lower prices than competitors.

Once the business-level strategy is determined, the company focuses on attaining competitive advantage by leveraging key building blocks such as quality, operational efficiency, innovation, and customer responsiveness. Using the Rolex example, innovation plays a crucial role in maintaining its competitive advantage. Rolex continuously innovates its watches with new technologies and materials, while maintaining the highest quality standards. This focus on innovation and quality is a key building block that supports Rolex's differentiation strategy.

Take another example, Blue Apron, which operates in the meal kit delivery industry. Blue Apron's corporate-level strategy might focus on expanding market share and increasing customer engagement through innovative meal solutions and convenient delivery services.

At the business-level, Blue Apron must decide on a strategy to realize this growth. Given its business model of delivering meal kits to customers, pursuing a cost leadership strategy might not be the most effective approach. Blue Apron's success hinges on its ability to differentiate itself from competitors by offering high-quality, fresh ingredients and unique recipes that cater to various dietary preferences and restrictions.

Once the business-level strategy is determined, Blue Apron focuses on attaining competitive advantage through key building blocks such as quality, operational efficiency, innovation, and customer responsiveness. Quality is a critical building block for Blue Apron, as it directly impacts customer satisfaction and retention. By ensuring the freshness and quality of its ingredients and delivering them in a timely manner, Blue Apron enhances its reputation and differentiates itself from competitors.

Innovation is another key building block for Blue Apron, as it constantly develops new recipes and meal options to meet the evolving needs and preferences of its customers. By offering innovative and diverse meal choices, Blue Apron enhances its value proposition and maintains a competitive edge in the market.

So what could happen in case the company misaligns its strategy tiers?

If Blue Apron's strategic tiers are misaligned, it could lead to several negative outcomes. For example:

■ Quality and Innovation: If the company were to pursue a cost leadership strategy at the business-level, it might prioritize reducing costs over maintaining the quality of its ingredients and meal offerings. This could result in lower-quality ingredients being used, leading to a decline in customer satisfaction and retention. Additionally, a focus on cost reduction might stifle innovation, as the company may be less inclined to invest in developing new recipes and meal options.

■ Differentiation: Misalignment between the corporate vision and the business-level strategy could result in a lack of differentiation for Blue Apron. If the corporate strategy emphasizes differentiation but the business-level strategy focuses on cost leadership, Blue Apron may struggle to distinguish itself from competitors offering similar, lower-cost meal kit options. This could lead to a loss of market share and competitive advantage.

■ Customer Responsiveness: A misalignment between the strategic tiers could also impact Blue Apron's ability to be responsive to customer needs and preferences. For example, if the corporate strategy emphasizes customer-centricity but the business-level strategy prioritizes cost reduction, Blue Apron may be less responsive to customer feedback and less able to adapt its offerings to meet changing customer demands.

Missing or misaligning the magnifying lenses

■ **Risk of Misalignment: Limited Resource Allocation**
  – Consequence: Misalignment among the three tiers of strategy can lead to inefficient resource allocation. When the corporate-level strategy is not effectively communicated or aligned with the business-level and functional-level strategies, resources may be allocated in a way that does not support the overall strategic objectives. This can result in wasted resources, duplication of efforts, and missed opportunities.
    • Example: Kodak. A once-dominant player in the photography industry, failed to effectively align their corporate-level strategy with their business-level and functional-level strategies. Despite having early knowledge of digital photography's potential, Kodak continued to heavily invest in their traditional film business while neglecting the emerging digital market. This misalignment in resource allocation ultimately led to Kodak's decline and bankruptcy as they failed to adapt to the digital revolution.

- ■ **Risk of Misalignment: Lack of Competitive Advantage**
  - – Strategic misalignment can hinder an organization's ability to develop and maintain a competitive advantage. When the different tiers of strategy are not aligned, it becomes challenging to differentiate the organization from its competitors and create unique value propositions. This lack of competitive advantage can result in market share erosion and decreased profitability.
    - • Example: BlackBerry. A leading smartphone manufacturer, experienced misalignment in their strategy during the rise of touchscreen smartphones. While the corporate-level strategy focused on maintaining their dominance in the business and professional market, the business-level and functional-level strategies did not effectively respond to the shift in consumer preferences toward touchscreen devices. This misalignment prevented BlackBerry from capitalizing on the changing market dynamics, leading to a significant decline in market share and loss of competitiveness.
- ■ **Risk of Misalignment: Inconsistent Customer Experience**
  - – When the three tiers of strategy are not aligned, it can result in an inconsistent customer experience. Each tier plays a crucial role in shaping the customer journey and delivering value to customers. Misalignment among these tiers can lead to fragmented or conflicting customer experiences, negatively impacting customer satisfaction and loyalty.
    - • Example: United Airlines. The company faced a notable incident of misalignment in their strategy when a passenger was forcibly removed from an overbooked flight. While the corporate-level strategy focused on maximizing profitability and operational efficiency, the business-level and functional-level strategies did not adequately prioritize customer satisfaction and experience. This misalignment resulted in a highly publicized incident that damaged United Airlines' reputation and customer trust.

Reasons for Misalignment in Organizations:

- ■ Lack of Communication and Coordination: Misalignment can occur when there is a lack of clear communication and coordination among different levels of the organization. Siloed decision-making and limited information sharing can hinder the integration and alignment of strategies.
- ■ Organizational Structure and Culture: Misalignment can be a result of organizational structures and cultures that inhibit cross-functional collaboration and hinder the flow of information. Hierarchical structures, bureaucratic processes, and cultural resistance to change can impede the alignment of strategies.

▪ External Environmental Factors: Rapid changes in the external environment, such as technological advancements, shifting market dynamics, or regulatory changes, can create challenges in aligning strategies. Organizations may struggle to adapt their strategies to the evolving landscape, leading to misalignment.

In conclusion, the risk of strategic misalignment among the three tiers of strategy is significant and can have detrimental consequences for organizations. Limited resource allocation, lack of competitive advantage, and inconsistent customer experiences are some of the risks associated with misalignment. Reasons for misalignment can stem from communication gaps, organizational structures, cultures, and external environmental factors. It is crucial for organizations to proactively address and manage these risks to ensure strategic alignment and maximize their chances of success in a dynamic business environment.

Toyota's Electrification Strategy

TOYOTA'S ELECTRIFICATION STRATEGY: PAVING THE ROAD TO AN ELECTRIC FUTURE

Toyota, a global automotive giant, is making significant strides in the electrification of its vehicle lineup, driven by stringent emission regulations, changing consumer preferences, and rapid advancements in automotive technology. As one of the leaders in the automotive industry, Toyota's strategy for electrification is comprehensive, aiming to meet both regulatory demands and consumer expectations.

Strategic Vision and Multi-Pathway Approach

Under the leadership of its new President, Koji Sato, Toyota has unveiled an updated electrification strategy that emphasizes the development of battery-electric vehicles (BEVs). Despite its commitment to a multi-pathway approach that includes hybrid and hydrogen technologies, electric cars are set to play a much more prominent role in Toyota's portfolio moving forward. By 2026, Toyota plans to launch 10 new fully-electric vehicles and expects to sell 1.5 million electric cars annually by then, with a target of 3.5 million units per year by 2030 (GreenCars, 2023a, 2023b; Toyota UK Magazine, 2023).

Toyota's multi-pathway approach demonstrates its flexibility and readiness to cater to different markets and customer needs. While BEVs are gaining significant traction, hybrids and hydrogen-powered vehicles still play a crucial role in Toyota's strategy. This diversified approach ensures that Toyota remains competitive across various segments and markets, adapting to regional differences in infrastructure and consumer preferences.

Next-Generation Platform and Global Reach

Toyota is developing a new, dedicated electric vehicle platform that will differ significantly from its current offerings. This new platform is designed exclusively for electric vehicles, promising to double the range of existing models and provide more passenger and cargo space. This shift to a dedicated platform represents a strategic move to enhance efficiency and performance in its electric vehicles. The company's global strategy includes the introduction of various models tailored to different markets. In 2023, Toyota plans to launch compact electric cars and fully-electric pickup trucks in Asia, with two new models slated for the Chinese market in 2024. Additionally, a three-row SUV designed for the American market will be produced in the U.S., with batteries sourced from Toyota's North Carolina plant. This dedicated EV platform, named e-TNGA, reflects Toyota's commitment to creating vehicles that maximize the benefits of electrification. By focusing on an EV-specific architecture, Toyota can optimize design and engineering processes to better meet the unique demands of electric vehicles, such as battery placement, weight distribution, and aerodynamics. This new platform is a critical component of Toyota's strategy to enhance the performance and appeal of its electric vehicles.

Investment in Battery Technology

Toyota has a long history of investing in battery technology. Since the establishment of Prime Earth EV Energy in 1996 and the Battery Research Division in 2008, Toyota has been at the forefront of developing advanced batteries. The company has committed nearly one trillion yen to battery research and production over the past 26 years, producing more than 19 million batteries. Moving forward, Toyota plans to increase its investment in batteries from 1.5 trillion yen to 2.0 trillion yen to develop more advanced, high-quality, and affordable batteries (Toyota UK Magazine, 2023). Toyota's investment in battery technology is not just about increasing production capacity but also about advancing battery performance and reducing costs. The company is exploring various battery chemistries and technologies, including solid-state batteries, which promise higher energy densities and faster charging times compared to current lithium-ion batteries. These advancements are crucial for making electric vehicles more practical and appealing to a broader range of consumers.

Focus on Hybrid Technology and Carbon Neutrality

While pushing forward with its BEV strategy, Toyota continues to invest in hybrid technology. New plug-in hybrid models are expected to achieve over 100 miles of full-electric range. This dual focus on hybrids and BEVs aligns with Toyota's long-term goal of achieving carbon neutrality by 2050. The company is also working on securing renewable energy sources and aiming for carbon-neutral manufacturing plants by 2035. Toyota's commitment to hybrid technology reflects its recognition of the varying stages of electrification readiness across different markets. Hybrids offer an immediate reduction in emissions and fuel consumption, making them an essential part of the transition to a fully electric future. By continuing to innovate in hybrid technology, Toyota ensures that it can offer a range of low-emission options to consumers, regardless of the pace of EV infrastructure development in their region.

Infrastructure and Charging Solutions

To support its electrification goals, Toyota is investing in the necessary infrastructure. The company has announced the construction of a battery plant in North Carolina and continues to expand its global production capabilities. This includes efforts to secure stable sources of lithium and other critical materials necessary for battery production (Toyota UK Magazine, 2023). Toyota recognizes that the success of its electrification strategy depends on the availability of reliable and convenient charging infrastructure. To this end, the company is also working on developing advanced charging solutions, including fast-charging technologies and home charging options. By addressing the infrastructure challenge, Toyota aims to make electric vehicle ownership more accessible and convenient for its customers.

Strategic Partnerships and Innovation

Toyota is leveraging strategic partnerships to accelerate its electrification strategy. Collaborations with companies like Prime Planet Energy & Solutions and efforts to innovate in areas such as solid-state batteries and next-generation battery technologies are central to its approach. By working closely with partners and investing in advanced technologies, Toyota aims to enhance its competitive edge in the rapidly evolving automotive landscape. These partnerships are crucial for sharing the risks and costs associated with developing new technologies. They also provide access to specialized expertise and resources that can accelerate the innovation process. Toyota's collaborative approach ensures that it remains at the forefront of technological advancements in the automotive industry.

Market Response and Future Outlook

Toyota's comprehensive electrification strategy is a response to increasing legislative pressure and the evolving automotive market. The company's goal to launch multiple new electric models and significantly increase its annual EV sales reflects its commitment to staying competitive. The shift to a dedicated EV platform, substantial investment in battery technology, and continued focus on hybrid vehicles position Toyota as a key player in the transition to a more sustainable automotive industry. The market response to Toyota's electrification strategy has been positive, with growing interest and demand for its electric and hybrid vehicles. Consumers are increasingly recognizing the benefits of electrification, including lower operating costs, reduced environmental impact, and enhanced driving experiences. Toyota's ability to deliver high-quality, reliable, and affordable electric vehicles is crucial for capturing a significant share of this expanding market. Looking ahead, Toyota's strategic initiatives are expected to drive significant growth in its electric vehicle sales. The company's focus on innovation, operational efficiency, and customer satisfaction will be key to its success in the competitive automotive landscape. By staying true to its core values and leveraging its strengths, Toyota is well-positioned to lead the industry into a more sustainable and electrified future.

Conclusion

Toyota's electrification strategy is a testament to its commitment to innovation, sustainability, and customer satisfaction. By adopting a multi-pathway approach that includes BEVs, hybrids, and hydrogen technologies, Toyota is addressing the diverse needs of its global customer base. The development of a dedicated EV platform, significant investment in battery technology, and strategic partnerships are all critical components of Toyota's plan to lead the automotive industry into a more sustainable future.

As the automotive industry continues to evolve, Toyota's proactive approach to electrification will ensure that it remains at the forefront of technological advancements and market trends. The company's focus on operational efficiency, customer experience, and environmental responsibility positions it as a leader in the transition to electric mobility. Through its comprehensive strategy, Toyota is not only meeting the demands of today but also paving the way for a more sustainable and electrified tomorrow.

SPECIAL NOTE: Leveraging AI for Strategic Advantage

Introduction to AI

Artificial intelligence (AI) refers to the simulation of human intelligence in machines that are programmed to think and learn like humans. These systems can perform tasks that typically require human intelligence, such as visual perception, speech recognition, decision-making, and language translation. AI is an umbrella term that encompasses various technologies, including machine learning (ML), deep learning (DL), natural language processing (NLP), computer vision (CV), and robotics.

ML is a subset of AI that enables systems to learn from data and improve their performance over time without being explicitly programmed. ML algorithms can analyze large datasets to identify patterns and make predictions. There are several types of ML, including supervised learning, unsupervised learning, and reinforcement learning. Supervised learning involves training a model on labeled data, while unsupervised learning deals with unlabeled data to identify hidden patterns. Reinforcement learning focuses on training models through trial and error, using feedback from actions to learn optimal behaviors.

DL is a more advanced subset of ML that uses artificial neural networks to mimic the human brain's functioning. DL algorithms require vast amounts of data and computational power to train deep neural networks, which consist of multiple layers of interconnected nodes. These networks can learn to recognize intricate patterns in data, making them particularly effective for tasks such as image and speech recognition.

NLP is a branch of AI that focuses on enabling machines to understand, interpret, and generate human language. NLP techniques are used in applications such as chatbots, sentiment analysis, language translation, and voice assistants. NLP combines computational linguistics, ML, and DL to process and analyze large volumes of text and speech data.

CV is another critical area of AI that deals with enabling machines to interpret and understand visual information from the world. CV technologies include image recognition, object detection, and facial recognition. These technologies are used in various applications, such as autonomous vehicles, medical imaging, and security systems.

Robotics is the field of AI that involves designing and building robots capable of performing tasks autonomously or semi-autonomously. Robotics combines AI technologies like computer vision and ML to enable robots to navigate environments, manipulate objects, and interact with humans.

In summary, AI encompasses a wide range of technologies and techniques that enable machines to perform tasks requiring human intelligence. By leveraging these technologies, organizations can enhance their strategic capabilities and achieve competitive advantages in various areas, including quality, innovation, customer responsiveness, and efficiency.

AI's Role in Supporting Strategic Decision-Making

At the corporate-level, AI can play a pivotal role in supporting strategic decision-making through advanced data analytics and insights. Organizations can use AI technologies such as ML and predictive analytics to analyze vast amounts of data, identify market trends, predict customer behavior, and optimize resource allocation. For instance, AI-driven market entry analysis can help companies assess potential markets and identify the best entry strategies. Additionally, AI can aid in optimizing resource allocation across different business units based on forecasts and simulations, ensuring that resources are deployed where they are most needed.

For example, predictive analytics, a subset of AI, involves using historical data to predict future outcomes. Companies can use predictive analytics to forecast market trends, customer demand, and financial performance. By leveraging these insights, organizations can make informed strategic decisions, such as entering new markets or expanding product lines.

Another example is NLP, which can be used to analyze customer feedback and sentiment. By processing and analyzing large volumes of text data from customer reviews, social media, and surveys, NLP can provide valuable insights into customer preferences and perceptions. This information can inform corporate strategies related to product development, marketing, and customer engagement.

At the business-level, AI can support strategies such as differentiation and cost leadership. Businesses can leverage AI technologies like ML, computer vision, and NLP to create personalized customer experiences or achieve operational efficiencies. For example, companies like Netflix use AI-driven recommendation systems to analyze user preferences and viewing history, enhancing customer engagement and loyalty. Similarly, Amazon employs AI-powered robotics and

ML algorithms to optimize its supply chain, achieving cost leadership through increased efficiency.

ML algorithms can be used to analyze customer data and segment customers based on their preferences and behavior. This segmentation can inform targeted marketing strategies, allowing businesses to tailor their offerings to different customer segments. By providing personalized experiences, companies can differentiate themselves from competitors and build stronger customer relationships. Computer vision technologies can be used in manufacturing and logistics to improve efficiency and reduce costs. For instance, automated inspection systems powered by computer vision can detect defects and anomalies in products, ensuring high-quality standards. In warehouses, AI-powered robots can streamline the picking and packing process, reducing labor costs and increasing operational efficiency.

Why AI Makes Sense at the Functional-Level

While AI provides significant benefits at the corporate and business-levels, its true potential is often realized at the functional-level. At this level, AI can directly impact the four building blocks of competitive advantage: quality, innovation, customer responsiveness, and efficiency. By focusing on functional-level strategies, organizations can leverage AI to enhance their capabilities in these critical areas, driving sustained competitive advantage.

■ Quality Enhancement through AI

AI can be used to improve product and service quality through advanced quality control and assurance processes. For example, Toyota has implemented AI-driven quality control systems that use real-time monitoring and predictive maintenance to ensure that products meet high standards. These systems can detect defects and anomalies early in the production process, allowing for immediate corrective actions and reducing the likelihood of faulty products reaching customers.

AI on Production Lines at Toyota:

Toyota, a global leader in the automotive industry, has long been recognized for its commitment to quality. To enhance its quality control processes, Toyota has integrated AI-driven systems that use real-time data from sensors installed on the production line. These systems continuously monitor various parameters, such as temperature, pressure, and vibration, to detect any anomalies that could indicate potential defects. By analyzing this data, the AI systems can predict when and where issues are likely to occur, allowing Toyota to take proactive measures to address them. This approach has significantly improved Toyota's ability to maintain high-quality standards, reduce waste, and increase customer satisfaction.

■ Driving Innovation with AI
AI fosters innovation within organizations by providing tools for rapid prototyping, testing, and iteration. Companies can use AI to accelerate the research and development (R&D) process, enabling them to bring new products and services to market more quickly. For example, Google has leveraged AI to develop innovative products such as Google Assistant and self-driving cars. AI-driven tools like generative design can create thousands of design options for new products, allowing companies to explore a wide range of possibilities and identify the most promising solutions.

AI at Google:
Google has been at the forefront of AI-driven innovation, using AI to develop groundbreaking products and services. One notable example is Google Assistant, an AI-powered virtual assistant that uses natural language processing and machine learning to understand and respond to user queries. Google Assistant can perform a wide range of tasks, from setting reminders to controlling smart home devices. Additionally, Google's self-driving car project, Waymo, uses AI to navigate complex road environments and make real-time driving decisions. These innovations demonstrate how AI can drive significant advancements in product development and create new market opportunities.

■ Boosting Customer Responsiveness with AI
AI plays a crucial role in enhancing customer service and engagement by enabling organizations to provide personalized experiences and instant support. AI-driven chatbots and virtual assistants can handle customer inquiries and resolve issues efficiently, improving response times and customer satisfaction. Companies like Sephora have used AI to enhance their customer engagement strategies, offering personalized recommendations and promotions based on customer preferences and behavior.

AI for Customer-Centricity at Sephora:
Sephora has successfully integrated AI into its customer engagement strategy through its AI-powered mobile app and in-store experiences. The app uses machine learning algorithms to analyze customer data, including purchase history and preferences, to provide personalized recommendations and promotions. For example, the app can suggest new

makeup products or skincare items based on a customer's past purchases and browsing behavior, and offer tailored discounts to encourage repeat purchases. Additionally, Sephora's AI-driven virtual artist feature allows customers to try on makeup virtually using augmented reality (AR) technology. These AI initiatives have helped Sephora enhance customer loyalty, improve customer satisfaction, and drive sales.

■ Achieving Efficiency with AI
AI can streamline operations and reduce costs by automating routine tasks, optimizing supply chains, and improving resource management. Organizations can use AI to identify inefficiencies and implement process improvements that drive cost savings. UPS, for example, has implemented AI-driven route optimization to reduce fuel consumption and delivery times, achieving significant efficiency gains.

Route Optimization with AI at UPS:
UPS has leveraged AI to optimize its delivery routes and improve operational efficiency. The company's AI-driven route optimization system, ORION (On-Road Integrated Optimization and Navigation), uses advanced algorithms to analyze data on package locations, traffic conditions, and delivery windows to determine the most efficient routes for drivers. By optimizing routes in real-time, ORION helps UPS reduce fuel consumption, lower emissions, and minimize delivery times. The system has reportedly saved the company millions of miles driven annually, resulting in significant cost savings and environmental benefits.

The intent here is not to suggest that AI should be excluded from strategy discussions at the highest levels, but to incorporate it into the right strategy discussions. When AI-enabled technologies are integrated into the functional-level of the strategy cascade, only then can AI deliver on its purpose. Only then can organizations enhance their competitive positioning, drive innovation, and achieve operational excellence. AI's ability to improve quality, foster innovation, boost customer responsiveness, and increase efficiency makes it a powerful tool for strategy deployment.

It is essential to recognize that AI is not a strategy in itself but a means to support and enhance strategic objectives at all levels of the organization. By leveraging AI effectively, organizations can navigate the complexities of the industry life cycle and achieve sustained success.

Chapter 12

Negotiating Your Strategy

Prelude

In this section, we will explore the concept of negotiation and its relevance to strategy. We will define negotiation as the process of reaching agreements through discussions and compromises between two or more parties. However, we will go beyond the traditional understanding of negotiation in the context of business deals or contracts and examine how negotiation applies to strategy development and implementation.

By viewing strategy as a negotiation, we recognize that strategic decisions involve trade-offs, conflicting interests, and the need to reconcile different perspectives within an organization. Strategy is not a static plan but an ongoing process of navigating dynamic environments, engaging stakeholders, and making choices that align with the organization's objectives.

The most important thing to understand here is that resources are not infinite and therefore, no organization can pursue all available strategic options to it....it must trade-off, and therefore, senior business leaders must negotiate with each other (and with external partners) over a limited amount of resources as they decide on trade-offs.

Even if trade-offs are not constrained by resources, the fact that trade-offs are pulled from different directions informs the need for some exchange and bargaining. Take the simple example of navigating a market growth strategy where senior

 DOI: 10.4324/9781003564133-15

business leaders are evaluating the regional options for expansion. It is likely that each region is led by a business leader. It is also likely that the organization does not have enough resources to expand in all regions simultaneously and at the same penetration levels.....so how is this handled? How does the organization make the necessary trade-offs to know where to expand and where not to expand? Certainly, many business planning and governance considerations are included in the analysis, negotiation should be one of them. It is a critical mechanism to enable an exchange.

To illustrate the art of negotiating strategy, we will draw parallels between the key elements of negotiation, such as understanding interests, exploring options, and finding common ground, and the strategic decision-making process. We will highlight how negotiation skills, such as effective communication, active listening, and problem-solving, can enhance strategy development and implementation.

In the context of this book, we are primarily concerned with the internal negotiations among senior business leaders as they navigate strategic options and decide on trade-offs and emphasize the importance of adopting a negotiation mindset when approaching strategy. This means recognizing that strategy is not a one-sided imposition but a collaborative process that requires engaging and aligning stakeholders, managing conflicting commitments, and finding win-win solutions that drive the organization's success.

The Art of Negotiation!

Negotiation is an essential skill in the business environment, enabling parties to reach agreements and make decisions in complex and dynamic situations. In the context of strategy development and deployment, negotiation plays a critical role in aligning interests, resolving conflicts, and making choices that drive organizational success. This section will provide an exploration of negotiation, its relevance in the business environment, and its indispensable role in the effective development and deployment of strategies.

Defining Negotiation

Negotiation is a process of communication and compromise between two or more parties with the goal of reaching mutually beneficial agreements. It involves a structured exchange of ideas, interests, and proposals to find common ground and resolve differences. Within a business context, negotiation encompasses both tangible aspects, such as price, terms, and conditions, as well as intangible elements, such as relationships, values, and long-term business objectives.

The Skillset of Negotiation

Successful negotiation requires a range of skills and qualities. Effective negotiators possess strong communication skills to articulate their perspectives and actively listen to the other parties' concerns. They are skilled in analyzing information, identifying underlying interests, and creatively generating options for mutual gain. Negotiators must also demonstrate empathy, emotional intelligence, and the ability to manage conflicts constructively.

The Criticality of Negotiation in Strategy

The essence of strategy lies in making choices and trade-offs to position an organization for success. And so, negotiation becomes paramount in the strategy process due to various reasons.

Resolving Conflicting Interests

Within organizations, different stakeholders have diverse interests, goals, and priorities. Strategic decisions often involve reconciling these conflicting interests to gain buy-in and build consensus. Negotiation helps business leaders navigate these differences, align perspectives, and forge a collective vision that supports the chosen strategic direction.

Managing External Relationships

Organizations operate in dynamic and interconnected environments where they interact with suppliers, customers, partners, and regulators. Negotiation skills enable business leaders to build and maintain fruitful relationships, negotiate favorable terms, and manage external stakeholders effectively. Negotiating alliances, contracts, and partnerships is crucial for securing resources, accessing new markets, and maximizing strategic opportunities.

Adapting to Uncertainty and Change

The business landscape is characterized by uncertainty, evolving market dynamics, and disruptive forces. Negotiation provides a flexible and adaptive approach to strategy by allowing organizations to respond to changing conditions. It facilitates the exploration of alternative options, the adjustment of strategic plans, and the renegotiation of contracts or agreements when circumstances demand it.

Leveraging Internal Expertise

Effective negotiation involves collaboration and drawing upon the expertise of diverse stakeholders within an organization. By involving employees, teams, and functional units in the strategy process, leaders tap into a wealth of knowledge and perspectives. Negotiation allows for inclusive decision-making, harnessing the collective intelligence and engagement of the organization to enhance strategy development and execution.

Google negotiating entry into the Chinese market:
When Google sought to enter the Chinese market, it faced complex challenges due to the country's regulatory environment and censorship requirements. Negotiations took place between Google's leadership and Chinese government officials to find a compromise that balanced Google's commitment to open access to information and China's concerns over censorship. The negotiation resulted in a limited version of Google's search engine operating in China.

Procter & Gamble' negotiating acquisition of Gillette:
In the merger between Procter & Gamble (P&G) and Gillette, negotiation played a vital role in aligning the interests of both companies. P&G negotiated the terms of the acquisition, including the exchange ratio, integration plans, and brand strategies. The negotiation process ensured that the merger created value for both parties, leading to the successful integration of Gillette's product portfolio into P&G's business.

Microsoft negotiating with software developers:
Microsoft's strategy of becoming a platform provider involved negotiations with software developers to build applications for its operating systems. By effectively negotiating partnership agreements, Microsoft secured the support and commitment of developers, ensuring a vibrant ecosystem of software applications that enhanced the value and competitiveness of its products.

Netflix negotiating amid shifting market landscape:
Netflix's evolution from a DVD-by-mail rental service to a streaming platform exemplifies the criticality of negotiation in strategic decision-making. In the early 2000s, as the market dynamics shifted toward digital streaming, Netflix recognized the need to adapt its business model. Through negotiation, Netflix secured licensing agreements with content providers to build a robust streaming library, negotiated with hardware manufacturers

to embed its service in devices, and negotiated partnerships with internet service providers to ensure smooth streaming experiences for its customers. These negotiations were instrumental in positioning Netflix as a dominant player in the streaming industry.

Regardless of the tier (or lens), negotiation is an indispensable skill for business leaders in the strategy development and deployment process. It enables the resolution of conflicting interests, the management of relationships, the adaptation to change, and the leverage of internal expertise. By embracing negotiation as a fundamental aspect of strategy, organizations can make informed decisions, achieve alignment, and navigate complex business environments effectively.

In the dynamic and complex business environment, strategy serves as the compass that guides organizations toward their goals. At its core, strategy is about making choices and trade-offs to position an organization for success. However, the ability to make effective strategic choices is contingent upon the organization's understanding and response to the signals emitted by the macroenvironment. This section will examine the critical role of negotiation in the strategy process, specifically in the context of choosing between signals from the macroenvironment. By examining the rationale and justifications for negotiation in strategic decision-making, we can appreciate its paramount importance and the value it brings to organizations.

The Essence of Strategy: Making Choices and Trade-Offs

■ The essence of strategy lies in the art of making choices and trade-offs. Organizations operate in a dynamic and uncertain business landscape where numerous opportunities and challenges emerge from the macroenvironment. These signals can be in the form of technological advancements, shifting consumer preferences, regulatory changes, or competitive disruptions. Successful strategic decision-making requires organizations to evaluate and prioritize these signals, allocating resources and efforts to seize opportunities and mitigate risks. However, this process of making choices necessitates negotiation as a critical tool to navigate the inherent complexities.

Negotiation as the Key to Navigating the Macroenvironment

■ The macroenvironment presents organizations with a multitude of signals, each vying for attention and resources. However, organizations cannot respond to every signal simultaneously. They must carefully assess and prioritize the signals that align with their strategic direction and capabilities.

This is where negotiation comes into play, enabling organizations to negotiate internally and externally to effectively choose between signals and make strategic trade-offs.

Negotiating Internally: Alignment and Resource Allocation

■ Internally, negotiation facilitates alignment among various stakeholders within the organization. Different functional units, teams, and individuals may have divergent perspectives and priorities. Negotiation brings these parties together to reach a consensus on strategic choices and trade-offs. Through negotiation, organizations ensure that resources are allocated to initiatives that best align with the organization's capabilities, goals, and values.

Negotiating Externally: Engaging the Macroenvironment

■ Externally, negotiation allows organizations to engage with the macroenvironment and negotiate with external stakeholders. Organizations negotiate with suppliers, customers, partners, and regulators to leverage opportunities, manage risks, and align interests. For example, negotiating contracts with suppliers helps organizations secure favorable terms, negotiate strategic partnerships, and navigate regulatory requirements. These negotiations enable organizations to access resources, gain market advantages, and effectively respond to the signals emitted by the macroenvironment.

In the strategy process, negotiation becomes paramount as organizations navigate the signals emitted by the macroenvironment and make choices and trade-offs. By effectively negotiating internally and externally, organizations align stakeholders, allocate resources strategically, and engage with the macroenvironment to seize opportunities and mitigate risks. Negotiation enables organizations to adapt to changing circumstances, capitalize on emerging trends, and position themselves for long-term success. By embracing negotiation as a core component of strategy development and deployment, organizations can navigate the complexities of the macroenvironment and make informed choices that propel them toward their desired outcomes.

Failing to negotiate your strategy, the pain of conflicting commitments

Negotiation plays a pivotal role in the effective development and deployment of strategies. However, failing to negotiate the strategy can have dire consequences for organizations. This section will examine the risks and consequences of failing to negotiate the strategy, specifically focusing on conflicting commitments, inefficient resource allocation, and overdiversification. By exploring these risks, we can understand the importance of negotiation in aligning strategic direction, optimizing resource allocation, and avoiding detrimental outcomes.

- ■ Risk 1: Conflicting Commitments and Misalignment in Strategic Direction
  - – Failing to negotiate the strategy can lead to conflicting commitments among different stakeholders within an organization. Each business unit or functional team may have its own priorities, objectives, and strategies, which can result in misalignment and lack of coherence in the overall strategic direction. This misalignment can lead to suboptimal decision-making and hinder organizational success.
    - • Example: Consider a multinational corporation with multiple business units operating in different regions. If each business unit pursues its own strategy without negotiation and alignment with the overarching corporate strategy, it can result in inconsistent branding, conflicting customer experiences, and inefficient use of resources. The lack of negotiation and coordination in strategic decision-making can create a fragmented organization, hampering its ability to compete effectively in the market.
- ■ Risk 2: Inefficient Allocation of Resources
  - – Effective negotiation is essential for optimizing resource allocation within an organization. Without negotiation, resources may be allocated haphazardly or based on individual preferences rather than strategic priorities. This inefficient allocation of resources can lead to missed opportunities, suboptimal performance, and reduced organizational effectiveness.
    - • Example: Consider a company that fails to negotiate resource allocation among its various business units. Each unit competes internally for investment, resulting in a siloed approach where units prioritize their own initiatives without considering the broader organizational goals. This lack of negotiation and coordination can lead to an imbalance in resource allocation, with some units receiving disproportionate funding while others struggle to achieve their objectives. Consequently, the organization may fail to leverage its full potential and may not effectively respond to market dynamics.
- ■ Risk 3: Overdiversification and Loss of Focus
  - – Negotiation plays a crucial role in strategic decision-making by helping organizations strike a balance between diversification and focus.

Without effective negotiation, organizations may fall victim to overdiversification, spreading their resources and efforts too thin across multiple initiatives or markets. This can lead to a loss of focus, diluted competitive advantage, and decreased organizational performance.

- Take the example of a consumer goods company that fails to negotiate its expansion strategy. The company ventures into numerous unrelated markets without careful consideration and coordination. As a result, it struggles to maintain its core competencies, loses its competitive edge, and fails to achieve sustainable growth. The lack of negotiation in defining the boundaries of diversification can stretch the organization's resources and hinder its ability to excel in any particular market.

Negotiation in strategic trade-offs is not about winning or losing but about collaboration and consensus-building. Business leaders must foster an environment of open dialogue and constructive debate where diverse perspectives are valued. By engaging stakeholders in the decision-making process, leaders can build consensus around trade-offs and ensure that decisions are implemented effectively.

A Special Note on the Importance of Communication on Strategy Effectiveness

Failing to articulate a clear strategy can have a significant impact on communication within the organization. Effective communication is crucial for successful strategy development and deployment, and its breakdown due to a lack of negotiation can lead to various challenges and consequences. When strategy is not effectively negotiated and communicated, there can be a lack of clarity and understanding among stakeholders. Without a shared understanding of the strategic direction, goals, and priorities, individuals may have different interpretations, leading to confusion, misunderstandings, and conflicting actions. This can hinder collaboration, coordination, and effective execution. For example, if the corporate-level strategy is not properly negotiated and communicated to business units, employees may have differing perspectives on the organization's priorities and how their work aligns with the overall strategy. This can result in disjointed efforts, duplication of work, and a lack of synergy among teams.

Additionally, an ill-communicated strategy can also perpetuate silos within the organization. Business units or functional teams may focus on their own objectives and fail to communicate and share information with others, leading to isolated decision-making and limited collaboration. In the absence of clarity around strategy, each unit may develop its own communication channels and methods, resulting in fragmented communication networks. This can hinder the flow of information, impede knowledge sharing, and limit the organization's ability to respond quickly to emerging opportunities or challenges.

Most importantly, effective communication on strategy involves seeking input and feedback from various stakeholders. When communication is overlooked, important voices and perspectives may be excluded from the strategy development process. This can result in a lack of diverse insights, missed opportunities for innovation, and decreased employee engagement. For instance, if functional-level strategies are not communicated with employees at appropriate levels and roles, valuable insights and ideas may be overlooked. Employees may feel disconnected from the strategy and become disengaged, leading to reduced motivation and lower productivity.

In terms of stakeholders, their involvement is critical to the success of the strategy process. So failing to include them can lead to resistance and opposition to the strategy. Without open communication channels, employees may feel excluded from decision-making, leading to skepticism, resistance, and a lack of commitment to the strategic direction.

When individuals do not feel heard or valued, they may become resistant to change, hinder strategy implementation, or actively work against the proposed initiatives. This can create a toxic work environment and impede the organization's ability to adapt and thrive. To mitigate the impact on communication and foster effective communication within the organization, it is crucial to prioritize negotiation as an integral part of the strategy development process.

So what does that mean? It means:

■ Establishing Open Communication Channels: Encourage open and transparent communication throughout the organization. Create forums for dialogue, feedback, and information sharing to ensure that all stakeholders have a voice and are kept informed about strategic decisions.

■ Seeking Input and Feedback: Actively seek input and feedback from employees at all levels and functions. Engage in meaningful discussions, listen to diverse perspectives, and incorporate valuable insights into the strategy development process.

■ Clarifying Expectations and Roles: Clearly communicate the strategic direction, goals, and priorities to ensure everyone understands their roles and responsibilities. Provide regular updates and share progress toward strategic objectives to maintain alignment and motivate employees.

■ Encouraging Collaboration and Cross-Functional Communication: Foster a culture of collaboration and cross-functional communication. Break down silos and encourage teams to work together, share knowledge, and collaborate on initiatives that drive the overall strategy forward.

■ By prioritizing effective communication and integrating negotiation into the strategy development process, organizations can overcome the communication challenges associated with a lack of negotiation and foster a collaborative, aligned, and engaged workforce.

Failing to communicate the strategy can have severe consequences for organizations. Conflicting commitments can lead to misalignment in strategic direction, inefficient resource allocation, and overdiversification, jeopardizing organizational success. Effective communication is essential in aligning stakeholder interests, optimizing resource allocation, and maintaining strategic focus. By recognizing the risks associated with failing to negotiate, organizations can prioritize negotiation as a core competency and drive their strategies toward long-term success.

Apple negotiating strategy for market expansion

In the early 2000s, Apple faced a critical strategic decision when considering its market expansion. At that time, Apple was primarily known for its Macintosh computers but desired to diversify its product offerings and compete in new markets.

The negotiation process within Apple involved discussions among top executives, including Steve Jobs, who played a pivotal role in shaping the company's strategic direction. The negotiation centered around two primary options: expanding into the mobile phone market or focusing on improving the existing product lines.

The conflicting commitments within the organization emerged between the product development team, advocating for enhancing the Macintosh line, and a group of executives who believed in the potential of entering the mobile phone market. During the negotiation process, the team led by Steve Jobs recognized the importance of tapping into the growing mobile phone industry. They understood that embracing innovation in the mobile market would enable Apple to reach a wider customer base and drive substantial growth. This perspective clashed with the traditional focus on improving Macintosh computers. Through intensive negotiations and analysis of market trends, Apple decided to enter the mobile phone market with the introduction of the revolutionary iPhone in 2007. This strategic move required significant investments in research and development, supply chain management, and marketing.

The negotiation process involved trade-offs and compromises. Apple had to balance the resources allocated to the Macintosh line while dedicating substantial investments to the development and marketing of the iPhone. This negotiation process led to the strategic decision of entering the mobile phone market while maintaining a commitment to ongoing innovation in the Macintosh line. The introduction of the iPhone proved to be a game-changer for Apple, propelling the company to unprecedented success. It allowed Apple to expand its market presence beyond computers and enter the lucrative world of smartphones. The negotiation process enabled Apple to reconcile conflicting commitments, aligning the organization's resources, and driving its strategic direction toward market expansion and innovation.

Amazon negotiating strategy for market dominance

Amazon, founded by Jeff Bezos in 1994, started as an online bookstore but quickly expanded its product offerings to become a global e-commerce giant. Over the years, Amazon faced strategic decisions related to its growth and market dominance. One significant strategic negotiation for Amazon was its entry into the cloud computing market with Amazon Web Services (AWS). Initially, AWS was developed as an internal infrastructure service to support Amazon's e-commerce operations. However, recognizing the potential of cloud computing, Amazon executives engaged in strategic negotiations to transform AWS into a separate business unit.

The negotiation process involved discussions among key stakeholders, including Jeff Bezos and other top executives. Conflicting commitments emerged between those who believed AWS should remain an internal support function and those who saw the opportunity to offer cloud computing services to external customers. Through extensive negotiations, Amazon decided to open AWS to external customers, transforming it into a leading provider of cloud infrastructure services. This strategic move required significant investments in data centers, technology infrastructure, and talent acquisition.

The negotiation process within Amazon involved addressing concerns about potential risks and conflicts with the existing e-commerce business. Trade-offs were made, and compromises were reached to ensure the success of AWS while maintaining a focus on Amazon's core e-commerce operations. The decision to expand into cloud computing through AWS proved to be strategically advantageous for Amazon. AWS grew rapidly and became a major revenue generator for the company, powering numerous websites and applications worldwide. The negotiation process allowed Amazon to reconcile conflicting commitments, adapt to market trends, and strategically position itself in the rapidly evolving technology landscape.

Microsoft negotiating strategy for cloud transformation

Microsoft Corporation, a global technology company, underwent a strategic transformation in response to changing industry dynamics and evolving customer needs. One significant strategic negotiation for Microsoft was its shift toward cloud-based services and the development of Microsoft Azure. As the technology landscape shifted toward cloud computing, Microsoft faced the challenge of adapting its business model to remain competitive. The negotiation process within Microsoft involved discussions among top executives, including Satya Nadella, who assumed the role of CEO in 2014. The negotiation centered around the company's strategic direction, particularly its cloud transformation. Conflicting commitments emerged between the traditional software licensing business and the emerging cloud computing market. The software licensing model had been the core revenue driver for Microsoft, while the cloud offered new opportunities for growth and innovation.

Through a series of negotiations, Microsoft made a strategic decision to invest heavily in cloud-based services and develop Microsoft Azure as its cloud computing platform. This move required significant investments in data centers, infrastructure, and talent to compete with other major players in the industry. The negotiation process involved addressing concerns about potential risks and challenges associated with the transition to the cloud. Trade-offs were made, and compromises were reached to ensure a successful transformation while maintaining the existing software licensing business.

The decision to embrace the cloud and develop Microsoft Azure proved to be a pivotal strategic move for the company. Microsoft successfully established itself as a leader in the cloud computing market, offering a comprehensive suite of cloud services to businesses worldwide. The negotiation process enabled Microsoft to reconcile conflicting commitments, adapt to changing market trends, and strategically position itself for long-term success in the digital era.

Lesson from a leader

Satya Nadella

One example of a business leader who successfully negotiated a strategy that benefited the organization is Satya Nadella, the CEO of Microsoft. When Nadella took over as CEO in 2014, Microsoft was facing challenges in adapting to the changing technology landscape and competition from companies like Apple and

Google. Under Nadella's leadership, Microsoft underwent a significant transformation, driven by a well-negotiated strategy. Nadella recognized the need for Microsoft to shift its focus from a primarily Windows-centric approach to a more inclusive and cloud-oriented strategy. He negotiated a new strategic direction that embraced cloud computing and services, expanding Microsoft's offerings beyond traditional software products. This shift was evident in the introduction of initiatives like Microsoft Azure, a cloud computing platform, and Office 365, a cloud-based productivity suite.

Nadella's negotiation of this new strategy involved multiple aspects. Firstly, he initiated a cultural change within the organization, fostering a growth mindset and encouraging collaboration among teams. This helped break down internal silos and fostered a more innovative and agile work environment. Secondly, Nadella negotiated strategic partnerships and acquisitions to strengthen Microsoft's position in key areas. One notable example is the acquisition of LinkedIn in 2016, which expanded Microsoft's presence in the professional networking and social media space.

Lastly, Nadella negotiated a shift in Microsoft's approach to software development, emphasizing a cloud-first, mobile-first strategy. This involved making Microsoft's products and services available across multiple platforms and devices, catering to the evolving needs of consumers and businesses. The successful negotiation of this strategy has had a profound impact on Microsoft's performance and market position. Under Nadella's leadership, Microsoft's market value has more than tripled, and the company has experienced significant growth in its cloud computing business, competing effectively with industry leaders like Amazon Web Services.

Chapter 13

Strategy Imperative: Thought Leadership, Blue Ocean, and Innovation

Defining the Term: Strategy Imperative

The strategy imperative is a fundamental concept that drives the direction and decision-making of organizations, aligning their efforts with core values, mission, and vision. It represents the critical and non-negotiable aspects of an organization's strategy that are essential for achieving its long-term goals and maintaining its competitive advantage in the market.

At its core, the strategy imperative serves as a guiding principle, directing the organization's actions and resource allocation toward its strategic objectives. It embodies the principles, values, and strategic priorities that an organization must adhere to, regardless of changing market conditions or competitive landscapes. The strategy imperative aligns with the core values and mission of an organization by acting as a north star, ensuring that every decision, initiative, and effort taken by the organization is in harmony with its fundamental purpose and principles. It serves as a strategic compass, keeping the organization on course and preventing it from straying into areas that may compromise its mission or values.

For example, let's consider a well-known tech company, Google. One of Google's core values is to focus on the user and provide the best possible user

DOI: 10.4324/9781003564133-16

experience. This value is embedded in Google's strategy imperative, driving its decision-making process at all levels of the organization. Every product, feature, or service Google develops is assessed against this imperative to ensure it enhances the user experience. This strategic alignment has not only resulted in Google's dominance in the search engine market but has also allowed the company to diversify successfully into other areas such as advertising, cloud services, and hardware.

The strategy imperative's influence on strategic decision-making is evident throughout an organization's hierarchy. From the C-suite to front-line employees, all individuals are guided by the same strategic priorities, ensuring coherence and synergy in their actions. For instance, consider a global retail chain with a strategy imperative to expand into emerging markets and cater to the needs of a diverse customer base. This imperative will inform the C-suite's decisions regarding market entry, product assortment, and pricing strategies. Simultaneously, store managers will be directed to tailor their inventory and marketing efforts to meet the specific demands of local customers. The strategy imperative fosters a cohesive approach to decision-making across the organization, enabling it to penetrate new markets effectively.

Moreover, the strategy imperative serves as a critical framework for evaluating and prioritizing strategic initiatives. When faced with various growth opportunities, organizations can use their strategy imperative as a lens to identify and pursue projects that align most closely with their core values and long-term goals. By prioritizing these initiatives, the organization ensures efficient resource allocation and prevents the diversion of focus on non-essential activities. To exemplify this, let's examine a healthcare organization with a strategy imperative to leverage cutting-edge medical technology to improve patient outcomes. When presented with different investment opportunities, such as expanding hospital facilities or implementing advanced robotic surgery systems, the organization would prioritize the latter, as it aligns more closely with its strategy imperative. This prioritization ensures that resources are channeled toward initiatives that directly contribute to the organization's mission and strategic objectives.

The strategy imperative is a function of thought leadership, blue ocean, and innovation due to their inherent characteristics and their interplay in driving successful organizational strategies. Let's define each term and then make logical arguments to propose their relationship as part of the strategy imperative.

Thought Leadership

Thought leadership refers to the ability of an organization or individual to provide innovative and insightful perspectives, ideas, and solutions that challenge conventional thinking and shape the industry's direction. Thought leaders are recognized for their expertise and influence in a particular domain. Incorporating thought leadership into the strategic imperative is essential for organizations aiming to thrive in an increasingly competitive landscape. The following logical arguments illustrate the significance of thought leadership in shaping strategy and driving organizational success:

a. Driving Innovation: Thought leadership stimulates innovative thinking and encourages organizations to challenge the status quo. By fostering a culture of thought leadership, organizations are more likely to generate groundbreaking ideas that lead to competitive advantage and market differentiation.

b. Building Credibility: Thought leadership enhances an organization's credibility and reputation as an industry expert. This credibility attracts customers, partners, and top talent, creating a virtuous cycle of success.

c. Navigating Complexity: In today's complex and dynamic business landscape, thought leadership provides organizations with the intellectual tools to navigate uncertainties and adapt proactively to market changes. It enables them to anticipate challenges and capitalize on emerging opportunities.

Blue Ocean Strategy

Blue ocean strategy involves creating uncontested market space by offering unique value propositions that diverge from traditional competition. It encourages organizations to explore new market segments and untapped opportunities instead of competing in crowded and highly competitive red oceans. Integrating Blue Ocean Strategy into the strategy imperative is vital for organizations seeking to innovate and thrive beyond traditional competitive boundaries. The following logical arguments highlight the importance of this integration in shaping effective strategies and driving sustained growth:

a. Market Differentiation: Blue ocean strategy drives organizations to differentiate their offerings, focusing on unique value drivers that set them apart from competitors. This differentiation allows companies to attract new customers and command premium pricing.

b. Sustainable Growth: By identifying and developing blue ocean opportunities, organizations can achieve sustainable growth and avoid the pitfalls of competing solely on price or features. Creating new market space allows for long-term growth even in mature industries.

c. Minimizing Competition: Embracing blue ocean strategy reduces the direct competition an organization faces, as it shifts its focus away from red oceans where competition is fierce. This reduces the pressure on pricing and allows for healthier profit margins.

Innovation

Innovation refers to the creation and implementation of novel ideas, processes, products, or services that deliver value to customers and drive organizational growth. The role of innovation in shaping organizational strategy cannot be overstated. By fostering a culture that prioritizes creative thinking and the development of new ideas, organizations position themselves to navigate challenges and seize opportunities. Below are compelling reasons for integrating innovation into the strategy imperative:

    a. Adapting to Change: Innovation is vital for organizations to adapt to rapidly changing market conditions, disruptive technologies, and evolving customer preferences. It enables organizations to stay relevant and thrive in a dynamic business environment.

    b. Continuous Improvement: Incorporating innovation into the strategy imperative promotes a culture of continuous improvement. It encourages organizations to seek better ways of doing things, refining processes, and enhancing customer experiences.

    c. Future-Proofing: Innovation is essential for future-proofing an organization. It enables companies to anticipate and respond to emerging trends, ensuring their relevance and success in the long term.

The Dynamics among Thought Leadership, Blue Ocean Strategy, and Innovation

The interplay among thought leadership, blue ocean strategy, and innovation is critical for the strategy imperative because thought leadership drives the generation of innovative ideas and concepts, inspiring the creation of blue ocean strategies that differentiate organizations in new market spaces. Blue ocean strategy, in turn, requires innovative thinking to identify and execute unique value propositions that lead to uncontested market spaces. Innovation fuels thought leadership, as organizations that continually innovate are more likely to establish themselves as industry thought leaders.

Thought leadership encourages a forward-thinking approach that embraces innovation and the pursuit of blue ocean strategies, setting the foundation for long-term success. In summary, the strategy imperative encompasses thought leadership, blue ocean strategy, and innovation as essential components of successful strategic decision-making. By embracing these elements, organizations can foster a culture of continuous improvement, differentiate themselves in the market, and adapt proactively to changing business landscapes. The interplay among thought leadership, blue ocean strategy, and innovation is a powerful force that drives the strategy imperative and positions organizations for sustainable growth and competitive advantage.

CASE STUDY: THOUGHT LEADERSHIP AND INNOVATION

Introduction

Strategy involves creating a unique and valuable position by making trade-offs and executing activities differently than rivals. This process is fundamentally an organizational challenge, making the development and reestablishment of strategies a leadership function. This inherent connection between strategy and leadership highlights the varying effectiveness of different leadership styles based on the strategic context. Innovation, the creation of new ideas, necessitates a specific form of leadership known as thought leadership, which is crucial for organizational success. Given the power of ideas to transform thinking, innovation and thought leadership become key differentiators enabling organizations to achieve their strategic positions in competitive environments. This paper emphasizes the importance of thought leadership in developing strategies geared toward innovation, addressing leaders and strategic managers to ensure the presence of thought leadership capacity for effective innovation strategies.

Thought Leadership

Thought leadership is a significant departure from traditional leadership, characterized as "the championing of new ideas rather than anything to do with managing people or helping a group achieve a goal" (McCrimmon, 2005, p. 1064). Thought leaders "inspire leadership; they ignite imaginations, explode old myths, and illuminate paths to the future that others can follow" (Butler, 2012, p. 1). Traditional leadership, which varies in style from charismatic to altruistic and transformational, involves authority over others and is essential for organizational structure. In contrast, thought leadership does not require managing others and is vital where innovation is crucial for organizational success (McCrimmon, 2005). Therefore, thought leadership should be integral to an organizational structure focused on innovation. McCrimmon (2005) identifies key characteristics of thought leadership, describing it as the promotion of new ideas rather than a role or position. Thought leadership qualities can be exhibited by non-managerial employees with revolutionary mindsets capable of championing new ideas. Thought leadership is egalitarian, ephemeral, non-hierarchical, and not easily monopolized. Unlike traditional leadership, which persists for the organization's life, thought leadership begins with a new idea and ends when the idea is ready for implementation, after which the thought leader moves on to champion other new ideas.

Innovation

Core competencies are essential for organizational performance and success (Goddard, 1997; Duysters & Hagedoorn, 2000). Despite variations in competencies based on organizational structure, innovation is a universally necessary core competence (Drucker, 1995a, 1995b). Innovation, a learned behavior (Dyer, Gregersen, & Clayton, 2011a; Dyer, Gregersen, & Christensen, 2011b), is a metric reflecting a company's growth prospects (Eccles, 1991). Broadly, innovation is an organization's inner capability, not limited to product or technology, optimizing new value propositions in processes, products, or business methods. Innovation spans disciplines including service, design, process, approach, methodology, or offering. A global organization defines innovation as creative thinking and developing new ideas, technologies, and processes to create differentiated products (Alhaddi, 2013). Extensive literature links innovation with leadership and strategy (Battistella, Biotto, & Toni, 2012; Stowe & Grider, 2014; Chalhoub, 2010; Innovation & Leadership, 2008). Consensus in the literature supports innovation as a driver for growth and positively impacts organizational performance. Consequently, organizations recognize the necessity of innovation for success in a global competitive environment (Chalhoub, 2010), elevating innovation as a top priority for executive leadership (Innovation & Leadership, 2008). Integrating innovation into strategic planning as a core value ensures long-term success (Alhaddi, 2013).

Innovation and Thought Leadership: A Duo

Research indicates a strong connection between thought leadership and innovation (Butler, 2012; McCrimmon, 2005). While similar, they are distinct; thought leadership is based on innovation. Innovation creates new ideas, and thought leadership champions them until ready for implementation. Once a new idea is accepted, traditional leadership ensures its successful implementation through project and operations management.

The cycle begins with an innovator creating a new idea. A thought leader then champions the idea until organizational acceptance, leading to the implementation phase overseen by traditional leadership through effective resource allocation. Drawing from literature, innovation and thought leadership are inseparable. Alhaddi (2013) demonstrated a strong connection between thought leadership and innovation in a global organization (Johnson Controls), where innovation was a strategic priority for long-term success. The analysis showed that the organization drives innovation through thought leadership, differentiating it from rivals and enabling it to achieve its strategic position. Johnson Controls defined thought leaders as innovators anticipating needs and proactively designing and providing solutions, a critical concept spanning multiple operational spaces.

Additionally, Chalhoub (2010) highlighted the cultural requirement of thought leadership and innovation in a global competitive environment. His theoretical framework for innovation drivers included dimensions like thought leadership, entrepreneurial culture, participative management style, performance evaluation criteria, and compensation mechanisms driving innovation and influencing organizational performance. Although significant research on integrating thought leadership into strategy is lacking, scholars have extended research on innovation in strategy literature. Stowe and Grider (2014) discussed strategies for advancing organizational innovation, suggesting that organizations should integrate innovation into strategies to cultivate a creative culture. Other research recommended developing strategies to embed innovation into organizational structures to establish an innovative culture foundation (Innovation & Leadership, 2008).

Practical Implementations for Organizations

Building on recent research and literature, this paper suggests practical recommendations for integrating thought leadership into innovation strategies at the organizational level. Addressing executive leaders and strategic managers, these recommendations aim to foster innovation and thought leadership as competitive advantages.

Foster a Culture of Innovation: Executive leaders should cultivate an organizational culture that promotes innovation and creative thinking. By raising awareness of innovation's critical role in organizational success, employees across functions will be inspired to think creatively. Promoting innovation through employee recognition, award systems, and compensation incentives can turn the entire workforce into an innovative engine.

Integrate Innovation and Thought Leadership into the Business Model: As the benefits of innovation and thought leadership become evident, strategists should incorporate them deeply into the business model.

Practitioners in strategic planning, communications, and human resources should develop strategies using innovation driven by thought leadership as a competitive advantage. For example, include the novelty and originality of ideas in the decision-making process for funding new investments.

Use Innovation and Thought Leadership as a Differentiation Strategy: Extensive literature shows a positive relationship between differentiation and organizational performance. Differentiation allows organizations to gain enduring advantages, improving performance over time (Razak & Llias, 2011; Heikkurinen, 2010; Tripathy, 2006). Leaders and strategists are advised to use the innovation-thought leadership duo as a differentiation strategy. Develop strategies targeting specific talent, customers, and stakeholders, and promote innovation and thought leadership in marketing campaigns to differentiate the organization from rivals, especially in a global competitive environment.

Chapter 14

Leadership Consideration: Ambidexterity

Defining the Term: Ambidextrous Leadership

In the dynamic landscape of business, leaders are continually challenged to steer their organizations through the complexities of changing industry dynamics. As we conclude this comprehensive journey through the intricacies of strategy across the industry life cycle, we examine an essential leadership consideration: ambidexterity. In this final chapter, we explore how organizational leaders can embrace ambidexterity to effectively navigate the shifting phases of the industry life cycle.

Defining Ambidexterity

Ambidexterity in the organizational context refers to the capability of an organization to balance and excel in both exploratory and exploitative activities simultaneously. Exploitative activities focus on refining and optimizing existing processes, products, and operations, while exploratory activities involve experimentation, innovation, and the pursuit of new opportunities. Ambidextrous organizations are adept at managing this duality, enabling them to adapt to changing circumstances, remain competitive, and drive growth.

Ambidexterity and Industry Life Cycle Phases

As organizations traverse the industry life cycle phases—embryonic, growth, shakeout, maturity, and decline—the demands on leadership evolve significantly. The application of ambidexterity becomes particularly relevant as companies transition between these phases.

1. Ambidexterity in the Embryonic Phase: In the embryonic phase of an industry's life cycle, innovation and differentiation are paramount. This phase is characterized by uncertainty, as new ideas and market opportunities are explored. Ambidextrous leadership in this phase involves finding a delicate balance between fostering innovation and managing the inherent risks associated with untested concepts.

   Leaders must create an environment that encourages experimentation and risk-taking. Teams need the freedom to explore novel ideas, which can lead to groundbreaking products or services. For instance, when the smartphone industry was in its embryonic phase, Apple's leader, Steve Jobs, embraced ambidexterity by fostering a culture of innovation. The creation of the iPhone revolutionized the industry, proving the power of an ambidextrous approach.

2. Ambidexterity in the Growth Phase: As industry transitions into the growth phase, the challenge for leaders shifts to scaling operations while continuing to innovate. Ambidextrous leadership during this phase necessitates the management of existing operations for efficiency and the pursuit of new opportunities for expansion.

   Amazon's growth phase is a prime example of ambidexterity in action. While expanding its online retail operations, the company invested heavily in new ventures like Amazon Web Services (AWS). This diversification allowed Amazon to capitalize on its infrastructure expertise, extending its market reach and becoming a leader in cloud computing.

3. Ambidexterity in the Shakeout Phase: In the shakeout phase, heightened competition forces leaders to differentiate their organizations while ensuring operational efficiency. Ambidextrous leadership involves finding innovative ways to streamline processes and simultaneously offering unique value to customers.

   Netflix's transition from a DVD rental service to a streaming platform exemplifies this approach. As competitors emerged, Netflix focused on optimizing its streaming services while investing in original content. This strategic ambidexterity enabled the company to navigate the shakeout phase successfully.

4. Ambidexterity in the Maturity Phase: The maturity phase calls for maintaining the status quo while exploring avenues for continued growth. Ambidextrous leadership requires optimizing core operations while diversifying into related markets or introducing new products.

   Procter & Gamble (P&G) demonstrates this ambidextrous approach by consistently innovating within its core product lines while expanding into new areas. P&G's acquisition of Gillette allowed the company to enter the shaving industry, diversifying its offerings and extending its maturity phase.

5. Ambidexterity in the Decline Phase: Even during industry decline, ambidextrous leadership has relevance. Leaders must allocate resources wisely, optimizing operations while identifying innovative strategies to extend the organization's lifespan or facilitate a graceful exit.

   Eastman Kodak's experience serves as a cautionary tale. Amidst the decline of film photography, Kodak failed to fully embrace digital photography and diversify its offerings. The absence of ambidextrous leadership hindered Kodak's ability to adapt to market changes and resulted in a decline from industry prominence.

Ambidextrous Leadership Across Three Tiers of Strategy

Ambidextrous leadership, the ability to balance and integrate opposing strategic directions, is not limited to a single level of strategy within an organization. Rather, it manifests across the three tiers of strategy: corporate, business, and functional. In each tier, organizations grapple with different, and sometimes conflicting, strategic objectives. Here's how ambidextrous leadership plays out at each level.

Corporate-Level Strategy: Balancing Growth and Business Model

At the corporate-level, ambidextrous leadership involves balancing growth initiatives with the optimization of the overall business model. Organizations must decide between pursuing growth by entering new markets, diversifying, or acquiring other companies, while simultaneously ensuring that the existing business operations remain efficient and profitable.

For example, consider Google's parent company, Alphabet Inc. While Alphabet explores moonshot projects like self-driving cars and advanced AI research for future growth, it simultaneously maintains Google's core business of online advertising and search engine dominance. This ambidextrous approach allows Google to experiment with innovative ideas while capitalizing on its established revenue streams.

Business-Level Strategy: Coordinating Differentiation and Cost Leadership

At the business-level, ambidextrous leadership involves coordinating two seemingly contradictory strategies: differentiation and cost leadership. Organizations must differentiate their products or services to stand out in the market, while simultaneously optimizing operational efficiency to reduce costs.

Apple's approach exemplifies this ambidexterity. While offering premium-priced, innovative products that are differentiated from competitors, Apple also focuses on cost optimization through efficient supply chain management and manufacturing processes. The seamless integration of these two strategies positions Apple as a leader in both innovation and profitability.

Functional-Level Strategy: Juggling Building Blocks

Functional-level strategy involves optimizing competitive advantages in four areas: quality, innovation, customer responsiveness, and efficiency. Ambidextrous leadership in this tier entails balancing the emphasis on these building blocks based on the organization's strategic priorities and the current industry context.

Toyota demonstrates this ambidextrous approach. The company is renowned for its quality-driven production system, but it also places a strong emphasis on innovation and efficiency. Toyota continuously refines its production processes while investing in R&D for hybrid and electric vehicles, showcasing its ability to manage diverse functional strategies cohesively.

In essence, ambidextrous leadership at all three tiers of strategy requires organizations to reconcile seemingly opposing objectives. It's about recognizing that each level has distinct challenges and goals, and the success lies in finding the delicate equilibrium between them. Successful organizations embrace ambidextrous leadership to adapt, innovate, and thrive across the dynamic landscape of corporate, business, and functional strategies.

Strategic Implications of Ambidextrous Leadership

Ambidextrous leadership has several strategic implications that align with the distinct characteristics of each industry life cycle phase. By embracing ambidexterity, leaders can:

- Mitigate Risk: Navigating the complexities of different phases requires a combination of risk-taking and risk-averse strategies. Ambidextrous leaders can make informed decisions based on a comprehensive understanding of their organization's capabilities and the external environment.
- Promote Agility: Ambidextrous leadership promotes agility by enabling organizations to adapt swiftly to changing market conditions. This flexibility is essential in all industry life cycle phases but becomes especially critical during periods of disruption.
- Foster Innovation: The exploration aspect of ambidexterity encourages a culture of innovation that fuels a company's ability to thrive in the long term. This is crucial in the embryonic and growth phases where pioneering ideas can set the foundation for future success.
- Ensure Sustainability: The exploitation side of ambidexterity focuses on optimizing current operations. This approach is crucial for maintaining stability during the maturity and decline phases, allowing the organization to efficiently manage resources and extend its lifespan.
- Enhance Competitive Advantage: Ambidextrous organizations are better equipped to differentiate themselves from competitors, ensuring they remain relevant even in fiercely competitive markets.

CASE STUDY: AMBIDEXTROUS LEADERSHIP AT JOHNSON & JOHNSON

Introduction

The world is experiencing a transformative era characterized by the convergence of physical, digital, and biological technologies. This period, known as the Fourth Industrial Revolution, is defined by rapid advancements and the blurring of boundaries between different domains. Unlike the previous industrial revolutions, which were driven by mechanization, electrification, and information technology, the fourth industrial revolution is fueled by artificial intelligence (AI), the Internet of Things (IoT), robotics, and biotechnology. These changes are reshaping industries and creating new opportunities and challenges for organizations.

Johnson & Johnson (J&J), a global leader in healthcare and pharmaceuticals, is navigating this complex landscape through ambidextrous leadership. By balancing the optimization of its core business with the exploration of innovative solutions, J&J is positioning itself at the forefront of the digital and biological transformation. This case study explores J&J's ambidextrous leadership approach, focusing on its strategic alignment, parallelism, and management of creative conflict.

Ambidextrous Organizations

Ambidextrous organizations excel at managing two distinct but complementary activities: exploitation and exploration. Exploitation involves refining and enhancing existing capabilities, while exploration entails pursuing new opportunities and innovations. This dual focus is crucial for organizations operating in rapidly changing industries, where the ability to innovate while maintaining operational efficiency is key to long-term success.

The healthcare and pharmaceuticals industry, in which J&J operates, is a prime example of a sector experiencing significant disruption. The rise of personalized medicine, digital health, and biotechnology is transforming the competitive landscape and challenging traditional business models. To navigate this environment, J&J has adopted an ambidextrous approach, balancing its legacy businesses with new growth areas.

Ambidextrous Leadership

Ambidextrous leadership involves balancing the optimization of current business models with the pursuit of future innovations. Leaders who excel in this area inspire their teams to innovate while maintaining operational efficiency. Alex Gorsky, Chairman and CEO of Johnson & Johnson, exemplifies ambidextrous leadership, guiding the company through its transformation in the face of the fourth industrial revolution.

Strategic Alignment

Ambidextrous leaders ensure strategic alignment by embedding core values that resonate across the organization. At J&J, this alignment is reflected in the company's guiding principles, which emphasize innovation, patient-centered care, responsibility, and integrity. These principles form the foundation of J&J's strategy, driving both its operational excellence and its innovative pursuits.

J&J's strategic vision encompasses a dual focus on enhancing its core healthcare business and pioneering new solutions in emerging areas. This vision is operationalized through initiatives such as Janssen Pharmaceuticals, the Johnson & Johnson Innovation Centers, and various digital health projects, which leverage the company's strengths in pharmaceuticals, medical devices, and consumer health to deliver integrated solutions to patients and healthcare providers.

Parallelism

J&J's leadership approach involves managing multiple time horizons simultaneously. This parallelism ensures that the company remains competitive in the present while preparing for future opportunities. J&J's commitment to parallelism is evident in its investment in both traditional and innovative technologies. For instance, J&J continues to refine its pharmaceutical and medical device businesses while aggressively investing in digital health and biotechnology. This dual strategy allows J&J to address current market demands and regulatory requirements while positioning itself as a leader in the next generation of healthcare.

Creative Conflict

Managing creative conflict is a critical aspect of ambidextrous leadership. At J&J, this involves fostering a culture where diverse perspectives are valued and constructive debate is encouraged. This approach drives innovation by challenging conventional thinking and promoting continuous improvement. J&J's emphasis on collaborative innovation exemplifies this approach. By encouraging employees at all levels to contribute ideas and challenge assumptions, J&J cultivates a culture of creativity and responsiveness. This commitment to collaborative innovation is complemented by J&J's willingness to experiment with new ideas, as seen in its development of advanced therapies and digital health solutions.

J&J's Strategic Initiatives: Janssen Pharmaceuticals

Janssen Pharmaceuticals, a subsidiary of J&J, represents a transformative approach to pharmaceutical research and development. By integrating cutting-edge science with patient-centered care, Janssen enhances efficiency, reduces costs, and improves outcomes for patients. This initiative reflects J&J's commitment to operational excellence and innovation.

Janssen's research focuses on six therapeutic areas: oncology, immunology, neuroscience, infectious diseases and vaccines, cardiovascular and metabolism, and pulmonary hypertension. These areas enable Janssen to address a wide range of unmet medical needs and drive advancements in personalized medicine.

J&J Innovation Centers

The J&J Innovation Centers are designed to accelerate the discovery and development of new healthcare solutions. These centers, located in major innovation hubs around the world, foster collaboration between J&J and external innovators, including startups, academic institutions, and research organizations. The Innovation Centers provide access to J&J's resources, expertise, and networks, enabling innovators to advance their ideas and bring new therapies and technologies to market. This initiative aligns with J&J's strategy of leveraging external partnerships to drive innovation and expand its impact.

Digital Health

J&J's digital health initiatives leverage data analytics, AI, and IoT to develop advanced healthcare solutions. This initiative aligns with digital megatrends, focusing on creating intelligent systems that can improve patient outcomes and streamline healthcare delivery. J&J's digital health solutions include connected medical devices, remote patient monitoring, and digital therapeutics. These solutions enable patients to manage their health more effectively, healthcare providers to deliver more personalized care, and the healthcare system to operate more efficiently.

COVID-19 Vaccine Development

J&J's response to the COVID-19 pandemic exemplifies its ambidextrous leadership and commitment to innovation. The company's rapid development of a single-dose COVID-19 vaccine, leveraging its expertise in vaccine research and development, showcased its ability to pivot quickly and address urgent global health needs. The vaccine, developed by Janssen Pharmaceuticals, received Emergency Use Authorization from regulatory agencies worldwide and has been a critical tool in the fight against the pandemic. J&J's collaborative approach, working with governments, healthcare organizations, and other pharmaceutical companies, underscores its leadership in addressing global health challenges.

Advanced Therapies

J&J is at the forefront of developing advanced therapies, including gene therapy, cell therapy, and regenerative medicine. These therapies have the potential to transform the treatment of various diseases by targeting the underlying causes rather than just managing symptoms. For example, Janssen is developing gene therapies for conditions such as hemophilia and retinal diseases, aiming to provide long-term or even curative treatments. Additionally, J&J's investment in cell therapy research is focused on harnessing the power of the immune system to fight cancer and other diseases.

Practical Implementations for Organizations

Drawing from recent research and literature, this case study suggests practical recommendations for integrating ambidextrous leadership into organizational strategies. Addressing executive leaders and strategic managers, these recommendations aim to foster innovation and operational excellence as competitive advantages.

Foster a Culture of Innovation: Executive leaders should cultivate an organizational culture that promotes innovation and creative thinking. By raising awareness of innovation's critical role in organizational success, employees across functions will be inspired to think creatively. Promoting innovation through employee recognition, award systems, and compensation incentives can turn the entire workforce into an innovative engine.

Integrate Innovation and Operational Excellence into the Business Model: As the benefits of innovation and operational excellence become evident, strategists should incorporate them deeply into the business model. Practitioners in strategic planning, communications, and human resources should develop strategies using innovation driven by ambidextrous leadership as a competitive advantage. For example, include the novelty and originality of ideas in the decision-making process for funding new investments.

Use Innovation and Operational Excellence as Differentiation Strategies: Extensive literature shows a positive relationship between differentiation and organizational performance. Differentiation allows organizations to gain enduring advantages, improving performance over time. Leaders and strategists are advised to use the ambidextrous leadership approach as a differentiation strategy. Develop strategies targeting specific talent, customers, and stakeholders, and promote innovation and operational excellence in marketing campaigns to differentiate the organization from rivals, especially in a global competitive environment.

Lesson from a Leader

Ajay Banga

Ajay Banga's leadership as the former CEO of Mastercard exemplifies effective ambidextrous leadership in the context of corporate, business, and functional-level strategies. He successfully balanced the challenges of expanding digital payments capabilities, optimizing global operations, and nurturing relationships with traditional financial institutions.

- Corporate-Level Strategy: Banga recognized the increasing trend toward digital payments and the importance of Mastercard evolving to remain relevant. He strategically pursued initiatives to position Mastercard as a leader in the digital payment landscape. This involved investments in technologies and partnerships that would enhance the company's digital offerings and secure its place in the future of financial transactions. At the corporate-level, Ajay Banga recognized the seismic shift toward digital payments and saw the need for Mastercard to evolve and stay competitive in this rapidly changing landscape. He implemented initiatives to expand the company's digital payments capabilities. This involved investments in technologies like contactless payments, mobile wallets, and secure online transactions. By focusing on innovation and technology, Banga aimed to position Mastercard as a leader in the digital payment industry, catering to evolving consumer preferences and market trends.
  - Leadership Characteristics: Banga's visionary leadership and strategic foresight were key to driving Mastercard's transformation into a digital payment powerhouse. He displayed the courage to embrace change, a willingness to take calculated risks, and a strong commitment to innovation. Banga's ability to communicate a compelling vision for the future of payments inspired his team and stakeholders alike.
  - Organizational Challenges: The challenge at the corporate-level was to balance Mastercard's legacy as a traditional payments company with its aspirations to be a digital innovator. Banga had to navigate the inherent tension between pushing for digital expansion while ensuring that the existing business and partnerships were not compromised.
- Business-Level Strategy: While driving digital innovation, Banga was also focused on maintaining Mastercard's core business relationships with traditional financial institutions. He understood the importance of providing value to existing partners while expanding into new markets. This ambidextrous approach ensured that Mastercard continued to serve its traditional customer base while strategically growing in new directions. While driving digital transformation, Banga didn't lose sight of Mastercard's

existing partnerships with traditional financial institutions. He understood the importance of maintaining relationships with banks and financial organizations that formed the backbone of Mastercard's business. Banga pursued a strategy that involved providing value to these institutions through innovative solutions, thus ensuring their continued support and loyalty.

– Leadership Characteristics: Banga's empathetic and relationship-oriented leadership style played a crucial role at the business-level. He was known for his ability to build strong partnerships based on trust and mutual benefit. His approachable demeanor and respect for the legacy business ensured that Mastercard's traditional partners felt valued and heard even as the company ventured into new territories.

– Organizational Challenges: The challenge here was to strike a balance between innovating for the future and honoring existing partnerships. Banga had to ensure that Mastercard's growth in the digital space did not alienate or undermine the relationships the company had built over decades.

■ Functional-Level Strategy: At the functional-level, Banga's leadership was apparent in the way he optimized global operations. He emphasized operational efficiency, cost-effectiveness, and the utilization of technology to streamline processes. This allowed Mastercard to effectively manage its expanding digital offerings while maintaining a high level of service for its clients. Ajay Banga's leadership extended to the functional-level by focusing on operational efficiency. He understood that Mastercard's growth ambitions would require the company to scale its operations effectively. He championed initiatives aimed at streamlining processes, reducing costs, and enhancing operational agility. This approach allowed Mastercard to support its expanding digital offerings without compromising quality or service.

– Leadership Characteristics: Banga's pragmatic leadership and keen attention to detail were evident in his functional strategy. He was known for his hands-on approach and willingness to roll up his sleeves to address operational challenges. His ability to inspire his team to embrace operational excellence contributed to Mastercard's overall success.

– Organizational Challenges: Scaling operations while pursuing digital innovation can strain an organization's resources and create operational bottlenecks. Banga had to ensure that Mastercard's operations were adaptive and efficient enough to support both traditional and digital payment services.

Ajay Banga's success as an ambidextrous leader stemmed from his visionary thinking, his ability to balance multiple strategic priorities, and his inclusive leadership style. He recognized that success hinged on maintaining Mastercard's existing strengths while simultaneously driving innovation and digital transformation. His leadership qualities of strategic foresight, relationship-building, and operational acumen made him a trailblazer in the payments industry.

Bringing It All Together

As we conclude our journey through the dynamic world of strategy, let's reflect on the insights we've uncovered and the pathways we've explored. We began by unraveling common misconceptions about strategy, recognizing it as a dynamic and adaptive process rather than a static plan. We dived into the essence of strategy, understanding it as a series of deliberate choices and trade-offs that shape an organization's competitive position and future trajectory.

Our journey then took us into the macroenvironment, where we navigated the complex interplay of external factors such as economic conditions, technological advancements, and regulatory forces. We embraced the concept of the organization as a Complex Adaptive System, acknowledging its ability to respond, learn, and adapt in the face of change. Guided by the industry life cycle, we charted a course through the stages of birth, growth, maturity, and decline observed in industries. Aligning strategies with the specific phase of the industry life cycle, we learned how organizations can position themselves strategically and seize opportunities for growth and success.

We then visited the concept of strategy as a series of interconnected magnifying lenses. Corporate-level strategy establishes the foundation and guides the overall direction, while business-level strategy refines and operationalizes that direction. The functional-level strategy focuses on specific functions to contribute to the organization's competitive advantage. Viewing these strategy tiers as complementary components enhances strategic coherence and drives effective execution. To enable the strategy process (development and deployment), it was necessary to maintain focus on the essence of strategy, trade-offs. Therefore, the art of negotiation in strategy requires strategists to navigate competing interests, conflicting commitments, and diverse perspectives within the organization. Effective negotiation builds consensus, drives stakeholder engagement, and increases the likelihood of successful strategy execution. It demands analytical thinking, strategic acumen, and effective communication skills.

Emphasizing the importance of thought leadership, blue ocean strategy, and innovation, we've highlighted the strategic imperatives for organizations. Becoming thought leaders, creating uncontested market space, and fostering a culture of innovation are key to staying ahead of the competition. Embracing these imperatives enhances strategic effectiveness and enables organizations to achieve sustainable success in today's dynamic business landscape.

If there is one thing we can't change, it is the natural evolution of everything around us. We are our organizations, and our organizations are our industries. And if there is one thing we must learn, then it is resilience during evolution. Just as the Monarch navigates vast distances and overcomes daunting obstacles through generations, so too do organizations; they must evolve and adapt in the face of ever-changing environments. In a world where uncertainty is the norm, and complexity is the challenge, the Monarch's journey serves as a potent symbol of resilience and an exemplar of how strategy is supposed to work.

May your strategies be as resilient and enduring as the journey of a Monarch!

Epilogue

The Ever-Evolving Landscape of Strategy

As we conclude our exploration of strategy through the lens of *Monarch: Resilience through Evolution*, it is crucial to reflect on the journey we have taken together. This book began with a clear understanding of what strategy is and is not, delving into the macroenvironment and recognizing organizations as complex adaptive systems (CAS). Throughout this journey, we have explored the dynamic interplay between an organization's internal capabilities and the external factors that influence its success.

The analogy of the monarch butterfly has been a constant thread, symbolizing resilience and adaptability. Just as the monarch navigates thousands of miles, crossing diverse terrains to reach its destination, organizations must navigate an ever-changing business environment. The butterfly's journey is not just a testament to endurance but also to the necessity of evolving strategies that respond to new challenges and opportunities.

A Recap of the Strategic Path

In Part I, we laid the foundation by discussing the broader ecosystem in which organizations operate. Understanding the macroenvironment is crucial for any strategic initiative, as it encompasses the economic, technological, social, and political factors that can impact an organization. Recognizing the complexity of these influences, we examined how organizations, like CAS, must be dynamic and continuously adaptive to maintain their competitive edge.

The industry life cycle, a critical concept discussed, highlighted how industries evolve from embryonic stages through growth, shakeout, maturity, and

DOI: 10.4324/9781003564133-18

decline. Each stage presents unique challenges and opportunities, requiring tailored strategies to navigate successfully. This cycle mirrors the life stages of the monarch, each requiring different forms of resilience and adaptability.

In Part II, we looked at practical strategies aligned with each stage of the industry life cycle. From disrupting during the embryonic phase to differentiating or leading in costs during growth, adapting to survive the shakeout, competing fiercely during maturity, and deciding whether to end the game or pivot during decline, each chapter provided a roadmap for strategic decision-making. These strategies are not static; they must evolve as the organization and its environment change.

Part III shifted focus to the implementation of strategy, emphasizing the importance of strategic alignment across the corporate, business, and functional-levels. Viewing strategy through these three magnifying lenses ensures that every part of the organization is moving in harmony toward common goals. We also discussed the critical role of negotiation in strategy, highlighting the need for continuous dialogue and alignment with stakeholders to achieve successful execution.

Lessons from the Monarch: Navigating with a North Star

Clarity of Purpose

The monarch butterfly's migration is driven by a clear and unwavering purpose: survival and reproduction. Similarly, organizations must define their North Star—a clear and compelling vision that guides all strategic decisions. This clarity of purpose ensures that every action taken aligns with the overarching goals of the organization.

Adaptability and Resilience

Throughout its journey, the monarch encounters various obstacles, from weather changes to predators. Its ability to adapt and remain resilient is crucial for survival. Organizations, too, must embrace adaptability and resilience, continuously adjusting their strategies in response to market shifts, technological advancements, and competitive pressures.

Strategic Alignment

The monarch's journey is not random; it follows a well-established migratory path. This alignment ensures that the butterfly reaches its destination efficiently.

Similarly, organizations must ensure that their strategies are aligned across all levels—corporate, business, and functional. Strategic alignment creates coherence and synergy, enabling the organization to move forward cohesively.

Continuous Learning and Innovation

The monarch's journey is a testament to the power of instinct and learned behavior. Over generations, monarchs have honed their migratory patterns. Organizations must foster a culture of continuous learning and innovation, encouraging employees to explore new ideas, embrace creativity, and drive the organization forward.

Navigating Complexity

The monarch's migration is a complex and multifaceted endeavor, much like the business environment organizations operate in. Recognizing the organization as a CAS helps leaders understand the interconnectedness of various elements and navigate the complexities with a holistic approach.

Holistic Approach

The monarch's journey is holistic, considering the entire ecosystem it traverses. Organizations, too, must adopt a holistic approach to strategy, ensuring alignment across all levels and integrating various functions and departments.

The Future of Strategy

As we look to the future, the landscape of strategy will continue to evolve. The fourth industrial revolution, characterized by rapid technological advancements and the fusion of physical, digital, and biological worlds, presents both unprecedented challenges and opportunities. Organizations must be prepared to innovate continuously, leveraging new technologies and adapting to new market dynamics.

Ambidextrous leadership will become increasingly important in this context. Leaders must balance the exploitation of existing capabilities with the exploration of new opportunities. This requires a mindset that embraces change, fosters innovation, and drives organizational transformation.

Final Thoughts

Monarch: Resilience through Evolution is not just a book on strategy; it is a call to action for leaders and organizations to embrace the journey of continuous adaptation and resilience. By understanding the macroenvironment, recognizing the life cycle of industries, and implementing strategies that align across all levels, organizations can navigate the complexities of the business world and achieve sustained success.

The journey of the monarch butterfly is a testament to the power of resilience and adaptability. As you continue your strategic journey, remember that success lies not just in reaching the destination but in navigating the path with agility, foresight, and an unwavering commitment to continuous evolution. Let the lessons from the monarch guide you as you lead your organization toward a future of endless possibilities.

Index

ADDITIONAL CASES

Warby Parker

Warby Parker, an eyewear retailer, is a prime example of a company that has effectively implemented a differentiation strategy in the highly competitive eyewear industry. Through its innovative business model and focus on affordability, Warby Parker has disrupted the traditional eyewear market and carved out a distinct position for itself. One key aspect of Warby Parker's differentiation strategy is its direct-to-consumer approach. By bypassing the traditional retail distribution channels and selling directly to customers through its online platform and brick-and-mortar stores, Warby Parker is able to offer high-quality, stylish eyewear at a fraction of the price of traditional luxury brands. This direct-to-consumer model allows the company to eliminate unnecessary markups and provide customers with greater value for their money.

Another crucial element of Warby Parker's differentiation strategy is its commitment to social responsibility. The company has integrated a strong social mission into its business model, aiming to make a positive impact on society. For every pair of eyeglasses sold, Warby Parker donates a pair to someone in need. This socially conscious approach has resonated with customers who value brands that prioritize both style and social good. Warby Parker has also differentiated itself through its innovative product design and customization options. The company offers a wide range of trendy and unique eyewear styles, allowing customers to find frames that match their personal preferences. Additionally, Warby Parker provides a home try-on program, allowing customers to select multiple frames to try at home before making a purchase decision. This personalized and convenient shopping experience sets Warby Parker apart from traditional eyewear retailers.

Furthermore, Warby Parker's emphasis on cutting-edge technology has played a significant role in its differentiation strategy. The company utilizes virtual try-on tools and advanced measurement techniques to enhance the online shopping experience for customers. By leveraging technology, Warby Parker has simplified the eyewear selection process, making it more engaging and accessible for consumers. A notable example of Warby Parker's successful differentiation strategy is its launch of the "Buy a Pair, Give a Pair" program. Through this initiative, Warby Parker addresses the global issue of limited access to eyewear by providing glasses to individuals in underserved communities. This program not only reinforces the company's social mission but also appeals to socially conscious consumers who want their purchase to contribute to a larger cause. Warby Parker's differentiation strategy has propelled the company to become a leader in the online eyewear market. Its focus on affordability, social responsibility, product design, customization, and technological innovation has resonated with consumers seeking fashionable eyewear at an accessible price point. By offering a unique value proposition, Warby Parker has gained a loyal customer base and disrupted the traditional eyewear industry.

IKEA

IKEA, the Swedish furniture retailer, is well-known for its successful low-cost strategy in the global market. The company has built its competitive advantage by offering affordable and functional furniture products to a wide customer base. IKEA's low-cost approach is reflected in several key elements of its business model and operations. First and foremost, IKEA focuses on cost-efficient sourcing and supply chain management. The company leverages economies of scale by working directly with suppliers and manufacturers to reduce production costs. IKEA designs its furniture to be flat-packed, optimizing transportation and storage space, which significantly lowers shipping costs. Additionally, IKEA strives to maintain long-term relationships with suppliers, ensuring consistent quality and cost-effective sourcing.

Another critical aspect of IKEA's low-cost strategy is its self-service model and in-store experience. By allowing customers to navigate and assemble furniture themselves, IKEA reduces labor costs and minimizes the need for additional sales personnel. The self-service concept enables customers to browse and choose products independently, creating a streamlined and cost-efficient shopping experience.

Furthermore, IKEA is committed to operational efficiency and cost reduction throughout its value chain. The company emphasizes lean production methods, reducing waste, and maximizing resource utilization. IKEA's warehouses are strategically located to optimize distribution and minimize transportation costs. The stores are designed to be functional and efficient, with standardized layouts and optimized use of space.

IKEA's low-cost strategy has resonated with consumers globally. By offering well-designed furniture at affordable prices, the company has attracted a wide customer base, including price-conscious individuals and young families. IKEA's success is evident in its strong market position, with a global presence and a loyal customer following.

Dollar General

Dollar General is a retail chain that operates discount stores offering a wide range of everyday essential products at affordable prices. The company has achieved remarkable success through its cost leadership strategy, catering to price-conscious consumers and differentiating itself from competitors. One key aspect of Dollar General's cost leadership strategy is its focus on maintaining low operating costs. The company achieves this through various measures such as efficient store layouts, optimized inventory management, and streamlined supply chain processes. Dollar General strategically chooses store locations in rural and small-town areas, allowing it to secure lower-cost real estate and take advantage of lower labor costs compared to urban areas.

Moreover, Dollar General leverages its purchasing power to negotiate favorable deals with suppliers and secure cost-effective sourcing of products. By procuring products in large quantities, the company enjoys economies of scale, reducing procurement costs and passing on those savings to customers. Dollar General's strong relationships with suppliers and its ability to offer a wide variety of products at low prices contribute to its competitive advantage. In addition, Dollar General implements a focused assortment strategy, carrying a limited but carefully curated selection of products that are in high demand among its target customers. This allows the company to optimize inventory levels, minimize carrying costs, and maximize sales per square foot of store space. By offering a limited selection of well-chosen products, Dollar General can efficiently manage its supply chain, reduce complexities, and maintain its cost leadership position.

Furthermore, Dollar General invests in technology and data analytics to enhance operational efficiency. The company utilizes advanced systems for inventory management, demand forecasting, and pricing optimization. By leveraging technology, Dollar General improves its supply chain operations, reduces costs, and ensures effective management of its store network.

The success of Dollar General's cost leadership strategy is evident in its widespread presence and financial performance. The company operates thousands of stores across the United States, predominantly in rural and underserved areas. Dollar General's ability to offer everyday essentials at competitive prices has resonated with its target customers, enabling it to capture market share and sustain growth. The example of Dollar General showcases how a business leader can successfully implement a cost leadership strategy by focusing on low operating costs, leveraging purchasing power, implementing a focused assortment strategy, investing in technology, and optimizing the supply chain. Through these strategic initiatives, Dollar General has established itself as a leading discount retailer, catering to price-conscious consumers and delivering value through its cost-effective business model.

Lesson from a Leader

Roberto Goizueta

Coca-Cola is a globally renowned beverage company that has achieved remarkable success by differentiating itself in the competitive beverage industry. One of the key factors behind Coca-Cola's differentiation strategy is its brand positioning and marketing efforts. The company has consistently focused on building a strong brand image and associating it with positive emotions, happiness, and shared experiences. Under the leadership of business leader Roberto Goizueta, who served as the CEO of Coca-Cola from 1981 to 1997, the company further emphasized its differentiation strategy. Goizueta recognized the importance of diversifying Coca-Cola's product portfolio beyond its flagship cola beverage. He led the company to introduce new product lines, including Diet Coke, Sprite, and Minute Maid, catering to different consumer preferences and expanding the company's market reach.

Furthermore, Goizueta spearheaded innovative marketing campaigns that helped Coca-Cola stand out from its competitors. The iconic "Share a Coke" campaign, for example, personalized Coca-Cola bottles with people's names, allowing consumers to connect emotionally with the brand. This approach not only differentiated Coca-Cola in the market but also created a sense of personalization and engagement with its customers. Another aspect of Coca-Cola's differentiation strategy lies in its commitment to innovation and product development. The company has consistently introduced new flavors, packaging formats, and variations of its beverages to meet evolving consumer demands. This focus on innovation has allowed Coca-Cola to differentiate its products and maintain a strong market presence.

Coca-Cola's success in differentiation is evident in its market position and brand recognition. The company has built a global network of loyal customers who associate Coca-Cola with refreshment, enjoyment, and a distinct taste experience. By consistently delivering on its brand promise and differentiating itself from competitors, Coca-Cola has become one of the most recognizable and valuable brands worldwide. The example of Coca-Cola highlights the effectiveness of a successful differentiation strategy under the leadership of Roberto Goizueta. By understanding consumer preferences, diversifying its product portfolio, implementing innovative marketing campaigns, and fostering a culture of continuous innovation, Coca-Cola has maintained its competitive advantage and established itself as a leader in the beverage industry.

BEYOND MEAT

In recent years, the food industry has seen a surge in demand for plant-based alternatives, driven by consumer preferences for healthier, sustainable, and ethical food options. Beyond Meat, a leading player in the plant-based meat industry, has been at the forefront of this shift. The company's mission is to create delicious, plant-based protein products that provide the same taste and texture as animal meat, promoting a more sustainable food system.

Beyond Meat's growth has been fueled by increasing awareness of the environmental impact of traditional meat production, such as greenhouse gas emissions, water usage, and deforestation. Governments and environmental organizations worldwide have advocated for reduced meat consumption, further propelling the plant-based market. In response, Beyond Meat has implemented a robust strategy to scale its operations, innovate product offerings, and expand its global presence.

Evolution of Plant-Based Meat

Early plant-based meat products often struggled with taste and texture, making them less appealing to mainstream consumers. However, advancements in food science and technology have significantly improved the quality of plant-based products. Beyond Meat, founded in 2009, launched its first product, the Beyond Burger, in 2016. This breakthrough product closely mimicked the taste and texture of beef, marking a turning point for the industry.

Beyond Meat's success is largely attributed to its focus on research and development (R&D). The company has continually improved its formulations, using ingredients such as pea protein, beet juice, and coconut oil to replicate the juiciness and flavor of meat. By 2020, Beyond Meat's products were available in over 80 countries, reflecting widespread consumer acceptance and market penetration.

Mass Production and Scaling Challenges

Scaling the production of plant-based meat presents unique challenges, including maintaining product quality, ensuring supply chain efficiency, and managing costs. Beyond Meat has addressed these challenges through strategic partnerships and investments. In 2019, the company partnered with food manufacturing giant Tyson Foods to leverage its extensive distribution network and production capabilities.

Additionally, Beyond Meat has invested in state-of-the-art manufacturing facilities to increase production capacity and improve efficiency. In 2020, the company opened its first European production facility in the Netherlands, aiming to meet the growing demand in Europe and reduce carbon emissions associated with shipping products from the United States.

Infrastructure and Market Expansion

Beyond Meat's expansion strategy involves building a robust infrastructure to support its global operations. The company has formed strategic alliances with major retailers and food service providers, including Walmart, Tesco, and McDonald's. These partnerships have enabled Beyond Meat to reach a broad consumer base and increase brand visibility. Furthermore, Beyond Meat has focused on diversifying its product portfolio to cater to different consumer preferences and regional tastes. In addition to Beyond Burger, the company offers plant-based sausages, meatballs, and chicken. This product diversification helps mitigate risks associated with market fluctuations and consumer trends.

Research and Development

Innovation is at the core of Beyond Meat's strategy. The company's R&D team continuously explores new ingredients and technologies to enhance the taste, texture, and nutritional profile of its products. In 2021, Beyond Meat announced a partnership with PepsiCo to develop and market plant-based snacks and beverages. This collaboration aims to leverage Beyond Meat's expertise in plant-based protein and PepsiCo's extensive marketing and distribution capabilities. Beyond Meat also invests in scientific research to support its claims about the environmental and health benefits of plant-based diets. The company collaborates with universities and research institutions to conduct studies on the impact of plant-based foods on human health and the environment.

Consumer Education and Advocacy

Beyond Meat recognizes the importance of consumer education in driving the adoption of plant-based diets. The company actively engages in marketing campaigns to raise awareness about the benefits of plant-based eating. By highlighting the environmental impact of meat production and the health advantages of plant-based diets, Beyond Meat aims to shift consumer behavior toward more sustainable food choices.

Challenges and Opportunities

Despite its success, Beyond Meat faces several challenges. The plant-based meat market is becoming increasingly competitive, with new entrants and established food companies launching their own plant-based products. Beyond Meat must continue to innovate and differentiate its offerings to maintain its market leadership. Additionally, the cost of plant-based meat remains higher than traditional meat, posing a barrier to mass adoption. Beyond Meat is working to achieve cost parity through economies of scale and advancements in production technology. As consumer demand grows and production efficiency improves, the price gap between plant-based and traditional meat is expected to narrow.

Beyond Meat's strategic approach to scaling its operations, investing in innovation, and expanding its market presence has positioned it as a leader in the plant-based meat industry. By addressing the challenges of infrastructure, cost, and consumer education, Beyond Meat aims to drive the widespread adoption of plant-based diets and contribute to a more sustainable food system. The company's journey reflects the broader trends and opportunities in the food industry as it navigates the shakeout phase, where adaptation and innovation are key to survival and growth.

Brief Opinion on AI

Why Having an Artificial Intelligence Strategy Is Not Intelligent

In today's fast-paced business environment, Artificial Intelligence (AI) is not just a buzzword—it's a strategic necessity. However, many companies make the mistake of viewing AI as a standalone strategy, which can lead to missed opportunities and wasted resources. AI could unlock tremendous potential for organizations, and sure it can help them realize their strategies…but in itself, is not a strategy.

Understanding AI

AI is a broad field that encompasses various technologies and applications aimed at simulating human intelligence. Machine learning, natural language processing, and computer vision are some of the key components of AI that are transforming industries. Understanding the capabilities and limitations of AI is crucial for businesses looking to leverage its potential. AI has the power to revolutionize how organizations operate, from streamlining operations to enhancing customer experiences. Today, it is not a challenge to see how AI plays a pivotal role in driving business growth and development by enhancing efficiency, improving decision-making, and enabling innovative products and services. Sure, AI excels in data analysis and pattern recognition, allowing businesses to extract valuable insights and make informed decisions (i.e., leveraging AI-powered analytics platforms like Tableau and Power BI to help businesses visualize complex data sets to identify trends, forecast demand, and optimize operations). But, AI also impacts the end user-facing front by revolutionizing customer service through chatbots and virtual assistants (i.e., Alex and Siri) and transforming industries such as healthcare and automotive with innovative solutions (think IBM's Watson and autonomous driving).

The Downsides of Chasing an AI Strategy

Enchanted by the endless possibilities of growing business with AI, many companies fall into the trap of viewing AI as a standalone strategy, believing that simply adopting AI technologies will lead to success (that could come in different forms and scales). However, this approach often results in disjointed initiatives that fail to deliver meaningful business results. Companies may invest heavily in AI technologies without a clear understanding of how they align with their broader business goals, leading to wasted resources and missed opportunities. Instead of chasing an AI strategy, companies should integrate AI into their existing strategic framework. But they must apply the right lens to AI, the "enabler" lens. This involves aligning AI initiatives with their broader business goals and identifying opportunities where AI can enhance (enable) existing operations and drive long-term value. By incorporating AI into their strategic framework, companies can ensure that their AI initiatives are well-aligned with their overall business strategy, leading to more impactful results. Before we embark on this journey to learn a bit more, we need to solidify our understanding of what strategy is.

So What Is Strategy?

Strategizing involves making trade-offs, a widely accepted concept among academics and industry experts. Developing a strategy is not a one-time event; it is a structured process that requires careful formulation and deployment. Despite the challenges and risks associated with changing a company's direction, some senior leadership teams recognize the need for change and work to persuade their organizations to follow suit. Strategy is formulated at three levels: corporate, business, and functional (also known as tactical).

At the corporate-level, the focus is on growth and the business model, often discussed with the board. Once growth objectives are identified, the business model to achieve that growth is established. Business-level strategy involves choosing between differentiation and cost leadership (or low cost) to deploy the business model and achieve growth. Many companies fall somewhere along the spectrum between these two extremes, known as the Efficiency Frontier.

Finally, at the functional-level, the focus is on defining the competitive advantages necessary to support the selected business-level strategy. Strategic alignment across these three levels is crucial for success. Academic scholars and industry experts agree on four key building blocks for developing competitive advantages: innovation, efficiency, quality, and customer responsiveness. Therefore, for any company to create and sustain competitive advantages, it must focus on one or more of these building blocks.

Integrating AI into Strategic Planning

To strategize effectively in today's rapidly evolving landscape, companies must consider how AI can be integrated into their strategic planning process. AI is not just a standalone strategy but a powerful enabler that can enhance each level of the strategy cascade—corporate, business, and functional.

At the corporate-level, AI can drive growth by enabling companies to innovate their business models. For example, AI-powered analytics can help identify new market opportunities or optimize existing processes, leading to increased efficiency and revenue growth. By integrating AI into their corporate-level strategy, companies can position themselves as leaders in their industries and drive sustainable growth.

At the business-level, AI can be used to differentiate products and services or achieve cost leadership. For example, AI-powered customer insights can help companies tailor their offerings to specific customer segments, increasing customer satisfaction and loyalty. Additionally, AI can help companies optimize their operations, reducing costs and improving profitability. By integrating AI into their business-level strategy, companies can gain a competitive edge and drive long-term value.

Finally, at the functional-level, AI can be used to develop competitive advantages in areas such as innovation, efficiency, quality, and customer responsiveness. For example, AI-powered automation can streamline processes, reducing errors and improving efficiency. By integrating AI into their functional-level strategy, companies can enhance their capabilities and better support their business-level strategy. This takes us to the right perspective on AI: it is one building block that can be leveraged to attain competitive advantages (sustained or transient), likely this building block is innovation. So what does this mean?

It means that senior leadership in organizations should apply the right lens to AI, it is an enabler for the attainment of competitive advantages through innovation. And when you employ it correctly, it should support the deployment of the strategy laddering up to corporate strategy.

So Why Having an "AI Strategy" Isn't Intelligent

As we step into the *era* of AI, many companies are quick to adopt what they perceive as an "AI strategy." Attempting at times to fit their business process (or offerings in general) into the AI box....in other words, to AI-wash their organizations. However, this approach overlooks several critical factors, making it far from intelligent. Why? Here, we lay out a couple of reasons.

Firstly, treating AI as a one-size-fits-all solution is a major misconception. AI is a tool, not a strategy in itself. It should be integrated into a broader strategic framework to deliver meaningful outcomes. Companies that rush into AI without aligning it with their overall business goals risk wasting resources on technology that does not address their specific needs.

Secondly, there's a danger of "AI washing"—using AI as a PR stunt without genuinely integrating it into core business operations. This superficial approach not only fails to deliver real value but also damages the company's reputation when customers and stakeholders realize the disconnect between promises and reality. Moreover, viewing AI as a standalone strategy ignores the complexity of strategic decision-making. Strategy development is a nuanced process that involves trade-offs and careful consideration of various factors. AI should be seen as an enabler of strategic objectives, not a strategy in itself.

In conclusion, approaching AI as a strategy is not intelligent because it oversimplifies the complexities of strategic decision-making, leads to superficial implementations, and fails to deliver meaningful outcomes. Instead, companies should integrate AI into their existing strategic framework, aligning it with their broader business goals to drive sustainable growth and competitive advantage.

Bibliography

Adner, R., & Kapoor, R. (2010). Value creation in innovation ecosystems: How the structure of technological interdependence affects firm performance in new technology generations. *Strategic Management Journal, 31*(3), 306–333.

Adobe Systems Incorporated: About Us. (n.d.) Retrieved from https://www.adobe.com/about-adobe.html

Aguilar, F. J. (1967). *Scanning the business environment.* Macmillan.

Ahmed, P. K., & Shepherd, C. D. (2010). *Innovation management: Context, strategies, systems, and processes.* Pearson Education.

Alasuutari, P. (1996). Theorizing in qualitative research: A cultural studies perspective. *Qualitative Inquiry, 2*(4), 371–384.

Aldrich, H. E., & Herker, D. (1977). Boundary spanning roles and organization structure. *Academy of Management Review, 2*(2), 217–230.

Alhaddi, A. (2013). Strategic management in a global context: The role of innovation and collaboration. *Journal of Business Strategy, 34*(1), 45–54.

Alhaddi, H. (2014). The influence of triple bottom line on strategic positioning: An exploratory case study on differentiation through image. *Journal of Management and Strategy, 5*(1), 55–72.

Alhaddi, H. (2014). The relationship between thought leadership and innovation: A look at strategy. *Journal of Business Administration and Education, 6*(2), 57–65.

Alvesson, M., & Kärreman, D. (2007). Constructing mystery: Empirical matters in theory development. *Academy of Management Review, 32*(4), 1265–1281.

Amazon. (n.d.). Amazon's mission and vision. Retrieved from https://www.aboutamazon.com/our-mission-and-vision

Amazon (n.d.). *How Amazon uses AI to optimize its supply chain.* Amazon.

Anderson, F. (1998). Environmental scanning and sustainable development: An introduction to the theory. *Scandinavian Journal of Management, 14*(3), 175–195.

Anderson, P. (1999). Complexity theory and organization science. *Organization Science, 10*(3), 216–232.

Anderson, P., & Tushman, M. L. (1990). Technological discontinuities and dominant designs: A cyclical model of technological change. *Administrative Science Quarterly, 35*(4), 604–633.

Ashby, W. R. (1956). *An introduction to cybernetics.* Chapman & Hall.

Ashby, W. R. (1962). Principles of the self-organizing system. *Journal of General Systems*, 3(2), 89–104.

Baghai, M., Coley, S., & White, D. (2000). *The alchemy of growth: Practical insights for building the enduring enterprise*. Perseus Books Group.

Barabási, A. L. (2002). *Linked: How everything is connected to everything else and what it means for business, Science, and Everyday Life*. Plume.

Barney, J. (1991). Firm resources and sustained competitive advantage. *Journal of Management*, 17(1), 99–120.

Barney, J. B., & Hesterly, W. S. (2018). *Strategic management and competitive advantage: Concepts and cases*. Pearson.

Barr, P. S. (1998). Adapting to unfamiliar environmental events: A look at the evolution of interpretation and its role in strategic change. *Organization Science*, 9(6), 644–669.

Battistella, C., Biotto, G., & Toni, A. (2012). From design driven innovation to meaning strategy. *Management Decision*, 50(4), 718–743.

Baumgartner, N. (2023, February 13). Toyota's new CEO pivots to electric vehicles with next-gen platform. *The Verge*. Retrieved from https://www.theverge.com/2023/2/13/23597619/toyota-electric-vehicles-strategy-new-ceo-platform

Blackberry's fall: A case study in how not to innovate. (n.d.) Retrieved from https://www.ivey.uwo.ca/cmsmedia/3775724/blackberrysfallrev.pdf

Blau, P. M. (1970). A formal theory of differentiation in organizations. *American Sociological Review*, 35(2), 201–218.

Bloomberg. (2013). Bloomberg game changers: Shantanu Narayen. [Video file]. Retrieved from https://www.youtube.com/watch?v=fkY1hBEJa9U

Bloomberg. (2018, October 15). The rise and fall of Sears in photos. *Bloomberg*. Retrieved from https://www.bloomberg.com/news/articles/2018-10-15/the-rise-and-fall-of-sears-in-photos

Boisot, M. H., & Child, J. (1999). Organizations as adaptive systems in complex environments: The case of China. *Organization Science*, 10(3), 237–252.

Bower, J. L., & Christensen, C. M. (1995). Disruptive technologies: Catching the wave. *Harvard Business Review*, 73(1), 43–53.

Brandenburger, A. M., & Nalebuff, B. J. (1996). *Co-opetition: A revolution mindset that combines competition and cooperation*. Currency Doubleday.

Brenner, S. N., & Molander, E. A. (1977). Is the ethics of business changing? *Harvard Business Review*, 55(1), 57–71.

Brett, J. M. (2014). *Negotiating globally: How to negotiate deals, resolve disputes, and make decisions across cultural boundaries*. John Wiley & Sons.

Brown, S. L., & Eisenhardt, K. M. (1998). Competing on the edge: Strategy as structured chaos. *Harvard Business Review*.

Brundtland, G. H. (1987). *Our common future: Report of the world commission on environment and development*. Oxford University Press.

Bughin, J., Catlin, T., & Hirt, M. (2018). *The technology fallacy: How people are the real key to digital transformation*. The MIT Press.

Burns, T., & Stalker, G. M. (1966). *The management of innovation*. Tavistock Publications.

Butler, G. (2012). *Think write grow. How to become a thought leader and build your business.* John Wiley & Sons.

Butler, J. (2012). Thought leadership: Real-world application of thought leadership for business success. *Business Strategy Review,* 23(2), 1–4.

Chalhoub, M. (2010). Innovation management and thought leadership-a cultural requirement in a global competitive environment. *The Journal of American Academy of Business, Cambridge,* 16(1), 240–245.

Chalhoub, M. S. (2010). Innovation management: Towards a theoretical framework. *Journal of Strategic Management Education,* 6(1), 23–36.

Chan Kim, W., & Mauborgne, R. (2017). *Blue ocean shift: Beyond competing – Proven steps to inspire confidence and seize new growth.* Hachette UK.

Chandler, A. D. (2014). *The visible hand: The managerial revolution in American business.* Belknap Press.

Charmaz, K. (2006). *Constructing grounded theory: A practical guide through qualitative analysis.* SAGE Publications.

Chesbrough, H. (2003). *Open innovation: The new imperative for creating and profiting from technology.* Harvard Business Review Press.

Chesbrough, H. (2010). Business model innovation: Opportunities and barriers. *Long Range Planning,* 43(2–3), 354–363.

Child, J. (1973). Predicting and understanding organization structure. *Administrative Science Quarterly,* 18(2), 168–185.

Child, J., & Mansfield, R. (1972). Organizational structure, environment, and performance: The role of strategic choice. *Sociology,* 6(1), 1–22.

Child, J., & Rodrigues, S. B. (2011). How organizations engage with external complexity: A political action perspective. *Organization Studies,* 32(6), 803–824.

Christensen, C. M. (1997). *The innovator's dilemma: When new technologies cause great firms to fail.* Harvard Business Review Press.

Christensen, C. M. (2011). *The innovator's dilemma: When new technologies cause great firms to fail.* Harvard Business Review Press.

Christensen, C. M., Raynor, M. E., & McDonald, R. (2015). What is disruptive innovation? *Harvard Business Review,* 93(12), 44–53.

Cilliers, P. (1998). *Complexity and postmodernism: Understanding complex systems.* Routledge.

CNBC. (2017, October 12). Sears just warned it may not survive. *CNBC.* Retrieved from https://www.cnbc.com/2017/10/12/sears-just-warned-it-may-not-survive.html

CNBC. (2018, October 15). Sears files for Chapter 11 bankruptcy. *CNBC.* Retrieved from https://www.cnbc.com/2018/10/15/sears-files-for-chapter-11-bankruptcy.html

Collins, J. (2001). *Good to great: Why some companies make the leap and others don't.* Harper Business.

Collis, D. J., & Montgomery, C. A. (2008). Competing on resources: Strategy in the 1990s. *Harvard Business Review,* 73(4), 118–128.

Crotts, J. C., Dickson, D. R., & Ford, R. C. (2005). Aligning organizational processes with mission: The case of service excellence. *Academy of Management Perspectives,* 19(3), 54–68.

Daft, R. L., & Lengel, R. H. (1986). Organizational information requirements, media richness and structural design. *Management Science, 32*(5), 554–571.

Daft, R. L., & Mackintosh, N. B. (1981). The evolution of organizational complexity: An empirical assessment. *Human Relations, 34*(7), 593–613.

Daft, R. L., & Weick, K. E. (1984). Toward a model of organizations as interpretation systems. *Academy of Management Review, 9*(2), 284–295.

Davenport, T. H., & Harris, J. G. (2007). Competing on analytics: The new science of winning. Harvard Business Review Press.

David, F. R., & David, F. R. (2020). Strategic management: Concepts and cases. Pearson.

Dervitsioyis, K. (2010). A framework for the assessment of an organization's innovation excellence. *Total Quality Management, 21*(9), 903–918.

Dixit, A. K., & Nalebuff, B. J. (2008). *The art of strategy: A game theorist's guide to success in business and life.* W. W. Norton & Company.

Doz, Y., & Kosonen, M. (2008). Fast strategy: How strategic agility will help you stay ahead of the game. *Harvard Business Review, 86*(10), 124–132.

Doz, Y. L., & Kosonen, M. (2010). Embedding strategic agility: A leadership agenda for accelerating business model renewal. *Long Range Planning, 43*(2–3), 370–382.

Drucker, P. (1995a). The information executives truly need. *Harvard Business Review, 73*(1), 54–62.

Drucker, P. F. (1963). *Managing for business effectiveness.* Harvard Business Review.

Drucker, P. F. (1995b). *Innovation and entrepreneurship: Practice and principles.* Harper Business.

Dubin, M. (2012). *Dollar shave club: The unboxing and first shave.* Harvard Business School Case Study.

Duysters, G., & Hagedoorn, J. (2000). Core competences and company performance in the worldwide computer industry. *Journal of High Technology Management Research, 11*(1), 75–91.

Dyer, J., Gregersen, H., & Clayton, C. (2011a). Picking the winners. What are the most innovative companies today, and tomorrow? *Forbes, 188*(2), 74–83.

Dyer, J. H., Gregersen, H. B., & Christensen, C. M. (2011b). *The innovator's DNA: Mastering the five skills of disruptive innovators.* Harvard Business Review Press.

Ebner, D., & Baumgartner, R. J. (2008). The relationship between sustainable development and corporate social responsibility. Corporate Responsibility Research Conference.

Eccles, R. (1991). The performance measurement manifesto. *Harvard Business Review, 69*(1), 131–137.

Eisenhardt, K. M., & Brown, S. L. (1998). Competing on the edge: Strategy as structured chaos. *Harvard Business Review, 76*(5), 94–101.

Eisenhardt, K. M., & Graebner, M. E. (2007). Theory building from cases: Opportunities and challenges. *Academy of Management Journal, 50*(1), 25–32.

Eisenmann, T., Christensen, C. M., & Bower, J. L. (2008). *Disruptive innovation: How to create and build a successful business model.* Harvard Business Review Press.

Electrify America. (2021). Our network. Retrieved from https://www.electrifyamerica.com/our-network/

Elkington, J. (1997). *Cannibals with forks: The triple bottom line of 21st century business.* Capstone Publishing.

Elkington, J., & Hartigan, P. (2008). *The power of unreasonable people: How social entrepreneurs create markets that change the world.* Harvard Business School Press.

Emery, F. E., & Trist, E. L. (1965). The causal texture of organizational environments. *Human Relations, 18*(1), 21–32.

Fahey, L. (1999). *Competitors: Outwitting, outmaneuvering, and outperforming.* Wiley.

Faulconbridge, J. R., & Muzio, D. (2015). Professional service firms, work and organization. In Laura Empson, Daniel Muzio, Joseph P. Broschak, and Bob Hinings (Eds.), *Oxford handbook of professional service firms* (pp. 15–31). Oxford University Press.

Fiss, P. C. (2007). A set-theoretic approach to organizational configurations. *Academy of Management Review, 32*(4), 1180–1198.

Foley, M. J. (2018). *Microsoft 2.0: How Microsoft plans to stay relevant in the post-gates era.* ZDNet.

Forbes. (n.d.). *Enhancing customer engagement with AI at Sephora.* Forbes.

Forbes. (n.d.). *Using AI for cost efficiency in manufacturing.* Forbes.

Galbraith, J. R. (1982). *Designing complex organizations.* Addison-Wesley.

Galenson, D. (2007). And now for something completely different: The versatility of conceptual innovators. *Historical Methods, 40*(1), 17–27.

Galunic, C. D., & Eisenhardt, K. M. (1994). Technological, strategic, and organizational designs for competence in dynamic environments. *Organization Science, 5*(2), 204–220.

Gavetti, G., & Rivkin, J. W. (2005). How strategists really think: Tapping the power of analogy. *Harvard Business Review, 83*(4), 54–63.

Gersick, C. J. G. (1991). Revolutionary change theories: A multilevel exploration of the punctuated equilibrium paradigm. *Academy of Management Review, 16*(1), 10–36.

Gerstner, L. V. (2002). *Who says elephants can't dance? Leading a great enterprise through dramatic change.* HarperCollins.

Ghoshal, S., & Nohria, N. (1989). Internal differentiation and the dynamics of growth within multiunit firms. *Academy of Management Review, 14*(3), 385–405.

Gibbins-Klein, M. (2011). Winning by thinking: How to create a culture of thought leadership in your organization. *Development and Learning in Organizations, 25*(1), 8–10.

Gilbert, C. G. (2005). Unbundling the structure of inertia: Resource versus routine rigidity. *Academy of Management Journal, 48*(5), 741–763.

Gladwell, M. (2002). *The tipping point: How little things can make a big difference.* Back Bay Books.

Gladwell, M. (2011). *Outliers: The story of success.* Back Bay Books.

Glaser, B. G., & Strauss, A. L. (1967). *The discovery of grounded theory: Strategies for qualitative research.* Aldine Publishing.

Goddard, J. (1997). The architecture of core competence. *Business Strategy Review, 8*(1), 43–52.

Goel, R. (2010). *Organizational commitment in Indian IT industry: An empirical study.* Lambert Academic Publishing.

Goldman Sachs. (2021). 2021 Annual Report. Retrieved from Goldman Sachs. https://www.goldmansachs.com/investor-relations/financials/current/annual-reports/2021-annual-report/

Google AI. (n.d.). *AI-driven innovation at Google.* Google AI.

Google AI. (n.d.). *Generative design in product development.* Google AI.

Google AI. (n.d.). *Google Assistant.* Google AI.

Google AI. (n.d.). *Waymo: Google's self-driving car project.* Google AI.

Google's AI division. (n.d.). *Machine learning for customer segmentation.* Google.

Grant, R. M. (2016). *Contemporary strategy analysis: Text and cases edition.* John Wiley & Sons.

Grant, R. M. (2019). *Contemporary strategy analysis: Text and cases edition.* John Wiley & Sons.

Greenbaum, R. L., Mawritz, M. B., & Eissa, G. (2012). Bottom-line mentality as an antecedent of social undermining and the moderating roles of core self-evaluations and conscientiousness. *Journal of Applied Psychology, 97*(2), 343–359.

GreenCars. (2023a). Toyota's electrification strategy. Retrieved from GreenCars. https://www.greencars.com/news/toyota-updates-electrification-strategy-promises-10-evs-by-2026

GreenCars. (2023b). Toyota updates electrification strategy, promises 10 EVs by 2026. Retrieved from https://www.greencars.com/news/toyota-updates-electrification-strategy-promises-10-evs-by-2026

Griffin, R. W., & Pustay, M. W. (2018). *International business: A managerial perspective.* Pearson.

Grinyer, P. H., Spender, J. C., & Scherer, A. G. (1988). The resolution of power struggles at the top. *Journal of Management Studies, 25*(2), 129–144.

Gupta, A. K., Smith, K. G., & Shalley, C. E. (2006). The interplay between exploration and exploitation. *Academy of Management Journal, 49*(4), 693–706.

Hambrick, D. C., & Fredrickson, J. W. (2005). Are you sure you have a strategy? *Academy of Management Executive, 19*(4), 51–62.

Hamel, G., & Prahalad, C. K. (1994). Competing for the future. *Harvard Business Review, 72*(4), 122–128.

Hansen, M. T., & Woollard, S. (2018). Cooperation, communication, and competition: The dark side of teams in dynamic environments. *Organization Science, 29*(5), 791–807.

Hartford, T. (2008). *Adaptive strategy: Profit from uncertainty.* MIT Sloan Management Review.

Heikkurinen, P. (2010). Image differentiation with corporate environmental responsibility. *Corporate Social Responsibility and Environmental Management, 17*, 142–152.

Hendry, J., Bradshaw, R., & Brown, I. (2003). Episodes as units of analysis. *Journal of Management Studies, 40*(2), 525–551.

Hidalgo, C. A. (2019). *Why information grows: The evolution of order, from atoms to economies.* Basic Books.

Hill, C. W., Jones, G. R., & Schilling, M. A. (2014). *Strategic management: Theory: An integrated approach.* Cengage Learning.

Hitt, M. A., Ireland, R. D., & Hoskisson, R. E. (2017). *Strategic management: Concepts and cases: Competitiveness and globalization.* Cengage Learning.

Hitt, M. A., Ireland, R. D., & Hoskisson, R. E. (2018). *Strategic management: Concepts and cases: Competitiveness and globalization.* Cengage Learning.

Hitt, M. A., Ireland, R. D., & Hoskisson, R. E. (2020). *Strategic management: Concepts and cases: Competitiveness and globalization.* Cengage Learning.

Hoffman, J. (2019). How McDonald's plans to win customers back. *CNBC*. Retrieved from https://www.cnbc.com/2019/10/25/how-mcdonalds-plans-to-win-customers-back.html

Holcomb, T. R., Sullivan, M. L., & Harrison, J. S. (2009). The dynamics of industry self-organization: Evidence from the video game industry. *Journal of Management Studies*, 46(7), 1197–1222.

Hsu, C. C., Rice, M. P., & Galbraith, C. S. (1983). Structural attributes and administrative strategies in hospitals. *Academy of Management Journal*, 26(2), 298–312. Retrieved from https://www.ups.com/us/en/services/knowledge-center/article.page?kid=aa595d89

Husted, B. W., & Salazar, J. J. (2006). Taking Friedman seriously: Maximizing profits and social performance. *Journal of Management Studies*, 43(1), 75–91.

Innovation and leadership: Executives fail to foster innovation. (2008). *Strategic Decision*, 24(5), 36–38.

Ionity. (2021). About Ionity. Retrieved from https://ionity.eu/en/about.html

Jarzabkowski, P., Balogun, J., & Seidl, D. (2007). Strategizing: The challenges of a practice perspective. *Human Relations*, 60(1), 5–27.

Johnson, G. (1992). Managing strategic change. *Strategy and Leadership*, 20(1), 26–30.

Johnson, G., Melin, L., & Whittington, R. (2003). Micro strategy and strategizing: Towards an activity-based view. *Journal of Management Studies*, 40(1), 3–22.

Johnson, G., Scholes, K., & Whittington, R. (2019). *Exploring strategy: Text and cases.* Pearson Education.

Johnson, G., Whittington, R., & Scholes, K. (2017). *Exploring strategy: Text and cases* (11th ed.). Pearson.

Johnson, G., Whittington, R., Scholes, K., Angwin, D., & Regner, P. (2021). *Exploring strategy: Text and cases* (12th ed.). Pearson.

Kahneman, D. (2011). *Thinking, fast and slow.* Farrar, Straus and Giroux.

Kaimann, H. (1974). Organizational structure and organizational effectiveness. In James G. March (Ed.), *Handbook of organizations* (pp. 171–216). Rand McNally.

Kanfer, R., & Ackerman, P. L. (1989). Motivation and cognitive abilities: An integrative/aptitude-treatment interaction approach to skill acquisition. *Journal of Applied Psychology*, 74(4), 657–690.

Kaplan, S. (2008). Framing contests: Strategy making under uncertainty. *Organization Science*, 19(5), 729–752.

Kenichi, S. (2023, February 13). Toyota's EV shift: 1.5 million electric cars annually by 2026. Nikkei Asia. Retrieved from https://asia.nikkei.com/Business/Automobiles/Toyota-s-EV-shift-1.5-million-electric-cars-annually-by-2026

Kiechel III, W. (2010). *The lords of strategy: The secret intellectual history of the new corporate world.* Harvard Business Review Press.

Kim, W. C., & Mauborgne, R. (2005). *Blue ocean strategy: How to create uncontested market space and make the competition irrelevant.* Harvard Business Review Press.

Kim, W. C., & Mauborgne, R. (2020). *Blue ocean shift: Beyond competing – Proven steps to inspire confidence and seize new growth.* Hachette UK.

Kodak's downfall isn't about technology. (n.d.) Retrieved from https://hbr.org/2012/01/kodaks-downfall-is-a-warning

Kotler, P. (2000). *Marketing management* (10th ed.). Prentice Hall.

Kotler, P., Kartajaya, H., & Setiawan, I. (2016). *Marketing 4.0: Moving from traditional to digital.* Wiley.

Kotler, P., & Keller, K. L. (2015). *Marketing management* (15th ed.). Pearson Education.

Kotler, P., & Keller, K. L. (2016). *Marketing management* (15th ed.). Pearson.

Kowitt, B. (2018). How McDonald's is using technology to transform customer experience. *Fortune.* Retrieved from https://fortune.com/2018/10/25/mcdonalds-technology-customer-experience/

Krames, J. A. (2004). *Jack Welch and the 4E's of leadership: How to put GE's leadership formula to work in your organization.* McGraw-Hill Professional.

Kurtzman, J. (1997). *Thought leaders: Insights on the future of business.* Jossey-Bass Publishers.

Lafley, A. G., & Martin, R. L. (2013). *Playing to win: How strategy really works.* Harvard Business Review Press.

Lashinsky, A. (2012). *Inside Apple: How America's most admired – and secretive – company really works.* Business Plus.

Laszlo, C. (2008). *Sustainable value: How the world's leading companies are doing well by doing good.* Stanford University Press.

Latham, G. P., & Locke, E. A. (2007). New developments in and directions for goal-setting research. *European Psychologist, 12*(4), 290–300.

Lawrence, P. R., & Lorsch, J. W. (1967). Differentiation and integration in complex organizations. *Administrative Science Quarterly,* 12(1), 1–47.

Lax, D. A., & Sebenius, J. K. (2006). *3D negotiation: Powerful tools to change the game in your most important deals.* Harvard Business Review Press.

Lax, D. A., & Sebenius, J. K. (2013). *3D negotiation: Powerful tools to change the game in your most important deals.* Harvard Business Review Press.

Lee, T. W. (1999). *Using qualitative methods in organizational research.* SAGE Publications.

LEGO. Retrieved from https://www.lego.com/en-us/aboutus/lego-group/the_lego_brand/our_brand

LEGO case study. Retrieved from https://www.ibscdc.org/Case_Studies/Strategy/LEGOs%20Turnaround%20Strategy/STR0098.htm

Levitt, T. (1960). Marketing myopia. *Harvard Business Review,* 38(4), 45–56.

Levitt, T. (2006). *The marketing imagination.* Simon and Schuster.

Lewicki, R. J., Barry, B., & Saunders, D. M. (2015). *Essentials of negotiation.* McGraw-Hill Education.

Liedtka, J., & Ogilvie, T. (2011). *Designing for growth: A design thinking toolkit for managers.* Columbia University Press.

Locke, E. A., & Latham, G. P. (1984). *Goal setting: A motivational technique that works.* Prentice Hall.

Locke, E. A., & Latham, G. P. (1990). *A theory of goal setting and task performance.* Prentice Hall.

Locke, E. A., Shaw, K. N., Saari, L. M., & Latham, G. P. (1981). Goal setting and task performance: 1969–1980. *Psychological Bulletin,* 90(1), 125–152.

Locke, R. M., Qin, F., & Brause, A. (2007). Globalization and the environment: Determinants of firm self-regulation in China. *Management Science,* 53(1), 118–133.

Lovette, T., & MacDonald, R. (2005). *Corporate social responsibility in the 21st century: Debates, models and practices across government, law and business.* Oxford University Press.

Luftman, J. (2011). *Managing the information technology resource: Leadership in the information age.* Pearson.

Luhmann, N. (1973). *Zweckbegriff und Systemrationalität. Überlegungen zur Theorie zweckrationalen Handelns.* J.C.B. Mohr.

Luhmann, N. (1975). Interaktion, Organisation, Gesellschaft: Geburtstunde der Systemtheorie. In F. Geyer (Ed.), *Niklas Luhmann. Beiträge zu einer Theorie sozialer Systeme* (pp. 24–36). Suhrkamp.

Luhmann, N. (1986). The autopoiesis of social systems. In F. Geyer & J. van der Zouwen (Eds.), *Sociocybernetic paradoxes* (pp. 172–192). Sage.

Luhmann, N. (1990). *Essays on self-reference.* Columbia University Press.

Luhmann, N. (1995). *Social systems.* Stanford University Press.

Luhmann, N. (1997). *Die Gesellschaft der Gesellschaft* (Vol. 1). Suhrkamp.

Maguire, S., Hardy, C., & Lawrence, T. B. (2006). Institutional entrepreneurship in emerging fields: HIV/AIDS treatment advocacy in Canada. *Academy of Management Journal,* 49(5), 981–998.

Marion, R., & Uhl-Bien, M. (2001). Leadership in complex organizations. *The Leadership Quarterly,* 12(4), 389–418.

Markides, C. (1999). *All the right moves: A guide to crafting breakthrough strategy.* Harvard Business Review Press.

Marshall, C., & Rossman, G. B. (2006). *Designing qualitative research* (4th ed.). SAGE Publications.

Mauborgne, R., & Kim, W. C. (2014). *Blue ocean strategy, expanded edition: How to create uncontested market space and make the competition irrelevant.* Harvard Business Review Press.

Mazzarol, T., & Soutar, G. N. (2008). *The global market for higher education: Sustainable competitive strategies for the new millennium.* Edward Elgar Publishing.

McAfee, A., & Brynjolfsson, E. (2012). Big data: The management revolution. *Harvard Business Review,* 90(10), 60–68.

McAfee, A., & Brynjolfsson, E. (2017). *Machine, platform, crowd: Harnessing our digital future.* W. W. Norton & Company.

McCrimmon, M. (2005). Thought leadership: A radical departure from traditional, positional leadership. *Management Decision,* 43(7/8), 1064–1070.

McDonald's Corporation. (2022). About McDonald's. Retrieved from https://www.mcdonalds.com/us/en-us/about-us.html

McGrath, R. G. (2001). Exploratory learning, innovative capacity, and managerial oversight. *Academy of Management Journal,* 44(1), 118–131.

McGrath, R. G. (2013). *The end of competitive advantage: How to keep your strategy moving as fast as your business*. Harvard Business Review Press.

Mckeown, M. (2014). *The strategy book: How to think and act strategically to deliver outstanding results*. Pearson.

McMillan, G. S., & Roberts, D. L. (1994). Using blue ocean strategy to overcome the growth and decline of the music industry. *Journal of Business Strategy*, 15(5), 37–42.

McQuarrie, E. F., & Munson, J. M. (1992). The strategy of decline. *The Journal of Marketing*, 56(4), 1–7.

Meadows, D. H. (2008). *Thinking in systems: A primer*. Chelsea Green Publishing.

Mezias, S. J., Grinyer, P. H., & Guth, W. D. (2001). The effects of sequential decision making on organizational outcomes. *Academy of Management Journal*, 44(5), 832–848.

Mintzberg, H., Ahlstrand, B., & Lampel, J. (1998). *Strategy safari: A guided tour through the wilds of strategic management*. The Free Press.

Mintzberg, H., Ahlstrand, B., & Lampel, J. (2008). *Strategy safari: A guided tour through the wilds of strategic management*. Free Press.

Mintzberg, H., Ahlstrand, B., & Lampel, J. (2009). *Strategy safari: A guided tour through the wilds of strategic management*. Pearson Education.

Mintzberg, H., Lampel, J., Ahlstrand, B., & Safarova, V. (2009). *Strategy bites back: It is a lot more, and less, than you ever imagined*. Pearson Education.

Mitchell, A. (2014). *Xerox's comeback story: How the iconic brand is reinventing itself*. Fortune.

Mitchell, R. K., Agle, B. R., & Wood, D. J. (1997). Toward a theory of stakeholder identification and salience: Defining the principle of who and what really counts. *Academy of Management Review*, 22(4), 853–886.

Moneva, J. M., & Ortas, E. (2010). Corporate environmental and financial performance: A multivariate approach. *Industrial Management & Data Systems*, 110(2), 193–210.

Montgomery, C. (2012). *The strategist: Be the leader your business needs*. HarperCollins.

Moore, G. A. (2002). *Crossing the chasm: Marketing and selling high-tech products to mainstream customers*. Harper Business.

Nadella, S. (2017). *Hit refresh: The quest to rediscover microsoft's soul and imagine a better future for everyone*. Harper Business.

Nassehi, A. (2005). Niklas Luhmann's theory of social systems and journalism as a social system. *Studies in Communication Sciences*, 5(1), 181–192.

Netflix. (n.d.). *How Netflix uses AI to deliver personalized experiences*. Netflix.

Netflix, Inc. (n.d.). Harvard business school case study: 9-607-138. https://www.hbs.edu/faculty/Pages/item.aspx?num=34596

Netflix: The Making of an Ecosystem (n.d.). Harvard business school case study: 9-713-493. https://www.hbs.edu/faculty/Pages/item.aspx?num=56185

New York Times. (2004, November 18). Sears and Kmart to merge. *New York Times*. Retrieved from https://www.nytimes.com/2004/11/18/business/sears-and-kmart-to-merge.html

Nike Official Website – About Nike. (2023). Retrieved from https://www.nike.com/

O'Keefe, M., Dye, A., & Hoffmann, M. (2020). *Thought leadership in action: A comprehensive guide to building your brand, elevating your profile, and creating thought leadership that lasts.* HarperCollins Leadership.

Ocasio, W. (2011). Attention to attention. *Organization Science*, 22(5), 1286–1296.

Osterwalder, A., & Pigneur, Y. (2010). *Business model generation: A handbook for visionaries, game changers, and challengers.* Wiley.

Ouyang, H. (2010). *Corporate social responsibility and firm performance: Evidence from China.* Lambert Academic Publishing.

P&G. (n.d.). Company strategy. Retrieved from https://us.pg.com/company/strategy/

Pache, A. C., & Santos, F. (2010). When worlds collide: The internal dynamics of organizational responses to conflicting institutional demands. *Academy of Management Review*, 35(3), 455–476.

Palmisano, S. (2009). The globally integrated enterprise. *Foreign Affairs*, 88(3), 127–136.

Peloton. (n.d.). Retrieved from https://www.onepeloton.com/

Pettigrew, A. M. (1985). *The awakening giant: Continuity and change in ICI.* Blackwell.

Porac, J. F., & Thomas, H. (1990). Taxonomic mental models in competitor definition. *Academy of Management Review*, 15(2), 224–240.

Porter, M. E. (1980). *Competitive strategy: Techniques for analyzing industries and competitors.* Free Press.

Porter, M. E. (1985). *Competitive advantage: Creating and sustaining superior performance.* Free Press.

Porter, M. E. (1987). From competitive advantage to corporate strategy. *Harvard Business Review*, 65(3), 43–59.

Porter, M. E. (1990). The competitive advantage of nations. *Harvard Business Review*, 68(2), 73–93.

Porter, M. E. (1996). *Competitive strategy: Techniques for analyzing industries and competitors.* Free Press.

Porter, M. E. (1996). What is strategy? *Harvard Business Review*, 74(6), 61–78.

Porter, M. E. (2008). *Competitive strategy: Techniques for analyzing industries and competitors.* Free Press.

Porter, M. E. (2008). The five competitive forces that shape strategy. *Harvard Business Review*, 86(1), 78–93.

Prahalad, C. K., & Hamel, G. (1990). The core competence of the corporation. *Harvard Business Review*, 68(3), 79–91.

Pringle, C. D., & Longenecker, J. G. (1982). The ethics of survival: A pragmatic approach to business ethics. *Business Horizons*, 25(4), 15–21.

QuantumScape. (2021). Our technology. Retrieved from https://www.quantumscape.com/technology/

Razak, M., & Llias, A. (2011). Seven unique differentiation strategies to online businesses: A comprehensive review of Malaysia Airline System (MAS). *Journal of Internet Banking and Commerce*, 16(2), 1–16.

Reeves, M., Haanaes, K., & Sinha, J. (2015). *Your strategy needs a strategy.* Harvard Business Review Press.

Reus, T. H., Lamont, B. T., & Ellis, K. M. (2009). A darker side of knowledge transfer following international acquisitions. *Strategic Management Journal, 30*(5), 447–467.

Ries, E. (2011). *The lean startup: How today's entrepreneurs use continuous innovation to create radically successful businesses.* Crown Business.

Roberts, P. W., & Dowling, G. R. (2002). Corporate reputation and sustained superior financial performance. *Strategic Management Journal, 23*(12), 1077–1093.

Roos, J., & Von Krogh, G. (1996). *Organizational epistemology.* Macmillan.

Rothaermel, F. T. (2019). *Strategic management* (4th ed.). McGraw-Hill Education.

Rumelt, R. (2011). *Good strategy/bad strategy: The difference and why it matters.* Crown Business.

Russell, S., & Norvig, P. (2016). *Artificial intelligence: A modern approach* (3rd ed.). Pearson Education.

Russo, M. V., & Fouts, P. A. (1997). A resource-based perspective on corporate environmental performance and profitability. *Academy of Management Journal, 40*(3), 534–559.

Schneider, C. Q., Wagemann, C., & Quaranta, M. (2016). *How to… use software-based text analysis in social science research.* ECPR Press.

Schoeneborn, D., Blaschke, S., & Kaufmann, I. M. (2014). Recontextualizing anthropomorphic metaphors in organization studies: The pathology of organizational insomnia. *Journal of Management Inquiry, 23*(4), 413–431.

Schreyogg, G., & Steinmann, H. (1987). The dynamics of organizational closure: A cybernetic model of organizational change. *Journal of Management Studies, 24*(4), 417–436.

Schumpeter, J. A. (1934). *The theory of economic development: An inquiry into profits, capital, credit, interest, and the business cycle.* Harvard University Press.

Schwartz, P. (1996). *The art of the long view: Planning for the future in an uncertain world.* Crown Business.

Scott, W. R. (1992). *Organizations: Rational, natural, and open systems.* Prentice Hall.

Scott, W. R., & Meyer, J. W. (1987). The organization of societal sectors. In W. W. Powell & P. J. DiMaggio (Eds.), *The new institutionalism in organizational analysis* (pp. 108–140). University of Chicago Press.

Senge, P. M. (1990). *The fifth discipline: The art and practice of the learning organization.* Currency Doubleday.

Sephora. (2023). AI-powered customer engagement at Sephora. *Sephora.* Retrieved from https://www.sephora.com/about-us

Shell, G. R. (2006). *Bargaining for advantage: Negotiation strategies for reasonable people.* Penguin Books.

Shell, G. R. (2019). *Bargaining for advantage: Negotiation strategies for reasonable people.* Penguin.

Siegel, D. S., Shepherd, D. A., & DeTienne, D. J. (2012). Managing decline: The role of organizational structure. *Strategic Management Journal, 33*(8), 857–877.

Siggelkow, N., & Rivkin, J. W. (2005). Speed and search: Designing organizations for turbulence and complexity. *Organization Science, 16*(2), 101–122.

Silver, N. (2012). *The signal and the noise: Why so many predictions fail—But some don't.* Penguin Books.

Silverman, D. (2001). *Interpreting qualitative data: Methods for analyzing talk, text, and interaction* (2nd ed.). SAGE Publications.

Simons, R. (2010). *Seven strategy questions: A simple approach for better execution.* Harvard Business Press.

Smaiziene, I. (2008). *Strategic management: Competitiveness and globalization.* Vytautas Magnus University.

Snow, C. C., Miles, R. E., & Coleman, H. J. (1992). Managing 21st century network organizations. *Organizational Dynamics*, 20(3), 5–20.

Snowden, D. J., & Boone, M. E. (2007). A leader's framework for decision-making. *Harvard Business Review*, 85(11), 68–76.

Stacey, R. D. (2007). *Strategic management and organizational dynamics: The challenge of complexity.* Pearson Education.

Stavros, J. M., & Sprangel, J. (2008). *Sustainable innovation: Building a green culture through appreciative inquiry.* Taos Institute Publications.

Stone, B. (2013). *The everything store: Jeff Bezos and the age of Amazon.* Back Bay Books.

Stowe, C., & Grider, L. (2014). Strategies for advancing organizational innovation. *Journal of Management and Marketing Research*, 14, 1–9.

Sull, D. N., & Turconi, S. (2008). Strategies for declining businesses. *Harvard Business Review*, 19(2), 4–11.

Surowiecki, J. (2005). *The wisdom of crowds: Why the many are smarter than the few and how collective wisdom shapes business, economies, societies, and nations.* Anchor.

Sutherland, S. (2013). *Think like a rocket scientist: Simple strategies you can use to make giant leaps in work and life.* Portfolio.

Swisher, K. (2002). *Microsoft: The plot to kill Google: How Microsoft generously tried to bail out yahoo! but left it in the hands of ignorant hacks.* Vox Media.

Taleb, N. N. (2007). *The black swan: The impact of the highly improbable.* Random House.

Taleb, N. N. (2012). *Antifragile: Things that gain from disorder.* Random House.

Teece, D. J. (2018). Business models and dynamic capabilities. *Long Range Planning*, 51(1), 40–49.

Teece, D. J., Pisano, G., & Shuen, A. (1997). Dynamic capabilities and strategic management. *Strategic Management Journal*, 18(7), 509–533.

Thompson, L. L., & Martin, R. (2010). *The power of negotiation: Skills to help you get what you want.* Harvard Business Review Press.

Tidd, J., Bessant, J., & Pavitt, K. (2005). *Managing innovation: Integrating technological, market, and organizational change.* John Wiley & Sons.

Toyota Global. (n.d.). Quality. *Toyota Global.* Retrieved from https://www.toyota-global.com/company/vision_philosophy/quality/

Toyota Motor Corporation. (2023, February 13). Toyota's electrification strategy and investment in battery technology. *Toyota Global Newsroom.* Retrieved from https://global.toyota/en/newsroom/corporate/38546973.html

Toyota UK Magazine. (2023). Toyota's roadmap to electrification. Retrieved from Toyota UK Magazine. https://mag.toyota.co.uk/toyota-unveils-full-global-electric-vehicle-line-up/

Treviño, L. K., den Nieuwenboer, N. A., & Kish-Gephart, J. J. (2014). (Un)ethical behavior in organizations. *Annual Review of Psychology*, 65, 635–660.

Treviño, L. K., Weaver, G. R., & Reynolds, S. J. (2006). Behavioral ethics in organizations: A review. *Journal of Management, 32*(6), 951–990.

Tripathy, A. (2006). Strategic positioning and firm performance (Doctoral dissertation). Retrieved from WorldCat Dissertations. (OCLC: 76043447).

Tsoukas, H. (1998). What is organizational knowledge? *Journal of Management Studies,* 35(3), 303–320.

Tushman, M. L., & Nadler, D. A. (1978). Information processing as an integrating concept in organizational design. *Academy of Management Review,* 3(3), 613–624.

Tushman, M. L., & O'Reilly, C. A. (1997). *Winning through innovation: A practical guide to leading organizational change and renewal.* Harvard Business Review Press.

Uhl-Bien, M., Marion, R., & McKelvey, B. (2007). Complexity leadership theory: Shifting leadership from the industrial age to the knowledge era. *The Leadership Quarterly,* 18(4), 298–318.

United Airlines' Crisis Communicators Failed. (n.d.) Retrieved from https://www.forbes.com/sites/micahsolomon/2017/04/11/united-airlines-crisis-communicators-failed/?sh=61277bea4b38

UPS. (n.d.). AI-driven route optimization at UPS. *UPS.* Retrieved from https://www.ups.com/us/en/services/knowledge-center/article.page?kid=aa595d89

Van de Ven, A. H., & Poole, M. S. (1995). Explaining development and change in organizations. *Academy of Management Review,* 20(3), 510–540.

Vernon, R. (1966). *The product life cycle and international trade.* Harvard University Press.

Vogelstein, F., & Stone, B. (2016). *War at the wall street journal: Inside the struggle to control an American business empire.* Random House Trade Paperbacks.

Vojak, B., Price, R., and Griffin, A. (2012). *Serial innovators: How individuals create and deliver breakthrough innovations in mature firms.* Research-Technology Management.

Volkswagen Group. (2020). Volkswagen group strategy. Retrieved from https://www.volkswagenag.com/en/group/strategy.html

Volkswagen Group. (2021a). Battery production at Volkswagen. Retrieved from https://www.volkswagenag.com/en/news/2021/03/battery-production.html

Volkswagen Group. (2021b). Volkswagen digitalization strategy. Retrieved from https://www.volkswagenag.com/en/news/2021/06/digitalization-strategy.html

Volkswagen Group. (2021c). Volkswagen ID. family. Retrieved from https://www.volkswagenag.com/en/news/2021/02/id-family.html

Volkswagen Group. (2022). Annual report 2021. Retrieved from https://www.volkswagenag.com/en/InvestorRelations/reports.html

Von Foerster, H., & Pörksen, B. (1998). *Understanding systems: Conversations on epistemology and ethics.* Kluwer Academic/Plenum Publishers.

Von Krogh, G., Ichijo, K., & Nonaka, I. (2000). *Enabling knowledge creation: How to unlock the mystery of tacit knowledge and release the power of innovation.* Oxford University Press.

Waddock, S. A., & Graves, S. B. (1997). The corporate social performance–financial performance link. *Strategic Management Journal,* 18(4), 303–319.

Waldrop, M. M. (1992). *Complexity: The emerging science at the edge of order and chaos.* Simon & Schuster.

Wang, H. (2010). Corporate social performance and financial-based brand equity. *Journal of Product & Brand Management*, 19(5), 335–345.

Watkins, M. D., & Rosegrant, A. (2007). *Breakthrough international negotiation: How great negotiators transformed the world's toughest post-cold war conflicts*. Jossey-Bass.

Weber, M. (1998). *Economy and society: An outline of interpretive sociology* (Vol. 1). University of California Press.

Weick, K. E. (1976). Educational organizations as loosely coupled systems. *Administrative Science Quarterly*, 21(1), 1–19.

Weick, K. E. (1979). *The social psychology of organizing*. Addison-Wesley.

Weick, K. E. (1995). *Sensemaking in organizations*. Sage Publications.

Weill, P., & Woerner, S. L. (2018). *What's your digital business model?: Six questions to help you build the next-generation enterprise*. Harvard Business Review Press.

Westerman, G., Bonnet, D., & McAfee, A. (2014). *Leading digital: Turning technology into business transformation*. Harvard Business Review Press.

Wheatley, M. J. (1999). *Leadership and the new science: Discovering order in a chaotic world*. Berrett-Koehler Publishers.

Whittington, R. (2006). Completing the practice turn in strategy research. *Organization Studies*, 27(5), 613–634.

Williamson, O. E. (1985). *The economic institutions of capitalism: Firms, markets, relational contracting*. Free Press.

Wolfe, R. A. (1988). Is there integrity in the bottom line: Managing obstacles to executive integrity. *Journal of Business Ethics*, 7(4), 273–284.

Worren, N. A., Ruddle, K., & Moore, K. (1999). From industry recipes to strategizing in the Canadian brewing industry. *Journal of Management Studies*, 36(6), 743–772.

Xerox Corporation. (2022). Xerox: About us. Retrieved from https://www.xerox.com/en-us/about

Yoffie, D. B., & Kim, R. (2010). Apple Inc. in 2010. *Harvard Business School Case*, 710–767.

Index

Pages in *italics* refer to figures and pages in **bold** refer to tables.

Printed in the United States
by Baker & Taylor Publisher Services